CE

SPENCER T

... A Biograp

D0286196

Born in Texas but most often a Californian
(UCLA '52), Larry Swindell has been a
newspaperman on both coasts, a Broadway
drama critic, and a magazine editor in
southern California. He is a free-lance writer
on the performing arts, and has conceived and
taught theater and film courses for the
University of California Extension at Irvine.
He is married to actress Eleanor Eby, and they
have four children. The Swindells now
inhabit a 200-year-old farmhouse in
Pennsylvania's Bucks County.

Spencer Tracy
. . . A Biography

Larry Swindell

CORONET BOOKS
Hodder Paperbacks Ltd., London

312464

Printed and bound in Great Britain for Coronet Books,
Hodder Paperbacks Ltd., St Paul's House, Warwick Lane,
London, E.C.4, by Cox & Wyman Limited, London, Reading
and Fakenham

PN
2287
.T7S9
1973

ISBN 0 340 16951 6

ACKNOWLEDGMENTS

An excerpt from *A Portrait of Joan: the
Autobiography of Joan Crawford* appears on
page 144 and is reprinted by permission of the
publisher, Doubleday & Co., Inc., New York.
The material on page 148 quoting Spencer
Tracy on the subject of Will Rogers is from
Will Rogers: a Biography, by Donald Day, and
is reprinted by permission of the publisher,
David McKay & Co., New York.

For Ellie
with love and appreciation

AUTHOR'S NOTE

I MET him twice. He was, by then, a legend of his profession who first had regaled my boyhood. I expected to come to *know* him during the biographical process, and to supplement fifteen years of personal research, I met or had contact with some two hundred persons variously 'close' to Spencer Tracy. I concluded that no one person really knew him . . . not *all* of him. So I have sought to synthesize the facts and opinions about his life and work.

By my design, his career provides the structure for this book. I have attempted to define, from an actor-star's viewpoint, the Hollywood 'system' during a vibrant era; and to follow the evolution of that system into a present day that does not augur new stars of Spencer Tracy's magnitude.

Many individual contributions will be apparent, but I must thank several persons who were particularly helpful: Charles Champlin, in whose Los Angeles *Times* office the idea for this book was born; Mrs. Spencer Tracy and Carroll Tracy, who found errors of fact that long had been part of the accepted record; a score of Tracy's directors, from Dr. J. Clark Graham to Chester Erskine of Tracy's years in the theater, and from John Ford to Stanley Kramer in films; Frances Fuller of the American Academy of Dramatic Arts; many librarians, but especially Lillian Schwartz of the Academy of Motion Picture Arts and Sciences, and Paul Myers and Rod Bladel of the Theater Collection of the New York Public Library; Elaine Alscher for her thesis notes on George M. Cohan; Joe Hyams for the loan of his personal Tracy file; Richard Altman, Richard DeNeut, and Pat McHugh for special assistance; Selena Royle Renavent for opening many doors; Howard Strickling of Metro-Goldwyn-

Mayer; and my wife, Eleanor, who, by suffering in something other than silence, assured the book's completion.

Grenoble Manor Farm,
Bucks County, Pennsylvania
December 29, 1968

CONTENTS

PROLOGUE

A STOCKY young Negro actor, D'Urville Martin, exploded in anger at the craggy, white-haired, sad-eyed Spencer Tracy.

'Stupid old man oughtn't be allowed out, he ought to be put away someplace, in a home or something!'

The drive-in bystanders egged him on. His hot-rod had been smacked by Tracy's car. Trembling in fury, Spencer Tracy shoved money into Martin's hands.

'All right! Here's fifty dollars . . . don't bother having the thing repaired, buy yourself a *new* one!'

Shaking with rage, Tracy got back into his car, and the director yelled 'Cut!' Stanley Kramer took a deep breath and called out, 'That's it!' He had his good 'take' for Scene 66 of the 117-scene *Guess Who's Coming to Dinner* . . . and now the picture was in the can.

Tracy got out of the car and shook hands with D'Urville Martin. The crowd cheered. The picture was finished at last.

As Stanley Kramer approached him, Tracy tried to smile. His eyes filled with tears. When they embraced, Tracy was sobbing. They hugged one another, and Kramer was weeping, too. So was Katharine Hepburn, who was at Tracy's side once again.

The finest acting career in motion pictures had come to a close. No one knew that in just two weeks Spencer Tracy would be dead; but in fact it was miracle that he had lived to finish his last picture.

When he died some would call it the end of an era, but Hollywood's glory had dimmed much earlier. Tracy called himself 'the last of the tribe' after Bogart and Cooper and Gable had died.

But who was this man that America, and the world, loved and would mourn? Was Spencer Tracy the screen's humanitarian conscience, or the town drunk, or both? Did his overt humility conceal excessive vanity? Was he, as he often confessed, 'putting one over' on everybody, or was he the great actor that other actors said he was? Did anybody 'know' this Spencer Tracy who had many acquaintances but avoided close friendships?

Did Stanley Kramer know him? Or did his brother, Carroll Tracy? Or did Louise Tracy, whose husband continued to revere her as a 'modern saint' during their long separation? And what of Katharine Hepburn?

On stage or before the cameras he was strong, mature, and restrained. Off the screen his private life was alternately tumultuous and cloistered. Jealous, unreasonably temperamental, but with extraordinary warmth and a dignity that transcended his quirks, he could walk with kings and yet keep the common touch.

A part of him, though, was always solitary. Four months after Spencer Tracy's death, Katharine Hepburn said, 'I think Spencer always thought that acting was a rather silly way for a man to make a living. But he was of such an emotional balance, you know, that he had to be an artist.

'Of course, he never realized this . . .'

CHAPTER ONE

THE MILWAUKEE YEARS: 1900–1920

VIOLENCE transformed Auburn Prison into a slaughterhouse. Inmates rebelled, sounding a furious keynote for the 1930's. They disarmed guards, murdered one prison official, captured the warden as hostage, and laid siege. Six hours and eight corpses later the riot was subdued. An aide to New York's Governor Franklin Roosevelt remarked that it was a hell of a way to begin a depression.

The Auburn calamity played on the morbid fancies of a nation in crisis. The public was chilled but at the same time excited by the disaster. Headline watchers in Hollywood responded swiftly. In the scenario department of Fox Films a project called *Up the River* was hastily formulated.

On Broadway, too, Auburn made its impact. A prison play with an all-male cast had been journeying toward opening night in New York with little chance of being a hit; the riot gave the play a topical flavor and underscored its theme of desperate rage. *The Last Mile* became the surprise success of the season, commercially and artistically.

The play was in the fourth month of its run when its leading actor was summoned to Hollywood. Thirty-year-old Spencer Tracy was leaving the play but would stay in jail: his assignment was to act in the movie *Up the River*.

Other actors in the play gathered at the Sam H. Harris Theater for special rehearsals to break in Thomas Mitchell as Tracy's replacement. They debated whether Spencer would ever return to the stage where he had finally begun to find success.

'They say it all the time,' stage manager Albert West grumbled. 'They're making just this one movie to see what it's like, then they're coming back to the theater. But it gets to them, first the easy life and then the money. They don't come back.'

'Oh, he'll be back. He'll *have* to come back,' Thomas Mitchell said. 'He doesn't have what they're looking for out there. Spencer is a fine actor, but he sure as hell can't make the grade in pictures!'

But Spencer Tracy did make the grade, and he made it with glory.

*   *   *

Spencer was born in 1900 in the family's apartment in Milwaukee. It was April 5, a clear spring day. John Tracy made the tavern rounds to celebrate the birth of a healthy new son with his Irish friends. He could certainly afford to stand his friends to a few drinks, for he managed well for his family.

People had once said that Carrie Brown had married beneath her station. The Browns had their roots in the East, and family records went back almost to the Massachusetts Bay Colony. An ancestor of Carrie's had founded Brown University. Carrie's graceful good looks suggested that she could have had her pick of many well-to-do young men of good family; but she chose instead a swarthy adventurer who was both Irish and Catholic, neither of which made him popular with her relatives.

She never regretted her choice. Whatever reservations others may have had soon disappeared, for he proved to be an exemplary husband. He had a good business sense, and not long after he took a job with the Sterling Motor Truck Company, he was made general sales manager.

John Edward Tracy, honest, religious, and physically very strong, was respected by the men and women of the local parish. He would have been happy indeed if one of his sons had chosen the priesthood. But if that was a lost hope, at least his sons could go into business with him. Tracy and Sons would be a good name for a trucking firm.

The last field that John Tracy would have chosen for a

son of his was a career in the theater. Years later Spencer would hear his father say that 'acting just isn't the way for a Milwaukee lad.' Yet the Milwaukee area and the south Wisconsin shore of Lake Michigan has produced fine American actors: Alfred Lunt; Frederic March; Orson Welles. As a boy however, Spencer Tracy never thought of becoming an actor. Although as an adult he was typically taciturn about his childhood, he would recall that 'I didn't give a thought to anything in those years, but I had a wonderful time.'

Prospect Avenue was the scene of the formative years of Tracy's Milwaukee boyhood. His parents moved out of the apartment and bought a handsome frame house on this tree-lined street. The house had a slate roof and a large porch — both status symbols at that time, and the address was a 'good' one. Prospect Avenue was near Lake Michigan, and on the right side of the streetcar tracks that ran down Farwell Street, to the west. He usually was working on some money-making scheme. If he was not 'saving' for something specific, he would take the street-car across the river to the penny arcade, for he was early smitten by the movies.

Spencer was a bright child who, according to his mother, walked and talked and fought early. His scrappy style was matched by a face well sprinkled with freckles and topped with thick, dull-copper hair. During their early childhood Carroll Tracy was guardian and protector of his younger brother. He also became Spencer's diplomat and conscience. Carroll's daily chore was getting Spencer out of fights, for he had a quick-flaring temper, although it subsided just as quickly. He liked to tease, and he liked to use his fists. Such a boy was bound to find his share of fights, particularly in a town of mixed racial and ethnic groups.

The Irish, whose stronghold was in the northeast part of the city, were few in proportion to the Germans and Poles who lived in the central and southern sections. Germans, Poles, Italians — Spencer would fight anybody. He most often fought the Irish. He was a smug rich boy or a lower class hoodlum, depending on whether he picked on the very poor shanty Irish, or the rich Irish from Shorewood, north of his neighborhood. But whoever he fought, the smart money would bet on Spencer.

John Tracy tried to be strict with Spencer, but he didn't really succeed. He was secretly proud of his boy's aggressiveness, so there would be a twinkle in his eye when he scolded him. Spencer felt that his father preferred Carroll, who was so reliable, but that his mother preferred Spencer, who wasn't. Spencer was too much of a tough little individual to become a mama's boy, but he did feel a strong, and typically Irish, bond with her.

Spencer's Milwaukee boyhood was spent sledding and skating on the river when the ice was barely firm, or skinny-dipping in waters where the current was dangerous, or building forts on the banks of the forbidden Kaykay — the Kinnickinnic Creek — where derelicts used to gather. But alas, the happy days were always threatened by school.

Most boys hated school but went; Spencer thought going to school a tragedy. He couldn't stand it. Often he would decide to run away. At the beginning of the second grade he begged his parents to let him stay home. He had heard rumors that the teacher was brutal and unfair. On the first day he could not be found. He had dressed and escaped through his bedroom window.

They found him late in the day, down in the rough South Side, playing happily with two urchins named Ratty and Mousie Donovan. Their father operated a saloon and he did not make them go to school. Ratty, the older boy, was about Spencer's size and, on seeing a strange face in his neighborhood, he picked a fight with him. The boys fought until they saw they were evenly matched and that the only way to end the fight was to become good friends. It was a blithe Spencer who was discovered by his parents, but he was overcome with remorse when he saw his mother crying. He promised his father that he would enter the second grade, and that he would never make his mother cry again.

Ratty and Mousie became Spencer's best friends, and Donovan's saloon was their headquarters. Spencer liked to hide under the counter to listen to the men talking. Ratty and Mousie seemed rodent in instinct as well as appearance. They had the run of the seamy side of Milwaukee, and taught Spencer what they knew.

Spencer would often leave the school grounds during recess to meet a gang of friends. In time his parents made the acquaintance of most of the truant officers of Milwaukee County. But through it all Spencer was likable. Even the truant officers admitted that. He could look pathetic and innocent, with his soft blue eyes and thick, unruly hair. Tears would glisten in his eyes; he would deliver a heart-broken apology and hang his head sadly until he was safely out of sight. Then he would break into a trot and look for new adventure.

His school attendance improved, but his performance did not. He was best at firing a spitball. The standard courses didn't hold his interest. His parents tried a succession of schools. They did not always withdraw him from a school — he was often expelled. He changed schools so often that he couldn't be promoted from year to year. He was kept back, and so, to add to his difficulties, he was older and bigger than his classmates.

Given a choice, Spencer would have quit school and gotten a job. But this was one time that he couldn't win his mother over to his side, for his father was determined that Spencer should have a good education. At last, Spencer managed to get an intermediate diploma from St. Rosa's Parochial School; it was about the fifteenth school he had attended.

Spencer became a Boy Scout, and developed an interest in athletics, particularly baseball, that he would never lose. He was competitive, and hated to lose. In fact, his interest in any activity would fade when he thought someone could outdo him, for he had to be the best. Wearing boxing gloves, he almost was, and he became the hero of the gym.

But early adolescence was not always smooth. Once he started a fire in the basement that almost burned down the Tracy home. Neighbors whispered that it was done willfully after a quarrel with his father. It was more likely that the fire was an accident that Spencer had difficulty explaining — he was probably trying out some cigarettes, which of course his parents had forbidden. But things began to look up about the time that Spencer began to think about girls.

He was not, however, an instant hit with girls. At the age of fourteen he developed a crush on an orange-haired girl who was impressed by the fact that Spencer was already shaving. For awhile they kept company, but when Spencer first tried to steal a kiss, he found himself in a fist fight. His true love's temper matched her fiery hair. Spencer said he was giving up women.

At this time Spencer liked to put on penny-admission plays in the basement. The plays weren't very original: he and his friends usually depended on movies they had seen to supply the plots. In fact, Spencer's real love was not his little theater but the movies. He once told a magazine interviewer: 'I wouldn't have gone to school at all if there'd been any other way of learning to read the subtitles in the silent films.'

When Spencer was fourteen he made the acquaintance of Bill O'Brien, a natural leader and organizer, from the more rough-and-tumble Tory Hill neighborhood. O'Brien saw that Spencer was allowed into the neighborhood gang. Older than Spencer by five months, William Joseph O'Brien was glib, smooth, and darkly handsome. He would sometimes talk about the theater. Spencer thought that hardly an interest for a male to be proud of, but he liked Bill nonetheless. In later years Bill would become famous as Pat O'Brien.

*   *   *

During Spencer's sixteenth year, there was a great change in his family's life. A new business opportunity opened up for John Tracy, but it meant moving to Kansas City, which they did. Carrie Tracy was not happy about the move, particularly because Spencer once again began having trouble with school. He was first enrolled in St. Mary's High School in Kansas City, but he quarreled with a teacher and had the

18

usual fist fights with other students, and was expelled. Then he entered Rockhurst High where his behavior was even worse. Fortunately, the Kansas City misery didn't last long: the business didn't live up to John Tracy's expectation, and six months later the family returned to Milwaukee.

They moved into a handsome apartment on Marietta Street in the old neighbourhood, near Prospect Avenue. Spencer picked up his old friendships, and hunted up Bill O'Brien. When he learned that O'Brien was attending Marquette Academy on a scholarship, he asked to go to the same school.

Marquette Academy, linked administratively to Marquette University, was a Jesuit prep school that had the best reputation in the state. Although it was more expensive than most other schools, the Tracys were so pleased to see Spencer enthusiastic about school that they quickly agreed to send him there.

He was seventeen when he entered Marquette Academy. He was just under five foot ten and had a good build. He had taken to parting his hair just barely off-center, like Douglas Fairbanks, and he kept it slicked down. He liked the students from the nearby girls' schools, and if he still felt shy and awkward with girls he was better at hiding it.

His school work as well as his manners showed vast improvement. To everyone's surprise, his grades were best in theological studies. Spencer first took a true interest in the Catholic church at the Academy, and it was there that he talked for the only time in his life about becoming a priest. He was still undecided about a career, when the United States finally entered the First World War. As the impact of the foreign war suddenly came closer to home, all thought of the future was centered in Europe. Like most young men in 1917, Spencer wanted to get 'over there' where the action was.

When classes started in the fall some seniors left for the service. Spencer, only a sophomore but older than his classmates, joined the line at the marine recruiting station. He neglected to lie about his age, and he was turned down for being under eighteen.

His mother loved him for his honesty, but Spencer was disgusted. Then Bill O'Brien stopped by the Tracy household a few days later in great excitement. He had joined the navy. He was going to see the world, and he thought that Spencer should come along, too.

'You don't have to lie about your age. Seventeen is all right, if you have your parents' consent.'

Spencer's mother was against the plan, but to no avail. His father decided he would let the boy join the navy on the theory that it would probably do him more good than harm. Then Carroll decided that he, too, would join. 'If Spence is going to be a sailor, someone has to keep him out of the brig.'

Spencer told his mother, 'If the Kaiser finds out we're all three in the navy the war can't last long.' He promised his parents that when he got back he would return to school and graduate.

Soon Carroll, Spencer, and Bill were off to war. They were trained at the Great Lakes Naval Training Center near Chicago. It was only eighty-five miles from Milwaukee, so they could get home on leave to parade around town in their uniforms. After training, Spencer was separated from his Milwaukee pals. They stayed; he was dispatched on special orders.

He was briefly at Lake Bluff, and then was sent to the Norfolk navy yard. His first look at the fighting ships in the harbor gripped him with the excitement of new adventures. But he never left Norfolk.

Once, just once, he got to take a ride on a whaleboat that sailed a few miles offshore. That was the extent of the Tracy maritime activity during a seven-month stay at the yard. For Spencer the Battle of Norfolk meant washing and tending ships, scrubbing urinals, and making his mark as a navy chowhand. He apparently did not meet a sailor named Humphrey Bogart who was also at Norfolk for a time. Earlier, though, at Lake Bluff, he had been entertained by a sailor named Jack Benny who, Spencer thought, was a pretty good violinist.

Seaman Tracy was mustered out shortly after the November Armistice and returned to a hero's welcome in Milwaukee that was, to him, downright embarrassing. His ten months in the navy had only put off school, and it was harder than ever now to go back to it.

After the first joys of coming home, Spencer chafed at the old routine. He felt older than his years, and wanted to be free of his family. The Norfolk tenure had given him long duty watches of solitude and reflection. Barracks life made him aware of his own natural advantages, and also how he had misused them. Tracy told the writer J. P. McEvoy, years later, that the months at Norfolk awakened him to the beautiful strength of his parents, and made him think for the first time how deeply he had disappointed them.

'I had never known ambition of any sort,' Tracy said. 'To my mind the best attainment was in doing nothing. I was that lazy. I still didn't know what I wanted to do, but I had at least decided I owed it to my parents not to settle for the usual.'

He came to see that the regimentation in the navy was necessary. And in life outside the navy as well as in it, there were the leaders and the followers, the winners and the losers, those who do things and those who are only affected by the doings of others. Spencer saw that his own father was among the doers, and realized how much he respected him. But these first good intentions of making his father proud were dashed by the realization that he couldn't do anything really well.

After completing his junior year at Marquette Academy in the spring, Spencer worked at odd jobs during the summer. In the fall, he was to enter the Northwestern Military and Naval Academy, located at Lake Geneva in the southern part of the state, about midway between Milwaukee and Chicago.

In the summer of 1919 he also began to attend the plays that toured through Milwaukee. He began to see that perhaps Bill O'Brien's acting ambitions weren't so stupid, after all. It seemed a good way out, he thought, if you could make a living at it; it certainly beat working. Bill O'Brien was filled with stories about how rich some actors were, but when Spencer tried this information out at the Tracy dinner table his family wasn't enthusiastic.

Spencer decided to say no more about it; but he was thinking about it when he entered the Northwestern Military and Naval Academy.

He was no ordinary new September cadet. He looked older than he was, and that was old enough. Northwestern had only a handful of nineteen-year-old veterans, and many of the cadets were only fourteen or fifteen. Tracy was assigned a dormitory room with a seventeen-year-old senior.

From the moment they met, Spencer Tracy and Kenneth Edgers hit it off. In no time they were best friends. John Tracy later said that the best thing that could have happened to his son was meeting Ken Edgers.

Edgers was from Seattle. Northwestern Academy collected enlistee cadets from all parts of the country, but he was perhaps the one farthest from home. He was well-to-do, but most of the cadets were that, although not all of them wore it so well. Spencer liked Ken's gentlemanliness which was not stuffy but casual and instinctive. He decided that Cadet Edgers would serve as the model for what he, Cadet Tracy, should become.

Edgers was a good talker, knowledgeable in practically everything, and he had the kind of ready wit that Tracy looked for in his friends. In the navy Tracy had been considered a solemn fellow, who liked to be by himself. Edgers, on the other hand, was always in good spirits and very outgoing.

All cadets were boarding students and no one left the campus except on general holidays. Tracy called it a bootcamp for bluebloods, but he thrived on it. Like the navy, it was geared to the kind of rigid discipline he knew he needed.

On the Thanksgiving holiday the Tracy family went to Lake Geneva. They met Ken Edgers and liked him immediately. Carrie Tracy invited Ken to spend the Christmas holidays in Milwaukee. She became his 'Wisconsin Mother', and 1919 was the first of three Christmas seasons Edgers would spend with the Tracys. They gave him full credit for the remarkable change that had come over Spencer, who was talking of going to college as if it were something he had always planned to do.

Although Spencer was serious about college, his father was afraid he would lose interest in it just as quickly as he had gotten it. But John Tracy counted on Spencer's friendship with Ken Edgers. He wrote Edgers' father in Seattle, suggesting that a small college like Ripon might be the right spot for both their sons. Mr. Edgers agreed, and both boys were to be enrolled in Ripon.

But Spencer's checkered academic career hounded him. Graduation from Northwestern in June would still leave him with too few course credits. He reluctantly agreed to make up the credits. He withdrew from Northwestern and returned to Milwaukee to cram.

He was still short a few credits when Ken Edgers entered Ripon in the fall of 1920. Spencer was impatient with what he thought was his slow progress, and no interesting jobs were available to distract him from the idea of going to college.

When Kenny Edgers spent Christmas in 1920 with his 'Milwaukee family' Spencer was delighted to hear how much his friend liked Ripon. Spencer's credits were finally in order, and he had been accepted for admission to Ripon at the beginning of the new semester in January. He said he wanted to become a doctor; actually he had something quite different in mind, but wanted to wait until he could try out the idea before he upset his family by telling them his plans.

The Milwaukee that he was leaving had changed since Spencer was a little boy. Most of the cobblestoned streets were now paved with asphalt, and the gaslights were gone from Prospect Avenue. Even in this hard-working industrial city the tempo was picking up; even in Milwaukee one could feel the arrival of the jazz age.

It was snowing when Spencer left Milwaukee. Uncertain but hopeful, he headed for Ripon, and a fresh start.

CHAPTER TWO

THE THEATER YEARS: 1921–1930

RIPON is a pleasant small town about ninety miles north-west of Milwaukee. Hidden in the cool lake country of central Wisconsin, it seems the ideal small college town.

Ripon College was the heartbeat of the community. The liberal arts college was seventy years old when Spencer Tracy entered as a freshman in January of 1921. It had been one of the first coeducational institutions in the Mid-west, and now had more than a hundred women students and several hundred men. There were several dozen war veterans, but they were mostly upper classmen. Ripon College was nondenominational, and the student body was largely Protestant.

Ken Edgers and Spencer were to be roommates again, in the West Hall dormitory. Les Werner, an upper classman who would become one of Tracy's good friends, told him all he needed to know: the Ripon girls were great, but there weren't enough to go around; Fond du Lac girls were not impressive, but they were plenty fast; the real charmers were in Oshkosh, a lively town filled with nice people who all went to bed at nine o'clock; the college, like its president, Dr. Silas Evans, was pretty stuffy on the surface, but you could find the action if you looked.

John Davies, whose dormitory room was next to Spencer's, was a leading actor in the plays put on at the college. He introduced Spencer to the drama teacher, J. Clark Graham, who was young and attractive like most of the Ripon faculty. Graham, Tracy guessed, should probably have been an actor. Instead, he was Ripon's one-man theater department, and he had helped the students put on plays such as *Come Out of the Kitchen* and *Sweet Lavender* with Jack Davies playing the lead.

Graham's first impression of Tracy was that he was more mature than most freshmen; he already had poise and a quiet dignity. Graham was especially impressed by Tracy's decisive, almost clipped manner of speaking, and he invited him to read for the spring play. Clyde Fitch's *The Truth*.

At tryouts, Tracy was nervous as he waited in the wings for his entrance. In a fluster to enter on time, he tripped over a music stand stored offstage with the orchestra's instruments. Tracy made his entrance somewhat out of character for the part.

'Gosh, I think I busted the drum,' he said. Everyone burst out laughing. Tracy salvaged his poise, and began the reading. Tracy was holding his script while saying his lines but he wasn't looking at it, even when listening to the other actors; he had memorized the lines while waiting in the wings, and now he delivered them in a voice that had strength and authority.

'Who *is* that?' Ethel Williams asked. She was one of the prettiest girls in the dramatic club, and it was assumed she would take the female lead in *The Truth*.

'I don't know who it is,' someone told her, 'but you're going to have a good chance to find out.'

In his letters home, Tracy scarcely mentioned having been cast in the leading role of the college play. He told them that he was having a good time at Ripon (he was), that the money was holding out nicely (it wasn't), that he was doing well in his classes (not really true), and that they were welcome to come to Ripon to see *The Truth* (they came).

The play was a Ripon sensation. Most people thought it was the school's best stage presentation to date. Tracy became a local celebrity. His mother was proud of him, but his father was worried. John Tracy wondered how far his son would carry his interest in the theater, but Spencer assured him that he wanted to be a doctor. Spencer winked at Carrie Tracy, for she had become interested in Christian Science.

Professor Graham, in praising Tracy for his performance in *The Truth*, suggested he find out as much about the theater as he could. He guided Tracy on which books to study and what to look for. Tracy would not be selective about it: he was hungry for anything and everything he could find that concerned acting or the theater. He had never been one to read for pleasure but now reading became his first passion in the dormitory. His playgoing experience was slight, and he learned that most of his West Hall friends knew more about the theater than he did. But he had seen Laurette Taylor in a touring production of *Peg O' My Heart* and had decided that her naturalness and sense of *being* the character she was playing onstage would be his own goal. He was satisfied that *The Truth* had pointed him in the right direction, and if he needed further persuasion it came from his mother. She wrote him that Bill O'Brien had put on a show called *The Fanciful Follies* that was a big success at Milwaukee's old Pabst Theater.

The term ended, summer came, and Tracy had an invitation from the Edgers family to go to Seattle with Ken. They first visited the Tracys in Milwaukee and planned a trip west through the Canadian Rockies that would include a stop at Banff and a visit to Lake Louise. That vacation was to be perhaps the only really carefree experience of Tracy's adult life; he had reached the age of twenty-one just before performing in *The Truth*.

The Edgers family had a house in Seattle and a cottage on Fox Island. The boys spent most of the time on Fox Island — fishing and boating, swimming, and digging clams. Tracy continued to cultivate his new penchant for reading, and discovered a magazine short story that he thought he could adapt into a one-act play. He spent hours at the typewriter in the cottage, working out his own adaptation of *The Valiant*.

Tracy and Edgers went up Mount Rainier, sailed out into the ocean, and acquired suntans. They sailed from Portland, Oregon, to San Francisco on the S.S. *Rose City*. They toured the Monterey peninsula, visited an aunt of Tracy's in San

Jose, and left San Francisco by train for Wisconsin, stopping off at the Grand Canyon, before returning to Ripon.

At college, Tracy, already well-known for his acting, was considered a good catch, but he played the field and didn't get deeply involved. In later years, his studio would say that the young Tracy could not overcome his shyness toward girls, but the West Hall gang wouldn't have agreed. Tracy had charm, and envious friends said that he had the ladies 'eating out of his ungrateful Irish palm'. That he did not date heavily was the ladies' disappointment, not his.

Periodically a West Hall group would take the train to Oshkosh, on Lake Winnebago, where the girls were eager for the attentions of college men. The boys were generally without much money. When they ran short they slept gratis in a hotel lobby where a friendly charwoman would supply pillows. They kept just enough money for the return fare to Ripon, but Jack Davies suspected that 'Spencer had plenty of money and didn't let on . . . he could have had a nice hotel room, but if we were going to rough it in a park or a hotel lobby, so was he.'

Davies had suggested that Tracy should consider taking the public-speaking course he was enrolled in, and so Tracy did. But he was less than happy about the instructor. Professor H. P. Boody had given him a rough time in a literature course, and their relationship had not improved when Boody saw Tracy play in *The Truth*.

'Anyone who can act as well as that is intelligent enough to do far better in his studies than you have, Mr. Tracy.'

Tracy could not take criticism gracefully, nor could he realize that people like Professor Boody were doing him a favor by being hard on him.

One day Boody told the public-speaking class to prepare some material with emotional content for an oral presentation. Tracy didn't do his homework, and the next day Boody called on him first. Tracy thought about it for a moment. He walked slowly to the platform, faced his audience, stared around mournfully, and finally spoke.

'I would like to tell you about . . . my sister.'

And he described his sparkling and enchanting sister, who had died in childhood. The class froze in attention. Jack Davies, who had met Tracy's parents and brother and had never known of the unfortunate sister, was startled. Some of the girls in the class were tearful as Tracy described her death, and Tracy's voice broke at the end. 'And that . . . was my sister.' Professor Boody was visibly shaken.

The class sat stricken. Should they applaud? In the past, they always had; this time they did not. After the class was over, Boody approached Davies, knowing he was Tracy's friend. He wondered if he should offer his condolences. Davies told the professor he would talk to Tracy.

'Say, Spence, I was sorry about what you told the class. So was Professor Boody, and he wanted you to know.'

Tracy looked incredulously at Davies.

'Are you kidding? Hell, I don't have a sister, not even a dead one. I was in a spot that's all.'

'Well, don't tell Professor Boody! He doesn't suspect that you're as good an actor as I *know* you are.'

Around the West Hall, Jack Davies was regarded as one of Tracy's best friends. They got along well, but Davies later said that although he 'always liked Spence, as everybody did, I never really felt close to him, because that was the way he seemed to want it . . . you had to go to Spence, he just didn't reach out.'

Other Tracy chums agreed that 'beyond the point of casual friendship Spence would put up barriers'. But although no one knew him well, except for Ken Edgers, many liked Tracy; he was elected president of West Hall for the winter quarter.

In describing Tracy and Edgers, Jack Davies remembered: 'Their military academy training was still with them. Their room would be in perfect order, clothes put away neatly, everything clean. Spence was very fussy about the way his clothes looked, and whether his shoes were polshed.'

Edgers' and Tracy's friendly competition in tidiness

29

reached a climax when Tracy noticed a pair of Edgers' shoes on his side of the room. He picked them up and tossed them out the window. Edgers promptly seized a pair of Tracy's shoes and did the same. Tracy grabbed an arm-load of clothes from Edgers's wardrobe. Out they went, Edgers reciprocated. And then there was no stopping them. Students coming from lunch at the Commons saw clothes floating down from the third floor of West Hall, and soon almost the entire student body had gathered to cheer. Hysterical with laughter, the two boys kept on until there was no clothing left in the room. Then Tracy tackled the bedding. Down it came, including the mattresses. The rugs came next. Finally the room was bare. The sophomores corralled some freshmen and made them carry everything up three flights and then put things in order.

In the fall, *The Valiant* was staged with Tracy as the doomed convict-hero ('Cowards die a thousand times before their death; the valiant never taste of death but once.'). That same year, the story had been professionally adapted into a one-act play, but it was Tracy's own unauthorized, nonroyalty version that was put on at Ripon. The result was another dramatic success. His parents again came to Ripon to see the show, and Spencer seized this moment, when his father was obviously proud of him, to announce his intention of becoming a professional actor. He added that he would rather do it sooner than later, and would quit school to try the stage once he was satisfied that he was 'ready'. That was too much for John Tracy, whose Irish temper exploded. He asked Jack Davies what he thought about his son's crazy idea of wanting to become an actor.

'Mr. Tracy,' Davies smiled, 'your son already *is* an actor.'

John Tracy plainly didn't like the idea, and that was that.

'Can you imagine that face ever being a matinee idol?' he asked, indicating his son. It was the era of the classic John Barrymore profile and the sensitive young faces of Wallace Reid and Richard Barthelmess. And the dark beauty of the newcomer,Valentino. No, they couldn't imagine. Spencer decided to let the matter rest for a while.

*   *   *

Intercollegiate debate was in its heyday, and little Ripon was an aggressive contributor to the national movement. The men on the college debating team were among the most important students on campus. H. P. Boody, who was mainly responsible for encouraging the activity at the college, had kept an eye on Tracy. After seeing *The Valiant*, he suggested that Tracy come out for debate.

Boody undoubtedly had a special interest in Tracy, who was often careless about studying and who, despite his apparent talent, seemed to go astray. Boody appeared to favor Tracy and to give him consideration that some of the other debators doubted he deserved. When Boody selected Tracy as one of the three members of the Eastern Debating Team, which would make a late-winter swing through the midwestern and eastern states and Canada for interscholastic competition, several of the boys felt slighted. But Boody was out to win as many debates as he could, and he needed Tracy.

Before going on the road with the debating team, Tracy and some of the other Ripon actors decided to make a try at professional theater. *The Truth* was long over, but it was fondly remembered. The students developed a scheme to take the play on a tour of the Wisconsin hinterlands. Most of the cast were still at the college; Ethel Williams, who had graduated, came back to resume her old role. They planned an ambitious intinerary of one-night stands during the Christmas holidays; bookings were confirmed, and refresher rehearsals were carried out. The Campus Players would perform at Stevens Point, Fond du Lac, Wisconsin Rapids, Shawano, Plymouth, Wausau, and Sheboygan.

The students wanted to take legitimate drama to towns that had not seen it. It seemed a good idea, but they would have to put up with some annoyances. One was an unusually harsh Wisconsin winter. The troupe collected a crowd of perhaps fifty people at Stevens Point, but at the other stops all they could expect was ten or twenty dedicated theatergoers. At Wausau only the janitor and his very large family showed up to see the play, gratis. The temperature stayed far below zero throughout the tour, but Tracy and Jack Davies stifled all talk about canceling the show. The Campus Players went broke and did not collect their salaries, but with true professional spirit, they saw to it that the show went on.

In Shawano the theater had no working heating system, and the young actors' hands were so numbed by the cold that they needed help buttoning their costumes. With teeth chattering, they joked that 'they shall see *The Truth* and *The Truth* shall make them freeze'.

In most of the towns they played in opera houses that had been dark for years. In Plymouth there was heat, but the ancient pipes coughed and sputtered throughout the performance. However, the audiences, albeit small, were full of appreciation, and reviewers were enthusiastic. The notices were displayed conspicuously at Ripon and the players were hailed for their feat.

The Ripon plays made Tracy aware of his extraordinary ability for memorizing printed material, and he decided to make the most of it. Perhaps he also wanted to get over a kind of intellectual inferiority complex he had acquired. Tracy would spend a few minutes each day at the college library, poring over old magazines. Then in the evening at dinner, he would casually ask, 'What do you know about the four horsemen of the Apocalypse?' or 'Chinese water clocks have an interesting history, don't you think?' When no one was able to contribute much to the conversation he would say with some smugness, 'Boy, are you stupid!' Then he would casually recite what he had learned that day.

Lois Heberlein happened to see Tracy in the library doing his secret research. After he left she looked at the article he had been studying. 'Mussel shoals of Louisiana!' She then briefed Kenny Edgers (her future husband) on all the facts in the article.

'All right, men,' Tracy said putting down his fork. 'What do any of you know about mussel shoals?'

'Mussel shoals!' The grinning Edgers allowed it was his favorite subject. If Spencer Tracy was so curious, he'd have to hear all about them. Tracy's forays in the library stopped abruptly.

Edgers and the Crimson Orchestra played for all the parties at the college and in the neighboring towns. Tracy was not cut out to be a musician, but he was such good company on the trips and in the bull sessions during intermissions that Edgers managed to get Tracy named 'financial manager' to justify his traveling with the orchestra. Contrary to rumor, Tracy never played the tuba in college; he *carried* the tuba. It was also his free ticket to all the football games.

While the debating team was making final plans for its three-week eastern tour, Tracy's parents visited the college to talk with Spencer's teachers about his future. His father still was opposed to his acting professionally and Professor Boody had a hunch that the boy was a born lawyer. But Dr. Clark Graham had a different opinion. Yes, Graham assured the Tracys, Spencer definitely had all the earmarks of a professional actor. He also doubted that Ripon could do much more toward preparing him for a theater career. John Tracy was afraid that Spencer would leave college for acting, then give up in discouragement, and have no college degree to help him get a regular job. Graham suggested that if Spencer decided to leave Ripon, he might consider a professional training school such as New York's American Academy of Dramatic Arts. He offered to write to the Academy. The reply was an offer for Tracy to try out. The eastern debating tour called for three days in New York, and Tracy decided that he would audition then.

On Washington's Birthday, 1922, the Eastern Debating Team left Ripon on the first leg of their tour. Besides Professor Boody, the team included Tracy, Harold Bumby, and Curtis MacDougall.

Bumby became a good friend during the debates. He was a

Ripon boy who seemed destined for success. He was the first speaker for the team. Tracy was the middle man, and Mac-Dougall who, like Bumby, had been on the team before, was last. MacDougall, it was generally agreed, had the quickest wit on campus and was the real 'brains' of the debating team, while Bumby was a skillful orator. Of Tracy, the *Crimson* yearbook said: 'he was perfectly at home on the platform and usually contented himself with hammering one or two main arguments ... his forceful presentation and stage appearance won him much applause.' The yearbook added, 'perhaps the local platform has never seen three men who worked together as well as Bumby, Tracy, and MacDougall.'

In Chicago, on the way to its first debate with Illinois Wesleyan at Bloomington, the team saw a performance of *The Claw* at the Blackstone Theater, and Tracy was enthralled by the acting of Lionel Barrymore.

'He wasn't acting at all, in the usual way,' Tracy said. 'Everything he did, his little movements and gestures, was so basic and natural that people didn't notice them. He coughed right in the middle of a speech, and it was part of the characterization. He was doing what Laurette Taylor did ... just being.'

Barrymore joined Miss Taylor at the top of Tracy's list, and after seeing *The Claw*, Tracy decided that his own acting was not nearly good enough.

The Ripon debators won two of three decisions on the tour and ended one debate in a tie. They traveled to Indianapolis, Buffalo, and Niagara Falls, and on into Canada with stops at Hamilton, Toronto, and at Montreal, where they were greatly impressed with the cathedral. Harold Bumby and MacDougall stood in the rear while Tracy walked up to the altar and knelt to pray. When he returned he winked at them.

'I just fixed the next debate.'

And they won the next debate.

Bumby felt that Tracy would have made a fine politician because 'he was one of those fortunate individuals whom everybody liked ... he did not make any great effort to be liked but was always his good, solid self.'

Bumby thought that he and Tracy would make a good team, and on the train from Boston to New York they discussed the possibility of entering business together. Tracy thought it could give him something to fall back on if he failed the acting audition.

He had chosen scenes from *The Truth* and *The Valiant* and had rehearsed them over and over for the audition, and in addition he had a well-memorized, personally interpreted Gettysburg Address. He also had the one-act script of *Sintram of Skagerrak*.

'It will be simpler if I flunk. If I pass the test, then I just won't know *what* to do.'

They arrived in New York on Sunday, and on the following morning Tracy arranged by telephone for a Tuesday audition with Mr. Sargent at the Academy. Bumby was taken ill and a doctor came to the hotel room to treat him, so Tracy explored the theater district alone. He walked for hours through the West Thirties and Forties where the playhouses were, and paused to absorb every poster, every stage photograph, every suggestion of the actor's world. Evening came and the lights went on, proclaiming old stars like John Drew and Mrs. Leslie Carter, who were completing their engagement in Maugham's *The Circle*, and young stars like Helen Hayes in *To the Ladies* and Katharine Cornell in *A Bill of Divorcement*. John Barrymore had opened in *Hamlet* and Tracy tried, and failed, to get a ticket. He settled for Al Jolson's long-run hit, *Bombo*, and when he returned to the hotel room he serenaded the suffering Bumby with an off-key version of *April Showers*. Bumby survived it, and the next morning felt up to going with Tracy to see Mr. Sargent. Tracy insisted on it; and he had to know there was an audience out there.

*   *   *

The American Academy of Dramatic Arts was located in the Carnegie Hall building and the identification plate visible from the street still read, 'The Sargent School of Acting'. Franklin Havens Sargent had founded his school in 1884 and over the years had developed it into the most nearly complete academy of theatrical training in the country. It had become a part of the Broadway Establishment. Producers and other theater professionals came to the student performances and helped support the school's operation with scholarships and other grants. Although Charles Jehlinger, as the school's director, had almost full control, Sargent still auditioned the prospective students.

The secretary ushered Tracy and Bumby into a small theater. Sargent was seated at his desk on the upstage portion of a small proscenium stage. A photograph of Jane Cowl — one of the more famous graduates — was on the wall behind his desk, and pictures of William and Cecil DeMille — also alumni — hung on another wall.

The lean, sharp-eyed Sargent was courteous. He mentioned Graham's letter, and he asked Tracy if he had brought along anything like a skit. Tracy brought *Sintram of Skagerrak* from his pocket and explained that the passage he had in mind needed two actors. Sargent agreed to read the minor part, and Bumby seated himself as an audience of one.

Tracy had selected an especially dramatic passage. At the end Sargent gave Tracy a long look and then said, 'Yes, yes, yes.' Sargent told Tracy he would be eligible for the new term beginning in June, but that if he wanted to enroll sooner he might be promoted more rapidly to senior status. Tracy asked Sargent if a lack of good looks would hurt his progress in the theater.

'Why, that's ridiculous. You're a good masculine type, and there never are enough of those, either here in the Academy or in the theater. A good voice is far more vital than a pretty face.' Tracy noticed that Sargent, who certainly did not have a pretty face, was still in splendid voice.

They shook hands. Tracy and Bumby left, and Tracy was quickly submerged in depression. It was natural with him when a decision had to be made.

He returned in triumph to Ripon after the successful debating tour, and he knew he could expect two more comfortable years as an undergraduate. But what then? He asked Boody for advice, and the professor advised him to stay in school until June and then look into summer stock in the Midwest.

Tracy wrote to his parents and his father wrote an affectionate letter back, saying that he was willing to cover the Academy tuition if that was what Spencer really wanted.

Harold Bumby suggested that a talk with his older brother could do no harm. Horace Bumby was a successful Ripon businessman and was regarded as a clear thinker and a sensible man. Tracy spent an evening in his home discussing the problem, and Horace told him he had no choice but to try the stage.

'You've got to get it out of your system, Spencer. You can never be completely satisfied unless and until you've given it a trial.'

That may have been what decided him, or it may have been that Kenneth Edgers was also leaving Ripon to enter the University of Southern California School of Dentistry.

In any event, the decision was made. But perhaps Tracy felt guilty about it, for he kept it a secret. Tryouts for the spring play were coming up, and he let people think that he would be available to perform again. He went through the season's final debate on March 20, which proved to be another triumph for Bumby, Tracy and MacDougall. Tracy was wet-eyed in accepting congratulations, for it was his last Ripon debate. That same week he withdrew from classes, without ceremony, and left before most of the West Hall gang knew what he had done.

'I felt guilty about it,' Tracy would recall, 'Because the place had been such an eye-opener for me. I was running away again, just as I had run away from home earlier. I was always running away from something.'

*   *   *

37

Spencer Tracy arrived in New York a few days after cele-
brating his twenty-second birthday with his family in Milwaukee. His father was gloomy about his son's prospects, but
Mrs. Tracy was sure that Spencer knew what he wanted to
do and that he would be a success.

The agreement between father and son was that Spencer
was to live on his monthly veteran's check of thirty dollars,
which would continue as long as he retained some kind of
designation as a student. Mr. Tracy would cover the tuition
of the American Academy of Dramatic Arts.

Spencer found a room on West 96th Street for two dollars
a week. It was 'about the size of a jail cell and furnished like
one, with a shared toilet and a shared bath that cost extra'.
He tried to stick to a tight budget, but after a few sparse
meals of sardines and crackers he would be forced to splurge.
Once he enjoyed a steak dinner in a midtown restaurant, and
then went to see the popular John Golden production of
Seventh Heaven. Then he took a cab back to his seedy West
Side room, and swore he would pinch his pennies.

At a local cigar store, Tracy ran into an old friend, Bill
O'Brien. They were delighted to find one another. O'Brien,
now called Pat, knew of a room for rent at 790 West End
Avenue, off 98th Street, that would do for two. The landlady
liked young actors and had been known to let them board on
credit.

Tracy recalled their room as a drab, sparsely furnished
twelve-by-twelve with twin iron beds and twin washstands
'with twin cracks'.

Pat O'Brien had been looking for acting jobs and had even
done a turn as a hoofer in a musical. He and Tracy had both
been accepted by Mr. Sargent at the American Academy of
Dramatic Arts. Spencer quickly decided that Pat knew
everybody in show business, or at least knew who the people
were who really counted. Pat O'Brien could tell tales of Al
Woods, Sam Harris, Arthur Hopkins, and William A. Brady.
Even then Pat was a superb storyteller and gave Tracy the
rundown on all the Broadway personalities.

At the Academy, Tracy was interviewed by Charles

38

Jehlinger, whom the students privately called 'Jelly'. Jehlinger, the Academy's director, read Franklin Havens Sargent's report of Tracy's audition. Sargent's notebook was filled with impressions of many young actors who later became famous. Sargent thought that Tracy had a good deal to learn, but recognized the special quality of his speaking voice.

More than twenty years later Charles Jehlinger remembered that 'if Tracy understood you — and he did almost always — he did what you asked of him immediately and decisively . . . he was a most responsive pupil.' Tracy did less well with the other teachers, for he was quickly bored with the drills in speech and movement. He learned fencing, but told Jehlinger that he would much rather act.

Most of the Academy students were girls in their late teens, wealthy New York debutantes for whom dramatic training was merely an extension of finishing school. With a few exceptions, they were more interested in finding husbands than in theatrical careers. The few male students were more serious about acting, and most were struggling to make ends meet.

Tracy had a crush on a dark beauty named Olga Brent who was one of the more dedicated young actresses, but he kept his passion a secret because he couldn't afford to woo her in style. Anita Damrosch, the daughter of conductor Walter Damrosch, was in his class, as was Kay Johnson, who was to appear in the Kaufman-Connelly *Beggar on Horseback* and make a career in early talking pictures.

Tracy's new friends included George Meeker and Charles Wagenheim, and the blond Sterling Holloway, with piccolo voice and funny face. Charles Callahan, a handsome Irish boy, never went on to a career in the theatre, but Tracy thought him the best all-around actor at the Academy.

Another student fascinated Tracy. The slick and genial Monroe Owsley, only twenty, was already wise to the ins and outs of theater life. Owsley usually had plenty of money and sometimes invited Tracy to help spend it. He knew jockeys who had tips on fixed races, girls in Brooklyn with liberal ideas, and doormen at Manhatten speakeasies. He told Tracy he had enrolled at the Academy not for the training, but for the connections. 'You have to push,' he said.

He claimed there were no more than a dozen Broadway offices that really had star-making power. Tracy thought Owsley was cynical, but he listened to him.

Owsley looked down on most of the Academy students, but welcomed Tracy's company because he considered Tracy the only student who was a better actor than himself. He grandly promised Tracy that he would help him break into the business. To Tracy's surprise, it happened.

Owsley got a walk-on in a Broadway play and, almost simultaneously, was offered a second one. He passed the word to Tracy. Owsley assured him it was a great non-speaking part: one of the robots.

Tracy didn't know what a robot was, but he had heard of *R.U.R.*, they play by the Czech dramatist Karel Capek now being produced by the Theater Guild. Aside from giving the word 'robot' to the English language, the science-fiction play was to become a classic.

Tracy saw the stage manager and obtained the part on a warm-body, no-audition basis. The salary was fifteen dollars a week. He went on stage immediately, without a rehearsal; he was told to do what the other robots did. Robot Tracy entered through a trapdoor at the beginning of the last act. He was to move mechanically and keep a poker face. There wasn't much challenge to it, but it was money and it was Broadway. When Tracy learned that another robot was leaving the play, he got Pat O'Brien to fill the spot. The big break was celebrated by a binge of thick steaks, instead of the standard Tracy–O'Brien menu of water, rice, and pretzels.

Toward the end of the run Tracy took over a minor speaking role and his salary was increased to twenty-five dollars. When a bigger role became available he tried for it, but was vetoed when one of the principals — England's Basil Sydney — claimed that Tracy lacked style. Defining style was standard procedure at the American Academy of Dra-

40

matic Arts and Tracy contributed his own definition: style, as he had just discovered, was an Oxford accent.

Pat O'Brien didn't finish the course at the Academy, but Tracy did. The seniors put on various short plays and scenes as a requirement for graduation. Tracy managed to be given several roles, and shared with Charles Callahan the distinction of being cast in five of the plays.

The scenes were presented in the Lyceum Theater the week before the Academy graduation ceremony in March of 1923. Invitations went out to most of the Establishment.

Tracy did best in the comedies. He was a hit in *The Wooing of Eve*, a short play that Hartley Manners had written for Laurette Taylor (then his wife). Tracy and Olga Brent acted superbly together in Harley Graville-Barker's *The Marrying of Ann Leete*. The most enthusiastic backstage congratulations were for Tracy, but Monroe Owsley, who was also in the play, was the real winner: a scout for Belasco signed him for a juvenile lead in a new comedy.

The Academy's special offering was Oscar Wilde's *The Importance of Being Earnest*, presented uncut. It was a roaring success with Callahan and Holloway as the male leads, and with Tracy in the character part of the minister. No producers or even agents showed any interest in Tracy, but there were encouraging words from some famous actors. Mr. and Mrs. Charles Coburn specifically praised Tracy in a note of congratulation to the Academy, and there was a report that Mrs. Fiske had been most complimentary. (On his twenty-third birthday Tracy attended his first Broadway opening, watching Mrs. Fiske from the balcony of the National Theater in *The Dice of the Gods*. He was glum about her performance, for he swore that he couldn't hear a word the lady said.)

With graduation came the end of the monthly veteran's allowance, and Tracy stood at a crossroads. He knew he could act, but he didn't know if he could earn a living at it. In later years he would recall the spring and early summer of 1923 as the most harrowing time of his life.

In the Broadway casting offices his own worst enemy was

Spencer Tracy. He was not rude on purpose, but his impatience and brashness did not sit well with the men in charge. A mounting prejudice against Irish actors didn't help. Tracy made the rounds but seldom got beyond the first interview.

Tracy paid a call at George M. Cohan's office and was unable to get past the secretary, but he left a photograph and biographical sketch with her. Very soon afterward the secretary telephoned Tracy with an invitation to read a part in a new Cohan production; it seemed that Cohan was already familiar with Tracy's acting. That puzzled Tracy, for Cohan had not attended the Academy plays (Cohan and Jehlinger were not on friendly terms) and it was unlikely that he had noticed Tracy in *R.U.R.*

When Tracy reported to the Cohan office, George M. glared at him and said, 'I don't know you at all.' Cohan had mistaken Spencer for Lee Tracy, also a relative newcomer. Spencer Tracy was not given a reading.

Both O'Brien and Tracy had a hard time of it. Jobs were few and hard to get in the theater. Tracy tried to take on Broadway, while O'Brien was willing to try bit parts with stock companies. Tracy would take on odd jobs when the money ran out. He was a door-to-door salesman briefly, and for a time he sold magazine subscriptions. He tried being a bellhop and a janitor, but would quit in disgust. If he wasn't going to act, he might as well go back to Milwaukee.

Clifton Webb once enlisted Tracy's aid in moving a piano for the musical star Irene Bordoni, and the story grew over the years until one could read that Tracy supported himself by moving pianos. Tracy did pick up a few dollars with boxing gloves, by sparring in a Bowery gymnasium.

Tracy and O'Brien helped each other out during these rough times. Luckily O'Brien was an irrepressible optimist and was able to pull Tracy out of a bad mood.

Since their measurements were almost identical, between them they had a substantial wardrobe. Both Spencer and Pat were known to wear beautiful pongee shirts, but never at the same time. O'Brien also had a full-dress suit that he inherited, in lieu of salary, from a stock company that went broke; Tracy purchased a half interest in the suit for five dollars. With the tuxedo, they could pick up jobs modeling — one at a time, of course.

As summer approached, the only job listings Tracy found at the Actors' Equity office were for out-of-town stock. And the only part he landed was a walk-on that lasted one week. Pat O'Brien finally took a job with a stock company in New Jersey.

Tracy's father had been urging him to return to Milwaukee, and Spencer may have thought about it. By June he was broke, behind in his rent, and his telephone had been removed. He could write home for money, or he could accept a small loan from his landlady. But Tracy was losing his confidence. Just when he decided to go home, he was unexpectedly rescued, and his career was on its way.

His landlady delivered a message from someone — Tracy never learned the identity of the caller — who had been trying to get in touch with him. A stock company being organized by Leonard Wood, Jr., son of the famous general, needed an actor for several parts.

Tracy checked at the Equity office and learned that Wood was in White Plains, where his troupe would be engaged for one month. Tracy gambled: he wired Wood, collect.

The younger Wood's career as a producer was brief and unsuccessful, but Spencer Tracy thought he was in a class by himself, a true gentleman, and the only person in show business he ever knew to accept a collect telegram.

A return wire was received later that day. Wood accepted Tracy for his company, and sent a money order for his first week's salary of forty dollars. He paid his rent and celebrated in style.

A few days later, when Tracy was in Grand Central Station, waiting for the train to White Plains, he spotted a young woman who had a good many suitcases. He followed her into the train and took a seat close to hers. Although their eyes never met, he sensed that she was just as aware of him.

43

Louise Treadwell was striking rather than pretty. She had neat, dark brown hair and a fair complexion. She was a Pennsylvanian by birth, and had attended Lake Erie College for Women before trying the stage. Within a few years she had a reputation as a promising young actress in stock. And she had a Broadway play to her credit.

She too had checked the call board at the Equity office, and among the actors assigned to the Leonard Wood company she found the name of Spencer Tracy. She thought the name suggested a solid sort of man who would be interesting to know.

At White Plains they introduced themselves and learned that they were both going to the Leonard Wood office. Louise Treadwell was the new company's leading lady. Tracy was to be less important — he was to take on bit parts.

The brief rehearsal period taught Tracy more than just his lines. He soon lost his awe of 'professional' actors, for most of Wood's players were less accomplished and much less idealistic than some of the students at the Academy. Tracy rebelled at the company's weaknesses and asked Wood for larger roles, but without success. Tracy did respect the leading lady, who managed to keep calm through all the chaos. In fact, he had fallen in love with Louise Treadwell and she with him.

Tracy always said later that Louise had been a big star who had no business getting entangled with an untried, undependable young actor. But Louise, for whom true stardom was as yet an unrealized hope, knew her man. Tracy had captured her heart and commanded her respect as well.

She told of Tracy's impact in his first assignment with the Wood company. The play was *The Man Who Came Back*, she was the leading lady, and Tracy's speaking part consisted of only one line: 'To hell with him!' Nonetheless, he never failed to get a burst of applause from the White Plains audience. Louise knew he was destined for bigger roles and she saw to it that it happened quickly. When the White Plains engagement ended she arranged to have Spencer Tracy included as part of the package in her next stock assignment. This time he would be her leading man.

Their booking was with the Repertory Theater of Cincinnati under Stuart Walker's supervision. Unlike Leonard Wood, Walker had spent most of his life in the theater and had made it pay. A Cincinnatian by birth, he had worked with a repertory company in Indianapolis before going to New York and organizing the Portmanteau Theater. He returned to Cincinnati to do classical repertory, but box-office pressures made him settle for a standard stock company, which put on mainly Avery Hopwood comedies. For Tracy it was a big step upward, and his salary was set at seventy-five dollars a week.

In the year 1923 the United States had a lively national theater and its name was stock. Although Broadway had the prestige, stock production was in its heyday, and it made playwriting a lucrative profession.

Every large city had its own stock companies, while the medium-sized towns entertained touring companies that traveled by bus from one town to another. The plays were mainly farces and comedies and most were written as formula pieces geared to conventional staging and easily portable scenery. Few stock companies employed stage designers; most acquired the flats, drops, and special props from theatrical warehouses that flourished in New York and across the country, and borrowed furniture and other props in each town in exchange for free passes to the performances.

Talking pictures, radio, and the Depression curtailed the life of stock theater, yet many, including Tracy, felt that stock companies had raised the quality of American acting to levels it was never again to achieve.

The directors in stock were mainly concerned with their deadline, and so the actors were thrown on their own resources. The company would be performing one play, rehearsing another, and learning a third one. However exhausting the schedule, it gave the young actor discipline.Tracy thrived on it.

45

Almost twenty years later Stuart Walker, then a movie producer for Paramount, admitted that he hadn't been aware of Tracy's potential, but he remembered him as a dynamo whose own application made the other actors push harder. Walker recalled that Tracy would have his part down pat by the first rehearsal call, and that other actors would be chagrined to find that he knew their parts before they did.

Tracy was always restless until a new part was memorized, and he was eager to get it on the stage. It was in his days in stock that he first developed the early-morning insomnia that plagued him the rest of his life.

Tracy was playing opposite Louise Treadwell in *Buddies* for Walker's Cincinnati company when he proposed marriage. Tracy later told different stories about his proposal. In every account, however, he expressed his amazement that Louise would have him — she accepted immediately — and his conviction that he did not deserve her. He felt that Louise had the stability he lacked, as well as all the qualities of a great lady.

It was not Tracy's style to wait. They were married as soon as they could get a license — the date was September 12 — and the show went on. This was one stock circuit marriage that didn't end with the season. And as for the problem of religion (Louise was an Episcopalian), Tracy could point out that his own father was happily married to a non-Catholic.

Tracy and his bride were both doing well in the theater, and they looked forward to a honeymoon on the road. Their plans changed abruptly when the promise of a break for Tracy brought them back to New York.

An agent named Maltby contacted Tracy through Stuart Walker about a part in a new Ethel Barrymore play. The producer was Arthur Hopkins, for whom Tracy had auditioned unsuccessfully before. Hopkins, a colorful and spirited character, was noted for high standards, and Tracy was apprehensive about reading for him. He got the role without an audition, however, when an aide of Hopkins, who had seen Tracy act, put in a good word for him.

Tracy joined the cast of *A Royal Fandango* during its eastern tryout tour, and by the time the play reached New York, Arthur Hopkins knew that he had a turkey on his hands.

Tracy's salary was almost a hundred dollars a week, but because the play's future looked dim, he and Louise rented an inexpensive apartment in Brooklyn. About the time of the play's opening, Louise learned that she was pregnant. Tracy was both delighted and terrified.

A Royal Fandango opened on November 12 at the Plymouth Theater and was panned by the critics. It was a silly comedy about a flirtatious princess and some stolen jewels. Tracy played a detective. A second detective was played by an older, but relatively unknown character actor who was also a graduate of the American Academy of Dramatic Arts. His name was Edward G. Robinson; his long friendship with Tracy began with the failure of Miss Barrymore's fandango, although it was the only time they ever acted together. In one of the more salty reviews, Tracy and Robinson were included in the critic's observation that 'the other players looked as if they had been picked up by the property man.'

Ethel Barrymore had involved herself with *A Royal Fandango* as a favor to playwright Zoe Akins, who had written Miss Barrymore's brilliantly successful *Déclassé* some years earlier. But on this occasion Miss Akins did not fare well. The play would have closed immediately but for the star's personal drawing power, which kept it running for three weeks.

Tracy used to say that the play and Miss Barrymore herself taught him some things he would always remember. He called her composure on the second night 'the best demonstration of class I ever saw.' The other actors arrived at the theater in despair at the reviews, and a child actor named Charles Eaton was crying. When Miss Barrymore arrived, she called the company together. She told them all to smile, relax, and get ready to do their best. 'The important thing is to know that you have done your best. If one knows that, the other disappointments don't mean much.'

Tracy and another actor, Jose Allesandro, watched in the wings as Miss Barrymore made her entrance on the second night, and 'we learned then what a star really is, or rather was, in the theater, and also something of a star's responsibility.'

Tracy said that Ethel Barrymore knew that she *was* the star and never forgot it for a moment, but that she was neither condescending nor haughty. The veteran Cyril Keightley, who was her leading man, looked down on the other actors, but Miss Barrymore made a point of being pleasant to everyone in the cast and crew.

Tracy had small chance for a real friendship with Miss Barrymore. But she remembered his admiration for Lionel Barrymore's acting, and when her older brother visited the Plymouth, she asked Tracy to her dressing room and introduced them. Tracy also met John Barrymore during the brief engagement of *A Royal Fandango*, before both Barrymore brothers went off to Hollywood.

Tracy also took to heart the advice that Ethel Barrymore customarily gave when advice about acting was requested: 'Be yourself.'

Miss Barrymore, he observed, did not bring new physical or vocal mannerisms to a role, but used her offstage style. A few years later, some actors in New York's Lambs Club were discussing Miss Barrymore's performance in *The Kingdom of God*, and William Boyd complained that Ethel's acting was too grand. 'Hell, that's not acting,' Tracy said, 'That's just Ethel.'

When the closing notice for *A Royal Fandango* was posted, Tracy started knocking on Broadway doors again, but without success. The only opportunity was in winter stock work. But at least it was a living. Shortly after the play closed, the Tracys took to the road again, playing in Pittsburgh and Winnipeg.

Even pinching pennies, they were short of money when Louise's advancing pregnancy made it no longer possible for her to work. Actors of the 1920's had few fringe benefits. Once again, Tracy faced a difficult decision.

Tracy's father advised trying some other sort of work. But Louise would not listen to any talk of Spencer giving up acting, even temporarily. Finally Tracy's mother, whose fondness for Louise had been apparent from the beginning, suggested a practical plan. Louise would stay with the Tracy family in Milwaukee and have her baby in their home, and Spencer would continue to work in stock until he could get another break.

The road lost its glitter for Tracy during his months of traveling alone. The other actors found him something of a tightwad and a loner. Tracy knew that mingling was expensive. Nor was there any stimulation in the cardboard roles he usually played. Tracy remembered how hard it was. 'You had to do it the long, hard way ... the trains were as bumpy as a frog's back, and the hotels were boot-camps for bedbugs and roaches.' He still couldn't manage his finances well and would squander dollars after he had hoarded pennies. He had only the consolation of doing his very best on the stage, and he made a point of that.

Tracy quit the road briefly to get to know his son. John Tracy was born in Milwaukee in June of 1924. He was a vigorous, healthy child, and his arrival made leaving home for another grind of stock doubly hard for Spencer Tracy.

*   *   *

In one-night stands or long runs, Tracy always considered himself a 'New York actor'. For some performers stock was what they wanted, and many companies used mostly local residents. A New York actor was not so much one who came from Broadway as one who was headed there, however dim his chances. Many New York actors never made it.

New York actors in professional stock stayed in touch with one another, with agents, and with all the Broadway theater gossip.

There was an Equity office in every city of reasonable size. The Broadway-oriented actors met there to pore over *Variety*. There Tracy saw old friends like George Meeker and

Monroe Owsley, and new ones like Fredric March and Brian Donlevy. He also kept in touch with several friends he and Pat O'Brien had known in New York.

Lynne Overman was one of those old friends, a one-time Milwaukeean who had been first a jockey and then an itinerant 'New York actor' for almost twenty years before he and Tracy became close friends on the road.

The two men shared an interest in prizefights, ball games, and motion pictures. Like many of the friends Tracy was most fond of, Overman was a good listener and naturally optimistic. He knew how to cope with Tracy's periodic glum moods.

Although Overman was finally able to work regularly and made a fair income in films, Spencer Tracy always thought that he was one of the unsung great actors of America. Tracy also claimed that he became a better actor during the brief time he was under Overman's watchful eye.

Tracy was called in as a replacement in a stock production of *The Nervous Wreck* when Overman left to take a Broadway part. Tracy arrived in Toledo for Overman's last performance, after which they spent the night working on the blocking for Tracy's part. Overman pointed out that Tracy telegraphed every physical move before he made it. Overman told him: 'Don't decide to make a move until you do it, and don't move at all unless it's instinctive.' Tracy claimed that Overman made him aware of instinct as an actor's ruling force.

In the midsummer of 1924 Lynne Overman was back on the midwestern road, another Broadway failure behind him. Once again he ran into Tracy. Overman knew of a possible opening for an actor with William Wright's company, in Grand Rapids, Michigan, a company with an excellent reputation. Overman sent a letter to Wright recommending Tracy.

* * *

Tracy visited his family in Milwaukee and was reunited with O'Brien, who was also home for a visit. Then Tracy

O'Brien, who was also looking for work, took the train to Grand Rapids. They spent the night sleeping on park benches and were not looking their best when they met the producer. William Wright was a little disappointed, for the two men weren't exactly elegant.

There was only one opening in the company. They were looking for a suave and handsome leading man. It looked hopeless for either Tracy or O'Brien. But Edwin Milton Royle, the playwright, was a friend of Wright's, and his daughter Selena was the company's leading lady. Royle thought the boys deserved a chance.

Tracy got the part. Wright grumbled that Tracy scrubbed and polished still didn't look like a leading man, but he hoped he might act like one. Thus began Spencer Tracy's association with Selena Royle who, except for Louise, was his first champion.

Selena was twenty, as vibrant as she was young, and certainly a temptation for even the most happily married young man. Many years later, recalling their propriety in an atmosphere that seldom demands it, Miss Royle concluded that 'acting gave us everything we needed, without the usual playing around'.

Tracy did well enough for Wright to sign him up as the leading man for the 1925 season. Wright picked his company members with care. He could afford to, for he paid his actors well. In choosing Tracy he may have been influenced by Edwin Milton Royle, who shared his daughter's enthusiasm for Spencer's acting.

Selena Royal acted with Tracy for several years, a period during which Tracy went through more than one personal crisis.

'There was no one I wanted to act with so much as Spence, and I know he felt the same way. We had our ups and downs, of course, but they were always resolved by good sense, and the pride we both had in doing the best job possible.

'All Spence had to do was walk on the stage and you knew he belonged there . . . he dominated it. It's so difficult to be natural on stage, but it's the only place where Spence *was* completely natural.'

She remembers that 'I was rather stuffy about staying in character. I was always scolding Spence because something unusual would happen and he'd be laughing, right on stage, completely out of character.'

Once Miss Royle was on stage in a scene with Porter Hall and Tracy. She had just made an entrance wearing some sexy silk pajamas. In the middle of her first speech, the elastic gave, and the pajamas suddenly fell to the floor. Porter Hall gaped and turned white; Selena pulled up the pajamas as she heard Tracy's boisterous laugh and roar of approval. She turned on him and yelled right back, 'Shut up, you damn fool!'

And he shut up. Miss Royle remembers that, naturally, they were a hit for the rest of the show.

Spencer's parents often made the trip to Grand Rapids to see him act, and finally even Mr. Tracy had to admit that his son was good at acting and should stick with it. When Tracy at last got this acknowledgment, he felt that he had ended his apprenticeship in the theater. When William Wright arranged for Tracy and Selena Royle to work a twenty-four-week fall-and-winter season of stock in Brooklyn, Tracy decided to reclaim his wife and infant son. He took them with him.

Tracy was the last person to discover that his son was deaf. Louise had found out in Milwaukee in September, 1924, when Johnny was three months old. He was a happy baby, in fact far more serene than other children. But Louise was alarmed by the fact that he cried so seldom, and she consulted a doctor. The diagnosis was that Johnny was totally deaf.

Days and weeks passed. Louise took the baby to a succession of ear specialists, but they all agreed that the affliction was permanent. She told some of Tracy's friends in the theater, including Selena Royle, hoping that someone could give her advice on how to tell Spencer. They all warned her that Tracy would take it badly.

Tracy learned of John's condition during the Brooklyn engagement. He was playing with him one afternoon, and the child was not responding to Tracy's words.

'Hey, this kid acts like he isn't hearing me!' It was the moment Louise Tracy had been dreading.

Tracy's first reaction was what his friends had feared. He fell apart. People said that when Louise found out about John's deafness she worried and took him to a doctor, and that when Spencer found out, he worried and went out to get drunk.

Tracy gave Louise full credit for the eventual successful education of his son. He wanted to help John but realized he 'was no damn good at it. I would come in after she had been working with the boy for hours and start undoing the good Louise had done. Maybe she had been working with him all day on a word like "shoe", showing it to him and saying the word over and over, trying to get him to read her lips. So I would pick up the damn shoe and throw it across the room and scare the poor kid half to death. I had no patience, and it's just amazing how much she had, and has.'

All he could do was pray, and Tracy did that more and more often. He had faith in God and in the power of money to help find a way out. He believed that somewhere there was a doctor, if he could afford his fee, who would be able to give John normal hearing. Failing that, he knew that proper training for a handicapped child would be expensive. He needed to strike it rich.

Louise once again reassured him. Money would help but she thought Spencer's best chance for it would be as an actor. She would not hear of his giving it up.

*   *   *

Although Tracy's success in Grand Rapids built up his ego, he was eager to make the big time. Only success on Broadway would bring in the kind of money he needed.

Earle Boothe, a retired colonel who wanted to produce plays on Broadway, saw a performance of Wright's company

and decided that Tracy was just the actor he had been looking for. He brought a script of a play called *The Sheepman*
to Tracy and offered him the lead. Tracy read it, liked it,
and wanted to do it. But he had to get out of his contract
with Wright. He asked to be released.

Tracy was not known for his tact. He was often blunt and
appeared rude when he was nonplussed or embarrassed. And
he never liked to ask favors of people. Whatever his true
feelings, to Wright, Tracy seemed selfish and ungrateful, and
Wright released him from his company with a good deal of
bad feeling.

The Sheepman opened and closed within a week of its
Stamford, Connecticut, tryout. It was a blow, and *The
Sheepman* was the closest Tracy was to get to Broadway for
another two years.

He settled for a job as the leading man for Frank McCoy's
Trent Stock Company in Trenton, New Jersey. He tried unsuccessfully to have his wife included in the package as the
female lead, for this time Louise was eager to get back to
work. But McCoy had a firm commitment to Ethel Remey,
whom Tracy never liked very much. McCoy had a strong
company that included Natalie Moorehead, Edward Rose
(who had been a classmate of Tracy's at the Academy) and
Leona Roberts, who would be with him at M-G-M some
years later. But McCoy's standards weren't as high as Tracy
would have liked, and he felt his career was moving backward.

The plays were a rehash of old stock favorites, or terrible
plays like *Chicken Feed, Wedding Bells*, and *The Family
Upstairs*. Ethel Remey seemed more concerned with her
hairdo than with her lines. Tracy didn't apply himself. He
slipped into a major depression. At home he was short-tem-
pered and would fly into a rage without real cause. He began
to drink more than he should. Indeed, some members of the
Treat Stock Company would have disputed Tracy's claim of
having never appeared on a stage drunk. Once he was reeling when he arrived at the theater; he had the title role in
George M. Cohan's *The Song and Dance Man*. Tracy liked

the play and that performance was said to be his liveliest of the season.

He stayed with McCoy into 1926, then returned to Grand Rapids for a reconciliation with the Wright Players. He gave his usual good performances, but his defeat didn't sit well with him. Over a three-year period he had performed more than fifty stage roles, but his career was at a standstill. He was gloomy, arrogant, even cruel.

Selena Royale was now in New York, a success as an ingenue. In mid-1926 she was given the lead in a new George M. Cohan play. The play was called *Yellow*, and when one of the secondary actors was fired, Miss Royale thought the part tailormade for Spencer Tracy. The problem would be to convince George M. Cohan.

She enlisted the aid of her father, whom Cohan respected as one of the theater's grand old men. After some skillful plotting on their part, Cohan agreed to give Tracy a reading, and Selena Royal knew that if Tracy read, he would make it.

Tracy arrived in New York on an August morning after a two-day train ride and read for Cohan. He started rehearsing his part after lunch.

By 1926 George M. Cohan was a bitter and battleworn man who disapproved of what was happening to the theater, both in its offices and on its stages. In 1919, Cohan, himself both an actor and a manager, had sided with the managers in the struggle that ended with the formation of the actors' union Equity Association. Cohan was stubborn in defeat, and refused to join. Because he was the king of American musical theater, and had been since the turn of the century the actors ruled that Cohan could continue his various careers without the additional humiliation of joining their union: it was a concession never granted to another performer.

Cohan remained bitter and unforgiving partly because he was a bad loser and partly because he resented the new theatrical fashions that were passing him by. His plays were hardy staples of stock, but the new drama critics paid no

attention to him at all. His old musicals were no longer performed, and his new ones were no longer successful.

But he remained George M. Cohan, the only one the theater had, and he was a power on Broadway. He was writing
less but producing more, and was still someone to reckon
with. And he exerted the singlemost positive influence on the
dramatic art of Spencer Tracy.

They got on well together once Cohan was satisfied that
Tracy was not going to bend over backward to please him.
Cohan knew about little John Tracy's deafness, which Spencer never mentioned, and Cohan's sympathy came through
despite his famous tongue-lashings. When Tracy and Cohan
were at their closest, they loved to insult one another; they
were both masters at needling remarks.

Basically, Cohan and Tracy were a lot alike. The young
Tracy had Cohan's brashness and bounce and nervous
energy. And Cohan could see much of what he once was in
Tracy's acting.

His respect for Tracy was evident during a remarkable
rehearsal of *Yellow* shortly before the play's opening. There
in the National Theater were Cohan's six leading actors:
Chester Morris, the leading man; Hale Hamilton; Shirley
Warde; Selena Royal; Majorie Wood; and Tracy. Cohan
was in top form, bellowing at all the actors except, for some
reason, Tracy, who thought Cohan might be saving the
worst for him.

Cohan liked to sit in the middle of the first row and direct
with his feet, which were propped on the orchestra railing.
Tracy was giving a line when Cohan thumped fiercely on
the railing with his shoes.

'Mister Tracy,' he called out, 'you are the best actor I
have ever seen.'

The rehearsal halted abruptly. Spencer stared out at
Cohan.

'What . . . what did you say?'

Cohan bellowed, 'I said, Tracy, you're the best god-
damned actor I've ever seen. Now, go ahead!'

So they went ahead. After rehearsal, Tracy was puzzled. He said to Selena, 'I wonder what made him say that?'

'He said it because he means it, you damn fool,' Selena answered, feeling a certain pride in having discovered the best actor George M. had ever seen.

The opening-night reviewers weren't as extravagant as Cohan, but they were more than kind to Spencer Tracy. And *Yellow* was a hit. It was a melodrama about a selfish young man who gets his girlfriend pregnant and leaves her. *Yellow* furthered the careers of all its actors, and made Chester Morris a sought-after leading man.

In those days the theater often was sound business, for a play could earn back its investment in a month. *Yellow* ran almost five months, and then went to Chicago for another four weeks. It meant almost five thousand dollars for Tracy, far more than he had earned before in a six-month period. Agents offered to represent him; producers sent him scripts to consider; he was welcomed into the Lambs.

Tracy and his wife lived modestly during these early days of success. They knew by now that in the theater bad days often followed close behind good ones, and of course their son's deafness was a never-ending worry. Tracy's success buoyed him, but at home he would still plunge into gloom more often than Louise liked to see.

And the tension in the household increased as Louise became more and more eager to return to the stage on her own. Tracy, driven by his own feelings of guilt over Louise's sacrifices for him, encouraged her, although he knew her plans might well conflict with Cohan's plans for his career. For Louise wanted to star with her husband in stock once again.

If Louise pushed Tracy back into stock against his wishes, as some claimed, she had her reasons. She may have been trying to recapture the happiness of their first year of marriage spent on the road, which, for all its financial hardships, was more companionable than their marriage had been since. Or she may have been afraid that the fastpaced Broadway world of buxom actresses, late nights on the town, and escape to the Lambs Club would tempt Spencer away from his life with her. And undoubtedly she did in her own way need to act once having tasted life on the stage it is hard to stifle the urge to act again.

George M. Cohan wanted Tracy to chart another course. Cohan could and would see that Tracy was employed without interruption on Broadway, and he thought about featuring Tracy in a musical. Cohan was aghast at Tracy's tone-deafness, but he believed he could train him to dance. Cohan was working on a new musical — his first in years — *The Merry Malones* — and he planned to star in it himself. Tracy was to join him in a role written just for him. But Tracy was signed up for another season of stock with the Wright Players, and his leading lady was Louise Treadwell.

Cohan promised Tracy that he would stay in touch. He was working on another idea for a comedy and would write one of the leads for Tracy.

*   *   *

In 1954, when the company of *Bad Day at Black Rock* journeyed to a desolate California desert town for shooting on location, the veteran Russell Collins remarked that it was the most miserable place he had ever seen.

'Then you've never been to Lima, Ohio,' Tracy muttered.

The little city of Lima, Ohio, is an attractive place today, but in 1927 it was a far cry from what Spencer Tracy was looking for. As a one-night stand for shows touring westward to Chicago, Lima was a standard joke among actors: if you gave them corn, everyone had succotash.

The Tracys were engaged for a four-month season. William Wright had decided to expand his stock operation, and Lima was a testing ground in the Midwest. Wright was delighted, for at that point most of his best actors had moved on and the only real talent he had was the character actor Porter Hall.

The season opened at the Faurot Opera House, and the first ad in the Lima *News* announced a 'season of high-class

58

stock, presented by a permanent company of distinguished New York players in great plays at small prices.' You could sit in the orchestra for seventy-five cents.

The first of the great plays was *Laff That Off* and it promised 'a clean laugh every twenty seconds'. The Wright Players offered a new production every Sunday, ranging from *The Whole Town's Talking* to *The Alarm Clock* and *Chicken Feed*. Avery Hopwood's *The Best People* returned again that season.

There were good houses at first, but there comes a point when even Lima rebels. The season was a financial disaster.

Tracy never accepted Lima. He was angry and sullen much of the time, and did not get to know the townspeople as the other actors did. He was humiliated by being there when Pat O'Brien showed up in Lima for a one-night booking of *Broadway*.

Still, Tracy wasn't one to shirk. He never gave less than his total effort on stage. But he kept hoping that Cohan wouldn't forget his promise.

Cohan didn't. The Tracys were preparing the eleventh production in as many weeks when word came from George M. that the comedy was written. Tracy's role was waiting, and Louise Treadwell's acting career was over.

More than one of the Wright Players felt that Louise Tracy was not a talented actress, but she made up for it with enormous ambition and hard work. She probably would have been fairly successful as an actress had she stuck to it. When she left Lima, her career as Louise Treadwell gave way to a quite different but very remarkable career as Mrs. Spencer Tracy.

*　　　*　　　*

Cohan's new play was *The Baby Cyclone*, a bit of fluff that nonetheless showed the old man's ability to stretch a long laugh from a thin joke.

The Baby Cyclone was specifically written for two actors: Spencer Tracy and Grant Mitchell, whom Cohan greatly admired.

The story involved a Pekingese dog and marital mixups stemming fron one husband mistakenly entering another's apartment. Tracy and Mitchell were cast as the husbands. Tracy knew Cohan well enough to tell him he didn't think much of what he had read. Cohan said, 'Don't read it, act it.'

During rehearsals Cohan gave Tracy advice. After one session that Tracy had thought went well, Cohan pulled him aside.

'Spencer, you have to act *less*.'

Cohan mentioned Grant Mitchell. 'What are Grant's mannerisms, his tricks of business? What does he *do*? I know you can't tell me.'

Tracy said that Grant Mitchell was an actor without mannerisms.

'Of course he has mannerisms, and you're a dead duck without them. That's Grant's style. He doesn't do anything, he only suggests. He doesn't pick his nose, doesn't even scratch it, for you'd notice that. He just gives it a quick rub you can hardly spot, and all those little touches add up to total characterization, and you are aware of *that*.'

Cohan brought up Walter Huston, who was often at rehearsals paying court to Nan Sunderland, whom he later married.

'Ever seen Huston act? He does something better than anybody else does, but you won't know what it is until I tell you, because you don't notice it. He listens, dammit, he listens! And how many actors you know listen today? All they do is talk and gawk.'

Tracy often quoted Cohan's standard advice to young actors. 'Take your hands out of your pockets and listen to the other actors.'

Tracy took the advice, and always credited George M. for his success.

Cohan insisted that something Tracy did better than Grant Mitchell or Walter Huston or anybody was glare. He boasted to a *Times* interviewer that Tracy could 'stare, glare, and finally scare the other actors, without batting an eyelash or making a peep.'

'Lynne Overman is a very great talent,' Cohan once sighed.

'Then why don't you write a part for him?'

'Tell me, Spencer: who does Lynne Overman look like?'

Tracy thought about it, and said that sometimes Lynnie did look a lot like George M. Cohan.

'That's it!' Cohan snapped. 'I couldn't stand to have him around.'

During the very first performance of *The Baby Cyclone* in the Boston tryout, Tracy tripped over some words in a long speech, and ruined the scene. Cohan was furious. Tracy explained that some words were so difficult to say together that he couldn't deliver them naturally.

'Then change the words, God damn it! Say it so it comes out right.'

Cohan never remembered the precise wording of anything he wrote unless it was a gag, and he assured Tracy that any playwright worth his salt would rather have his play done well than literally.

Tracy took a more liberal approach to the playwright's lines, and in consequence was good at ad-libbing on stage. Cohan was disgusted that so few good actors could ad-lib.

One night during the Boston engagement a noisy crowd gathered outside. Tracy and Cohan left the theater at eleven thirty and found the Boston Common filled with thousands of shouting, screaming people. It was August 23, 1927, and in half an hour Sacco and Vanzetti would be executed at Charlestown Prison. The violent demonstration against this injustice made a deep impression on Tracy, as it did on the world.

True to Cohan's prediction, *The Baby Cyclone* was a hit. It played 184 performances in Henry Miller's Theater and once again a successful Chicago engagement followed. Tracy got top reviews. Grant Mitchell and the rest of the cast — Nan Sunderland, Georgia Caine, and Natalie Morehead — also did well.

Tracy had arrived. The brutal stock days were behind for good, and the next step was stardom. Already word was going around Broadway that Spencer Tracy was a solid actor — but not star material. Cohan told Tracy to relax and enjoy himself, the glory would come.

In New York, Tracy now spent more and more time in the Lambs Club on West 44th Street. Among the various private club for actors, the Lambs was the largest and the most famous. It dated back to Edwin Booth, who founded it. In the Lambs Club, Tracy knew actors, comics, writers, and all the characters who collect around the fringes of theater life.

Tracy needed to be around people; he knew everybody but never got really close to many. His real friends at the club, when they were in town, were Pat O'Brien and Frank McHugh.

His way of living and his emotional outlook changed after his parents moved to New York. After various ups and downs, Mr. Tracy was working for General Motors, and had been transferred to New York. Mrs. Tracy was glad; she could see her son in *The Baby Cyclone*, and also help out with three-year-old John.

Tracy gradually began to adjust to his son's deafness, and there was less tension in the household. There was no doubt, however, that John's condition had changed Tracy. To most of the Lambs he was entertaining, but definitely not happy. Chester Morris, who frequently had dinner with Tracy during the run of *Yellow*, thought the boy's deafness had 'affected Spence's whole career, and had changed him and aged him almost overnight . . . all due to frustration because he couldn't make Johnny a normal kid.'

*   *   *

After the Lima fiasco, Louise Tracy threw herself into helping her husband's career. It was apparent that someone would have to guide him, for Spencer Tracy was neither well organized nor aggressive. As he moved closer to success, his individuality and his impatience with conventional behavior became more and more obvious.

No actor worked harder, once he had been given a part.

But many actors of lesser stature landed better parts by being smart about it. In interviews and auditions Tracy was often impatient and rude, and his quick temper was famous. Most actors learned to take rejection in stride, but Tracy took every rebuff as a slur on his ability.

It usually took some friend's efforts to land Tracy a good part. And when times were good, Tracy would let things slide. During *The Baby Cyclone* Louise asserted herself. Cohan wanted to keep Tracy in comedy. Louise made Tracy give some thought to whether being typed in light comedy was what he really wanted. She was afraid that Spencer's powers as a dramatic actor would atrophy, so she urged him to try for serious roles.

By Tracy's own account it was always Louise who kept him going in those days in New York. She believed in him at a time that he had stopped believing in himself as a serious dramatic actor.

His chance came after *The Baby Cyclone* closed.

In 1928, William A. Brady (in whose home Tracy met, for the first time, a young actor named Humphrey Bogart) was planning a chicago production of Sidney Howard's *Ned McCobb's Daughter*. The play was a true comedy, not a farce. There were no jokes and no punchlines — the humor was gentle, and the setting was Down East Maine. For the first time Tracy had a good solid part to act. The play opened at the Princess Theater in Chicago to unanimous rave reviews, but small audiences. After three weeks the play closed. But it had been time well spent for Tracy. He found work on a really fine play particularly satisfying, and was also buoyed up by the strong encouragement John Cromwell, the director-star, gave him.

Spencer Tracy felt a new sense of confidence and a new pride in his work. After his return to New York, most of the roles he tried for were in plays marked by breadth of character and artistic dimension.

*   *   *

All the talk in the Lambs Club was of the new phenomenon,

talking pictures. The Warner brothers were issuing their first feature-length, all-talking and sometimes singing, movies in the wake of the Vitaphone success with *The Jazz Singer*.

Most of the Lambs either feared that the Vitaphone would fail, or feared that it would succeed. Talking pictures would mean more work for actors; on the other hand, what would they do to the stage? Tracy thought it would be a long time before pictures affected his own life, and he didn't get involved in the arguments. And he had other things to think about, and new unhappiness.

*   *   *

John Edward Tracy, always the most vital and robust of men in Spencer's eyes, was dying of cancer.

In New York they had been closer than ever before — they often went off to have dinner together before Spencer's evening performances. After learning of his father's condition, Spencer spent less time with the Lambs and more with his parents.

But he could not afford to stay out of work. Fortunately George M. Cohan had a spot for him, although it was only as a cast replacement. It was a comedy-drama entitled *Whispering Friends* and Tracy took over the male lead for William Harrigan. The play was only a fair success, and was the last assignment Tracy had with Cohan.

During one performance Tracy was aware of Cohan hovering in the wings, and when he saw Cohan's sticken face after the act curtain, he knew his father was dead.

He played the final act. The show had to go on; and more than that, Spencer was still trying to prove something to his father. Tracy's family was proud of him, and his father obviously had taken pleasure in his success in New York. But Spencer Tracy knew that his father died still doubting that acting was a respectable and honorable way of life.

*   *   *

The loss of his father carved more lines in Tracy's craggy

64

face and deepened his feelings of dejection. And once again the course of his career slowed to a standstill. After going out with *Whispering Friends* for a limited tour, he returned to New York and more frustration.

There was, for awhile, some demand for his services. Scripts with good roles were offered to him, but he became overly cautious. He was afraid of making some terrible mistake, and was unable to make a decision.

In later years Tracy often admitted he never could evaluate a script properly. He passed up several plays that became hits. He tried for a leading role in *Gods of the Lightning*, a tragedy based on the Sacco-Vanzetti case, and thought he had it. But after an argument with Hamilton MacFadden, the producer-director, the part went to Charles Bickford. *Gods of the Lightning* was not a financial success, but it was well received by the critics. It also gave Bickford the reputation that sent him off to Hollywood.

Now Tracy's unemployment became a matter of grave concern. His savings were soon exhausted. So in December of 1928 he gave in once more and worked in stock.

As usual it took a friend, this time Pat O'Brien, to help Tracy again get settled on the stage. The booking was in Baltimore with a company that was being organized by Lester Bryant, a Lambs Club acquaintance. (Pat also found a spot for Frank McHugh.) Bryant's company could not pay well, so Tracy's satisfaction was in finally sharing the professional stage with Pat O'Brien.

It was a bleak Christmas in Baltimore. The first production, *Tenth Avenue*, couldn't compete with a musical at another theater, *Boom Boom*, featuring Jeanette MacDonald and Archie Leach (whom Mae West, four years later, would transform into dashing Cary Grant). Lester Bryant's troupe hoped for better times in Mrs. Sparrow's theatrical boarding house.

Help came from Boston. George Meeker, a friend of Tracy's since Academy days, was back on the stage after a year in silent pictures in a drama about returning war veterans called *Conflict*. While the play was trying out in

65

Boston, one of the leads canceled out — his name was Clark Gable. Meeker had the director, Edward Clarke Lilley, contact Tracy and give him the part.

Conflict showed promise on the road, but except for the actors, the crew and management were novices in professional theater, and it showed. When the New York critics panned *Conflict*, Tracy was jolted; from the first reading he had thought it was terrific.

It opened in March of 1929 at the Fulton Theater. The cast, including Tracy, Meeker, McHugh, Edward Arnold, Albert Dekker, and Dennie Moore, agreed to a salary cut in hopes of keeping the play running. But *Conflict* gave up after thirty-seven performances.

Shortly after its opening, Tracy and the playwright, Warren Lawrence, decided to take on the critics. They collected all the bad notices and made the rounds of the newspaper officers. They took on the reviewers one by one, and the mercurial Tracy was able to win some points.

But once again Tracy was out of work, and out of money, Selena Royle got him a brief booking in Providence, but it didn't last.

'They said I had no sex appeal,' Tracy remembered. 'The matinees were strictly for the women, and nobody was coming to the matinees.'

Driving him back to New York, Selena Royle saw Tracy more distressed than she had known he could be. The confidence he had gained with Cohan had disappeared, and he was at the breaking point. Once more he was talking about giving it all up and leaving the theater. Even his sense of humor was gone. He told Selena he was going to read for a new play called *The Last Mile*, and that if nothing came of it, he was through.

There were delays in getting *The Last Mile* ready for production, but Tracy got work almost immediately. He was in three bad plays — *Nigger Rich*, which folded after two weeks, *Dread*, which also closed promptly (when Tracy told friends at the Lambs that he was going to Atlantic City with *Dread*, Ring Lardner said, 'Spence, I don't blame you'), and

66

Veneer, a lackluster play that limped along for a month after Tracy took over the lead.

Many call the twenties the greatest days of the American theater, and although the material Spencer Tracy worked on wasn't often memorable, he did in the space of six years work for the greatest producers — Arthur Hopkins, George M. Cohan, the Shuberts, William A. Brady, and Sam Harris, among others. Yet when he finally made his big break, it was with unknowns. In fact, most of the company was younger than he was. The producer of *The Last Mile* was twenty-seven-year-old Herman Shumlin. Chester Erskine, his director, was only twenty-three. The author, also twenty-three, was a little-known Broadway actor named John Wexley, and the idea for the play, laid in a prison's death house, had been inspired by a magazine story called *The Law Takes Its Toll* that had been written by a condemned prisoner named Robert Blake, just before his execution.

The Last Mile received scant notice by the Broadway people during its preparation. Nor did it much impress Spencer Tracy after he won the lead. Tracy had felt enthusiastic about too many bad plays to be fooled again. He told George M. Cohan about the play and Cohan was not optimistic; he thought Tracy was drifting too far from comedy. Sam Harris, however, was intrigued by *The Last Mile* and booked it into his theater.

Tracy's reluctance about playing the role of Killer Meers was matched by young Chester Erskine's reluctance to give it to him. Erskine, too, thought of Tracy primarily as an actor suited to light comedy.

'But I had already been impressed by the knowledge that Spencer usually had work,' Erskine would recall. 'He was seldom without an acting job for a long period, and he always was treated very kindly by the reviewers, even in plays that were obviously weak. He was a very employable actor.

'Herman Shumlin seemed to want Tracy, but left the final selections entirely to me. Spencer had a substance that other actors lacked, so he became the choice.'

Tracy cast his lot with *The Last Mile* during the last days of 1929. George M. Cohan was disappointed. He wanted to revive *The Song and Dance Man* in the spring, with Tracy, who had played it in stock, taking Cohan's old role. Tracy told Cohan to keep the thought warm: the way things had gone all year, he'd soon be available.

*   *   *

The Last Mile tried out in Hartford in January, and went went badly. The Auburn prison riot — the new year's first big story — hit the papers while the play was in Connecticut. When the play opened in New York on February 6, 1930, a prison break had been written into the second act.

'The play was being rewritten every day until it opened,' Chester Erskine said, 'and was quite different from what we began with. But the reshaping was not influenced by current events.'

Just before the opening, Tracy was sure that *The Last Mile* was going to be a flop. He begged his friends at the Lambs to stay away from it. Nonetheless Pat O'Brien went on opening night and saw 'a one-man performance of amazing power, of near greatness.'

The critics praised the play's fine acting, but didn't single out Tracy especially. The critics knew Tracy and the sort of job he did, and their response to his portrayal of Killer Meers indicated that he performed much as they had expected him to. Tracy did not need a generous press as much as he needed a sturdy play, and at last he had that. The play was a hit.

John Wexley was hailed as a playwright of exceptional promise, and Chester Erskine's staging was acclaimed. For Herman Shumlin, the triumph marked the beginning of a great career as a producer and director that continues to this day. But looking back, *The Last Mile* was more Spencer Tracy's play than anyone else's.

Tracy turned thirty when *The Last Mile* had been running two months. Then, after another two months as Killer Meers, he left the play for an assignment in Hollywood. He

68

was once more in jail: the movie, triggered by the Auburn riot, was called *Up the River*. It was then that Thomas Mitchell predicted that Spencer Tracy wouldn't make the grade in pictures.

CHAPTER THREE

THE TALKIES CALL: 1930–1933

In the late 1920's there seemed small likelihood that Broadway and Hollywood would ever meet. Movies were entertainment for what H. L. Mencken called 'the moron majority'. The stage was special; it was an art form. Even in the tank towns where Spencer Tracy played stock the first-nighters dressed formally like the best New Yorkers. D. W. Griffith made the movies respectable, but it still seemed sure that the distinction between stage and screen would be kept, and that legitimate theater would remain the higher art.

After a brief and unsatisfactory experience in films in 1916–1917, George M. Cohan said that a stage director had to be an artist, but a movie director had only to be an engineer. If you could write plays, you didn't supply movie scenarios or write their titles ... unless you were broke. That was how matters rested until the day a grinning, blackfaced Al Jolson assured a startled movie audience, 'You ain't heard nothin' yet!'

Robert E. Sherwood, then the nation's foremost movie critic, saw *The Jazz Singer* and, writing in the old *Life*, said the silent movie was on its way to oblivion. The transition began in earnest late in 1928 and was virtually completed in the spring of 1929. During this period Hollywood was jolted by the realization that the silent screen stars were now as obsolete as the subtitles of the silents.

Some of the screen's more popular stars began in legitimate theater. Mary Pickford and the Gish girls were hired as children by Belasco. Douglas Fairbanks had been a promising leading man on Broadway before trying films. But most of the stars — the Gilberts, Novarros, and La-Rocques; the

Talmadges, Bows, and Negris — were without stage experience and, for various reasons, probably could not have met a theatrical challenge.

The crudeness of the early talking pictures presented an unfair challenge to movie actors who, trusting neither the recording equipment nor their own communicative powers, would shout and scream the simplest lines and turn the script into a sputtering mess. In late 1928 Paramount produced a blackmail drama called *Interference*, based on a contemporary play, and much was made of the fact that the four principal players — Evelyn Brent, Clive Brook, William Powell, and Doris Kenyon — had been selected on the basis of their considerable stage experience. Their trained speaking voices were such an improvement that all the Hollywood studios took note.

At the dawn of 1929 the Broadway theater had an exceptional number of young actors who, like Tracy, had learned their craft in stock and were on the threshold of stage stardom. They became the prime targets of the film companies. Although leading stage stars of the day were also lured into movie careers, the studios preferred actors who were younger and less expensive, who could be shaped by the studio, who had enough training to use their voices well, but whose most important attribute was a beautiful face.

Hollywood called Irene Dunne, Barbara Stanwyck, Bette Davis, Claudette Colbert, Miriam Hopkins, Jeanette Mac-Donald, Joan and Constance Bennett; and Frederic March, James Cagney, Robert Montgomery, Paul Muni, and Edward G. Robinson. The studio scout and his distant cousin, the Hollywood agent, invaded Broadway. They swarmed in theater lobbies and were admitted to dressing rooms. They received potential film stars in the most expensive hotel suites. They had the money.

In 1929 alone, more than a thousand film tests were believed to have been made in and around Manhattan. The bait was a long-term contract with an option-renewal clause. Stuart Erwin noted that when he went to Hollywood, most of the train's through passengers seemed to be actors. Many of Spencer Tracy's friends answered the call. Chester Morris, who went out in the first wave, was one of the first to succeed.

Tracy knew many who were going west, and tales of the money they were making made him think about joining them. He told George M. Cohan that he didn't really care about movie work, but that he wanted to get in on the money while it was just sitting there. Cohan knew that Tracy was thinking of Johnny.

'If I can help you I will, Spencer. But they'll try to ruin you.'

'I'd like them to have that chance,' Tracy said.

'They're still after me,' Cohan said, 'but I'll freeze in hell before I make a talking picture.' (He yielded, not long afterward, to make *The Phantom President* for Paramount.)

But they weren't after Spencer Tracy. No talent scout rapped on his door, nor were the actors' agents optimistic about being able to peddle Tracy's 'worn linoleum mug' to the studios.

The movie bug bit Tracy while he was in rehearsal for *Conflict.* He and Edward Arnold, after working late into the night, went to the Lambs Club. They were having a drink with some of the regulars, and were joined by Donald Meek, who was starring in a Broadway comedy called *Broken Dishes.* Meek, an aptly named man, had had a busy day. Before giving his evening performance, he had spent the day at the Paramount studio getting ready for his role in *Hole in the Wall,* which was to be the first all-talking picture filmed in New York.

Tracy asked Donald Meek how he could possibly make a movie while occupied with a play, and Meek explained that Paramount had arranged it that way; the leading roles in *Hole in the Wall* were being taken by Edward G. Robinson and Claudette Colbert, who also had commitments on the stage.

Although most of America's film industry had long been based in Hollywood, the Paramount company — the largest in the world at the time — continued to operate a mammoth studio in Astoria, Long Island, that produced approximately half the company's feature films. Early in 1929 new and improved recording equipment was installed at Astoria, giving Paramount an advantage over other film companies in the battle for Broadway talent. They could use actors who were still fulfilling their stage contracts. By night Jeanne Eagels could play *Her Cardboard Lover* on the stage, while Herbert Marshall was down the street in another theater, performing in *The High Road*. But in the daytime, except for matinees, Miss Eagels and Mr. Marshall were in Astoria, working on a talkie version of *The Letter*. Miriam Hopkins, Kay Francis, and Ginger Rogers all started their film careers on Long Island while working on Broadway, as did Charlie Ruggles and Mary Boland. It was the best of both worlds: the gratification of the stage and the easy money of the movies.

Donald Meek remembered that a third leading role had not yet been cast, so Tracy wangled his way in to see Emerson York, the casting director.

'It's a juvenile — middle twenties. You're much too old for the part.'

'I'm twenty-eight.'

'Some other part, maybe. I'll keep you in mind.'

Tracy never heard from Yorke, but he did learn from Donald Meek that his age had not been the reason. Yorke didn't consider Tracy attractive enough. An actor named David Newell was given the part. Tracy was angry about it and swore he'd break into the movies as a matter of principle.

During the run of *Nigger Rich* he managed to get a screen test with M-G-M. It took all of half a day, 'most of it spent getting into character make-up.' He never saw the test and never heard from M-G-M.

After *The Last Mile*, he might have expected the film studios to take an interest. But by 1930 the talkie fever was dying down, the 'raid' was subsiding, and some actors were returning to New York, their movie options unrenewed. While Tracy was in the first flush of his new success, both

Fox and Universal invited him to test for films, but nothing came of it.

At the Fox Movietone studio in Manhattan he was rigged up as a sailor, given a scarred face and a beard, and a script that mainly required him to grunt. He never heard from Fox.

For Universal he did a scene from *Broadway*, the George Abbot play that the studio had filmed as an early talkie. When the makeup crew was finished with him, the mirror revealed an older man. He was being tested in the part that Otis Harlan had played in the movie. Tracy knew Harlan; he was probably in his sixties, maybe older. Tracy never heard from Universal.

Not without bitterness, he decided to put the movies out of his mind. At the Lambs Club someone suggested Pathe.

'Gee, that's right,' Tracy said. 'They may need a new rooster.'

His first offer of movie work came from one of the Lambs Club members — he seemed to live there — Arthur Hurley, who directed Vitaphone shorts for Warners. Hurley shot one-reelers and two-reelers, mostly comedies but also love stories and cops-and-robbers yarns. He used the Vitaphone studio in Brooklyn, but shooting went on all over town, usually on the run.

Shortly after *The Last Mile* opened, Tracy played a hoodlum in a two-reeler called *Taxi Talks*. He was stabbed to death by May Methot, who played his moll; later she would become the wife and famous sparring partner of Humphrey Bogart. Tracy did not especially like the results, nor did Louise, who noted in a letter to her sister that 'Spencer doesn't photograph very well, so for the present, I'm afraid, we'll have to forget about talking pictures.'

His work in *Taxi Talks* took only one day, as did his second stint, which is nameless — it did not acquire a Vitaphone serial number and apparently was never released. His third Vitaphone effort was *The Strong Arm* and cast Tracy and Henry O'Neill in parts very similar to the ones they played in *The Last Mile*. It was a one-reeler but took two whole days to make.

In his last Vitaphone labor, *The Hard Guy*, Spencer Tracy had star billing, as a consequence of his growing renown with *The Last Mile*. By the time it was released to theaters, Tracy was on his way to Hollywood.

Making Vitaphone shorts was a slaphappy procedure. Story ideas were developed by a resident crew who threw the scripts together rapidly. Production took two days or at most three days. The shorts were edited quickly and mechanically and were rushed out as fast as possible. Several would make a 'program' supporting a lightweight feature-length film. (The advent of double features systematically killed off the short feature some years later.) Some of the shorts were of remarkably fine quality, for the speed with which they were put together gave them spontaneity and energy. Not even Arthur Hurley could track the progress and travels of the many featurettes he brought into being, but he considered them good screen tests for the actors, because the studio get an audience reaction to a face or personality. But Tracy heard nothing from Warners. If there was an audience reaction to his Vitaphone efforts, nobody told him.

At Paramount, John Cromwell had signed with the studio as an actor but had switched to directing. Because he was familiar with the New York scene, he was asked by the casting department to recommend any actors he thought were especially talented. Cromwell, who had directed and acted with Tracy in *Ned McCobb's Daughter*, searched his memory 'and came up with two names, one a character actor I knew, and the other Spencer Tracy. I rather went overboard for Spencer, as I was one of the directors who were sick to death of the collar-ad type and longed to cast a *man* in a leading part.' But time passed, nothing happened, and Tracy did not even know someone was campaigning for him. No wonder, then, that he was skeptical when John Ford started talking to him about playing in a movie called *Up the River*.

Up the River, based on the Auburn prison riot, was the brainchild of Robert Yost of the story department of Fox studios. The company had just taken Maurine Watkins as a staff writer and she was unassigned; she herself had written a smash play called *Chicago*. Miss Watkins produced an outline that excited studio boss Winfield Sheehan and Yost. They would make *Up the River* one of the major productions of the year.

Only two of Fox's directors were major talents, and since Frank Borzage's schedule was committed well in advance, John Ford was assigned to *Up the River*. Ford was in high favor for the sensational preview reaction to an all-male film called *Men Without Women*. A Fox press release announced that John Ford would direct *Up the River* with a cast of popular Fox favorites which was the customary way of saying that no roles had been cast.

By the time Ford was available for his new assignment, the script had bogged down. Ford did not like the fragment he saw, and Maurine Watkins got busy on a rewrite. No one knew when production would begin, so casting was out of the question. Fox sent John Ford to New York to look over the new plays and, with luck, to find a potential star or two.

Ford arrived in New York on a Monday and found theater tickets waiting for him at the Fox headquarters: six plays for six nights. His Monday night ticket was to *The Last Mile*.

The other tickets for the first week would go unused: Ford went to the Sam H. Harris Theater every night for the entire week.

Later he said, 'What impressed me the first time was the direction. I thought that the staging was absolutely brilliant. The way the play got its great forward motion was through sheer direction, and being a director myself, I knew I had to see it again. So I got a ticket for the next night and forgot all about whatever play I was supposed to see.'

By the Tuesday performance he became aware of Spencer Tracy.

'More than anything else I was tantalized by his movement. I don't think many people were ever conscious of Spence's bodily discipline. After seeing the play twice I still didn't have a good impression of what he looked like, and

77

aside from knowing that he had a fairly good voice it failed to register for me in terms of its quality. But his catlike agility was something extraordinary. He made every movement sharp and meaningful, and didn't waste a single turn.'

When Ford returned to see *The Last Mile* for the third time, it was to study Tracy, and 'that was when I saw that he had it all ... the consummate power of an actor.'

Ford saw Tracy in his dressing room after the performance. Tracy remembered that George Meeker had said good things about Ford, and Tracy suggested the Lambs Club for a nightcap.

'And that,' Ford would remember, 'turned out to be quite an evening. More than an evening. I think we stayed at the club until about four o'clock.'

They hit it off because Ford was Tracy's kind of man: a gruff but companionable Irishman with no pretense. By 1930 he had already made his mark on the movies. His energy was translated into tremendous vitality in his films. He was still in his teens when he directed his first film for Universal in 1914. And his greatest professional accomplishments were still to come.

That night Ford and Tracy didn't talk about pictures or directing.

'Hell, no, we were having too good a time.' Ford was amazed to see so many Irishmen. 'Bill Frawley was there, and Allen Jenkins. And that was the night I met Pat O'Brien. Pat got to telling Irish stories — he was spinning the yarns even then, and nobody else is really in his class — and then Spence pointed to a fellow who was sort of holding court, and said there was the greatest Irishman of us all. And I looked over and saw John McGraw.' Although McGraw's Giants were going through some bad days, no one forgot his ten pennants. 'So we spent a few hours talking about baseball,' Ford remembers.

When the Lambs reeled out of the club before dawn, Ford paid another tribute to *The Last Mile*. Someone said if he liked the play so much, he should see it again. And Ford did, the next night.

'From then on I was watching a good friend act. Some of the actors maybe were up and down but Spence was always the same, which was to say that to my mind, he was perfect. That's when I decided I wanted him. It wasn't so much for *Up the River*. If I had been about to start some other picture, I know I would have wanted to get Spence in it.'

When Ford introduced the subject of movie work, Tracy was not particularly impressed.

'I made a test for Fox,' he told Ford. 'If they had wanted me they could have met my price.'

Ford reported his find to the Fox office in New York and met resistance. Spencer Tracy? Sure, they'd heard of him. No, he wouldn't do.

'Tracy tested for us. He's not much good ... and he's ugly.' Spencer Tracy, they said, had a certain ability but was too young for character parts, which was all he was suited for. The test was uncovered from a morgue that also contained terrible showings of Clark Gable and Jean Harlow, both of whom had been refused Fox contracts. Ford saw Tracy as the bearded pirate, and was enraged.

'That's just a collection of props! Tracy looks fine, not pretty, but interesting — but you've got to uncover him to see it!'

Ford arranged for Tracy to meet the Fox executives in New York and coached him to ask for seven hundred and fifty dollars a week.

Tracy asked Herman Shumlin for a leave of absence to make a film for the Fox company.

Tracy was firm. 'I need the money.'

The producer told Tracy he would agree to giving him six weeks off — provided a suitable actor could be found to take over the role of Killer Meers. Tracy said six weeks would be plenty. After all, if a one-reeler could be shot in two days, a feature shouldn't take more than a month.

That was in June. Thomas Mitchell left a vacation at Montauk to take over the Meers part.

'Poor Tommy, he just couldn't get into that part,' Chester Erskine recalls. In all fairness to Mitchell, he was the only actor ever faced with replacing Spencer Tracy on Broadway.

*   *   *

The contract was signed in Fox's New York office. Tracy was taken by surprise when they offered eight hundred a week. He gulped, and asked for a thousand. He got it.

Afterward his mood swung from enthusiasm to worry. The money, he reasoned, was incredible. Did he really deserve it?

'Why didn't Arthur Hurley's people think I was so great? They may think I stink for pictures . . . and maybe I do.'

It exasperated Louise, but she was used to it. She also knew that Tracy's worrying spurred him on.

At the Lambs Club there was a party of sorts at which Tracy became sentimental, then depressed. He admitted that he was terrified, and sure he was making a horrible mistake.

He *knew* it was a mistake when his train left Pennsylvania Station for the long trip west. He found himself sharing a seat with an actor named J. Edward Davis. He was going to Columbia to make his first picture, *Madonna of the Streets,* with Evelyn Brent. Davis showed Tracy a newspaper review of a new picture called *The Big House.* It was a rave notice for Chester Morris and Robert Montgomery and Wallace Beery, and the picture was based on the Auburn prison riot. M-G-M had made it.

'Fox will probably cancel your picture now,' Davis said cheerily. 'They do that all the time in Hollywood.'

Tracy listened to Davis all the way to Hollywood. The trip took six days.

He arrived on a warm morning late in June. He was met at the Los Angeles station by two bronzed youths from Fox who chauffered him to the Hollywood Hotel. After he was settled, he was driven to the old Fox studio on Western Avenue.

Tracy met the general manager, Ed Butcher. 'Jack Ford's done a real sales job on you, and this guy Beauregard Humphries says you're all right, too.'

'You mean Humphrey Bogart?'

'That's the boy, Bogart,' Butcher said. 'He's going to be in your picture.'

The rest of the picture wasn't yet cast, as there were problems with the script. Tracy tried not to show his impatience. 'Where is Mr. Fox's office?' he asked.

'Didn't you know? He's not here anymore. We sacked him two months ago.'

Tracy had never paid much attention to Hollywood's struggles at the top.

'Did you take his place?' Tracy asked Butcher.

'I'm just the general manager,' Butcher said, smiling. 'Winnie Sheehan's in charge now. He's the production chief. I think you'll like him.'

Tracy told Ed Butcher he would like Sheehan a lot if Sheehan would get the picture moving.

Butcher introduced Tracy to the head of wardrobe and to the makeup man.

He also got a quick tour of part of the studio and saw workmen milling about, and the complicated array of lights and camera machinery.

John Ford arrived late in the morning. The sets were no closer to readiness than the script. But Ford had picked his leading lady, Claire Luce, also signed for her first picture.

Ed Butcher gave Tracy an Oldsmobile roadster to use, and told him to draw a salary advance from the paymaster. Tracy said he liked the way they operated.

The first week passed without a scene being shot. Tracy roamed freely about the studio at Ed Butcher's suggestion, 'to get acquainted with your new line of business'.

Tracy worried about all that wasn't happening, and about everything he heard. The people at the studio talked as if he would be spending the balance of his life there, but his commitment was for six weeks only, two of which had already been wasted in traveling and in waiting for things to get started. There was no indication when shooting would begin. He reminded Ed Butcher and the other Fox people of his obligation to *The Last Mile*, and finally realized they just didn't take a commitment to a stage play very seriously.

He did use this chance to poke around behind the scenes, exploring the movie business from the inside. He would question technicians and bystanders, asking them what they did and how they did it. He looked in on other pictures that were being made on the Fox lot. He met Raoul Walsh, Irving Cummings, and Henry King, all of whom would eventually direct him. He met old, fading actors like Hobart Bosworth, Beryl Mercer, and Tyrone Power the elder, and young and rising actors like Joel McCrea, Joan Bennett, and Maureen O'Sullivan. Walsh introduced him to Marion Michael Morrison, a green but likable fellow out of U.S.C. who was making *his* first film, as John Wayne.

On the set of *Lightnin'* he met Will Rogers, who surprised Tracy by knowing all about him. He still followed the New York theater closely, and knew about *The Last Mile* and of Spencer's earlier tutelage under his good friend, George M. Cohan. Will Rogers invited Tracy to lunch at his table, which was something of an honor.

They were great friends from the start. Tracy said he still hadn't met Winnie Sheehan. Rogers said he would take care of that.

'You'll like Winnie,' Rogers said, 'everybody does. Of course, liking people is a professional speciality with me, but Winnie blackmails me into loving him.' Rogers was an enormous success in talking pictures and had a long-term Fox contract of fantastic financial proportions. Tracy, who had been awestruck at the thought of making five thousand dollars for just one picture, found it difficult to comprehend that some actors earned that much in a week.

Will Rogers introduced Tracy to Winfield Sheehan and Frank Borzage; they would be of critical importance to the first phase of Tracy's movie career.

Sheehan looked like an Avery Hopwood butler: a kindly round face, with thin hair parted down the middle and pasted down on his temples. He didn't look much like a studio boss. Sharp-featured, ruddy Frank Borzage looked somewhat like Spencer Tracy. Leaving their table, Will

Rogers remarked that Winnie Sheehan had a lot of problems and was not to be envied.

Will Rogers was the king of the Hollywood polo crowd. He played in the matches at the Riviera Country Club and also had a field of his own at his ranch. On his first Hollywood Sunday, Tracy visited the club and watched the polo matches. He fell in love with the game and with sunny southern California. He decided that Louise and Johnny were going to have the benefits of California, however temporarily, and he rented a small house on Franklin Avenue. His wife and son joined him at a time when *Up the River* was almost down the drain.

Sheehan considered scrapping the picture. The script was awful, and M-G-M's *The Big House* didn't help. If it came to losing Tracy, Sheehan was for letting him go, but Ford was determined to make the picture, and to make it with Tracy playing the leading role of 'St. Louis'. Sheehan gave the go-ahead at least, but downgraded *Up the River* from 'special feature' to 'programmer' status. This reduced the shooting schedule (which, in effect, had already been accomplished), and put budged limitations on all departments, including promotion.

Tracy had now been hanging around the studio for almost a month, and was due back in New York in just three weeks.

Tracy asked for a script. Ford said he would not need one. 'Since Metro made the picture we wanted to,' he said, 'we'll have to make a different one . . . but we can have some fun doing it.'

He had decided to play it for laughs and to depend a good deal on improvising new scenes and dialogue. This bright thought originated with William Collier, Senior, a cheery anachronism in show business. He had been a performer for more than fifty years, and was a vaudeville headliner before movies were thought of. He had performed with Weber and Fields and had written sketches for them, and he had also worked with George M. Cohan, and with Mack Sennett in the early days of Hollywood. Collier found Maurine

Watkins' serious script unintentionally funny, and felt that what it needed was not rewriting but a good goosing.

'Ford told me to just remember that St. Louis was a comic,' Tracy said, 'and that was all he had to tell me.'

St. Louis was one jailbird and Dannemora Dan was another and together they were supposed to bring to mind Quirt and Flagg in Sing Sing. Warren Hymer, a lizard-eyed youth not long out of Yale who played morons almost exclusively in films, was Dannemora Dan.

The straight-man accomplice would be played by young Humphrey Bogart — on the set Spencer started to call him 'Bogie', which was to become Hollywood's most famous nickname. Bogart was working on two pictures at the same time on adjacent sets, and Warren Hymer was doing three. Movie actors, Tracy thought, should all have bicycles.

Tracy picked up his convict costume and was also fitted for a proper suit — his first indication that St. Louis would not be a jailbird throughout the film.

John Ford recalls that when Tracy played his first scene for the movie camera, he knew that the actor's entire performance was going to be right on the button. 'There was no awkwardness at all. Spence was as natural as if he didn't know a camera was there, or as if there had *always* been a camera when he acted before. His speech was decisive. He knew a straight line from a laugh line. If he had a chance for a laugh, he played it in a way that would get it.'

Both Ford and Tracy detested multiple 'takes', for spontaneity is lost with repetition.

Tracy said, 'If you want it from me the first time, you'll get it the first time.' When a second take was required, the offender was hardly ever Tracy.

Towards the end of his career Tracy remarked that of all his films, none was more enjoyable to make than *Up the River*, not because it was the first but because it was the quickest, and its feeling of camaraderie was extraordinary. The good fellowship provided the funniest and best-remembered sequence in the film — one that certainly was not in the Maurine Watkins script.

Ford and Tracy liked to talk baseball, as did Bogart and Hymer, but Bill Collier was a rabid fan. He told dozens of baseball anecdotes that grew like fish stories in the retelling, and at the last minute a prison ball-game sequence including Collier's zany recollections was put into the film.

Tracy remained adamant about keeping his commitment to *The Last Mile* and Ford worked his company long hours and a full final weekend to get it all in the can. Tracy wound up his assignment in mid-August. Not all of his scenes had been shot, but time had run out. He was before the cameras on a Wednesday morning for his final scene, and on an eastbound train that same afternoon. He arrived in New York the following Monday and was on the stage of the Ambassador Theater — the new residence of *The Last Mile* — for the eight-thirty performance.

He had spent the train ride trying to forget the character of St. Louis and to remember Killer John Meers. Tracy never liked good-byes, and the only farewell was to his wife and son, who would return to New York on a later train.

Variety noted that Spencer Tracy's return to *The Last Mile* had given its box office a new spurt. People would ask him about the movie he had made, but he wouldn't say much; it was hard for him to make up his mind about it.

There had been no discussions, aside from the usual gossip, of a possible term contract with Fox. That would rest on the outcome of the first picture. With his family back in New York, Tracy lost touch with the West Coast. He concentrated once again on his responsibilities to the stage.

But in Hollywood things were moving fast. The major studios in 1930 were factories that didn't take long to grind out a picture. *Up the River* was processed in a matter of days, edited in a week, and its rough cut shown at the studio two weeks after Tracy left California. A preview was scheduled in San Bernardino in late September. Most of the studio brass attended, from Sheehan on down. They were taken by surprise by the enthusiasm of the preview audience. The film credits weren't responsible, for the cast was made up largely of unknowns. But five minutes after the movie began it was obvious it was a success.

Sheehan saw the reaction at the preview, and started to work on a contract for Tracy.

Up the River was released nationally on October 30, 1930. The critical reaction was distinctly favorable. Nothing in the picture's slim promotional material indicated that the picture was Tracy's first, and Richard Watts, Jr., in the *Herald-Tribune,* accepting Tracy as an old pro in the movie business, said that Spencer Tracy gave his 'usual' excellent performance.

By the time the reviews were all in, Tracy had reached an agreement with Fox. He had only to complete his obligation to *The Last Mile*.

On January 18, 1931, Fox Films announced that Spencer Tracy had been signed for five years (with options) and that the first film under his new contract would be the super musical, *Skyline*.

'Five years seems like an awfully long time,' he told a newspaper interviewer, 'but I'm going to give it a try. I'll be back, though, because acting is my line, and this is where acting is.'

Pat O'Brien had been lured into films by Howard Hughes and was a hit in *The Front Page*. Frank McHugh, in the same picture, was also in Hollywood to stay. James Cagney and James Gleason were there, and the growing list of Lambs in Hollywood included Frank Morgan and William Boyd. The film colony now claimed, along with Chester Morris and John Cromwell, Grant Mitchell and Walter Huston. Tracy's friend from the Academy, Monroe Owsley, was 'typed' as a weakling brother after scoring a hit in the film version of *Holiday*. Tracy told Lynne Overman in New York that he felt like the last rat to leave the ship; he wasn't leaving home, just trying to catch up with it.

This time the Tracy family went to Hollywood together.

*   *   *

The first impression Tracy had of the film colony was that everyone in it was young. The new industry had no old tradition; and there were no Belascos, no Shuberts, not even an Al Woods or a George M. Cohan. Everyone in Hollywood, Tracy concluded, either was thirty, like the already powerful Hal Wallis, Darryl Zanuck, and Irving Thalberg, or acted thirty, as Will Rogers did on a polo field.

And everyone seemed to have money. There was confidence in the air: the Depression that paralyzed New York hadn't seemed to reach the Far West. 'This is the safest business to be in at the moment,' Frank Borzage told Tracy. 'Times are getting hard all over the world, but people feel better if they can go to the picture show and hear Will Rogers tell them everything's going to be all right.'

Borzage and Rogers were Tracy's first good friends in Hollywood. He would usually lunch with one or both at the Fox commissary, and they showed him Hollywood life outside the studio, telling him to take the part he wanted and leave the rest alone.

The part he wanted was the Riviera Country Club, not for the golf but for polo. He took up riding shortly after his second arrival in California, pursued it with a fierce passion, took polo lessons, and soon was playing regularly in the Sunday matches at the Riviera. He was a precise horseman, but something of a daredevil, and he got better and better. Soon he was one of the best players on the scene.

For Tracy the Riviera was like an outdoor version of the Lambs Club, with the added asset of pretty ladies. The Riviera also was somewhat more tolerant than the Lambs of a tipsy guest, and the Sunday evening get-togethers after polo were merry. Tracy fitted comfortably into a group that included Borzage, Rogers, Zanuck, Tim Durant, Fred Bailes, Neil McCarthy, Tommy Hitchcock, Jack Holt, and the senior Doug Fairbanks.

The Hollywood he chose to ignore was the network of nightclubs, parties, and speakeasies. Hollywood has always encouraged free and easy sex, but Tracy ignored the studio's matter-of-fact call-girl service and establishments like the high-class whorehouse on Wilcox Avenue, Tracy preferred the polo field and quiet evenings at home — something he and Louise had not had much occasion to experience in the past.

The earliest months of their Hollywood residence were, for Tracy, the happiest in many respects. Tracy's Fox contract would net him, as a minimum, at least $70,000 annually — more than he had collected in his entire career as a legitimate actor. Life was getting to be more comfortable.

At the same time, the money made Tracy nervous. How could he manage such large sums? He had no experience or interest in the task, so he asked his brother Carroll to come from Milwaukee to manage his income. Soon their widowed mother also came west to be with 'her boys' and the family was together once again.

Tracy's most persistent worry was that the money would vanish as quickly as it had come to him. He worried so about failing in films that he began to believe it was inevitable.

'This mug of mine is as plain as a barn door,' he would say. 'Why should poor people want to pay thirty-five cents to look at it?'

His apprehension was not unjustified. Every day he heard studio gossip of options not being renewed. Fox had dropped Humphrey Bogart after his fourth picture; he had not caught on. Tracy figured it could happen to him.

Louise did not worry. She was much more adaptable than Spencer, able to make the best of any situation. She adjusted her plans to their improved income. Her main concern was their son John.

When John was a baby, the Tracys had dreams that a large sum of money could buy a miracle. Now they had the money, but it couldn't help. But Louise had nevertheless discovered her special cause. Children who are deaf do not have to remain mute; they can talk and understand the language they can't hear. Louise had explored all the theories of education for the deaf, had consulted virtually every leading specialist, and in the process had become a specialist herself. Now that there was some money in the bank, she could put this knowledge to some use.

John Tracy did, indeed, thrive in California. It was hard to pull him away from the swimming pool, and he showed signs of being as athletic as his father. Louise was delighted with how normal he was emotionally, and how responsive. John was mentally alert, and he was inventive; he did not talk distinctly — one had to be patient listening to him — but the breakthrough had come. He was reading lips and knowing what others said, and when he talked, he knew what he was saying.

Tracy's interest in his son grew. At the studio and at the country club, Tracy began to talk of his son's accomplishments with an easygoing paternal pride. He never mentioned the boy's deafness, however; his friends came to regard the subject as taboo.

'It wasn't that Spence was ashamed of the boy,' a close friend explained. 'He was ashamed of himself. No matter what anybody or any doctor said, Spencer was convinced he was at fault. Having a son who was not entirely normal made Spencer feel he wasn't normal . . . wasn't a complete man.'

The cause of John Tracy's deafness probably was due to an illness Louise contracted during her pregnancy. Tracy finally accepted the thought that he was not responsible, but by that time his sense of guilt had plagued him so long that he never was able to leave it behind completely.

* * *

Any new idea in the movie business quickly became a fad. The first all-talking picture was a backstage musical, so hardly a picture was made by any studio that wasn't an all-talking, all-singing, all-dancing extravaganza. The next craze was 'photographed stage plays' and just about every decent play — and many poor ones — was filmed during the first three years of the talkies. The last important film of 1930, Warner Brothers' *Little Caesar*, introduced gangsters, bootleggers, racketeers, and other types who strayed far from the law but were still good to their mothers. Warners followed their first triumph with *The Public Enemy*. The title roles were taken by Tracy's former New York pals, Edward G. Robinson and James Cagney, both relative newcomers to the movies, and neither one a matinee idol. In early 1931 gangster films took over every lot and influenced the style of an era. And most important to Spencer Tracy, the gangster hero didn't have to be good-looking.

When Spencer Tracy reported to Fox Films as a contract actor, he was told that he was going to become a 'tough guy'. He was withdrawn from *Skyline* and was assigned the principal role in a melodrama entitled *Quick Millions*.

Winfield Sheehan summoned Tracy to his office and outlined the campaign. After Tracy's success in *Up the River*, the studio was banking on him to be its big new star for the year. It was a lucky accident they had Tracy; they hadn't been looking for a tough guy, but now they needed one. Paramount had George Bancroft, Metro had Beery, Warners had Robinson, and Fox needed an equivalent. There was McLaglen, but the public wanted him in comedy. The picture called *Quick Millions* was to get special promotion and Tracy's name was to appear above the title — star billing. And more, Sheehan started to talk about a new contract — a 'better' one.

Needless to say, Tracy was enthusiastic about *Quick Millions*. In addition, Rowland Brown, who was to direct *Quick Millions,* had also written it, and the final script Tracy studied was obviously a strong one. Tracy looked forward to getting into the character of 'Bugs' Raymond, an amiable, basically honest truck driver corrupted during the Depression by money and the lust for power. 'Bugs' Raymond gets into the rackets, becomes a powerful gangster, and meets a violent death. The plot wasn't unique, but there was honesty in Brown's writing, and good characterization of the hero. And Brown directed the film with crispness and economy. The finished print was hard-hitting and vivid. The Fox executives were pleased.

Tracy was told that his next picture would be a change of pace, a comedy called *A Girl in Every Port.* After he saw the script he faced Sheehan.

'What happened to the tough guy?' he demanded. 'This comedy, if you can call it that, is crap.'

Sheehan gave his bland smile and said he hoped Tracy didn't expect every script to be as solid as *Quick Millions*.

'Of course I do,' Tracy said. Fuming at Sheehan would become a regular ritual.

'Spence, gangster pictures aren't such a sure thing anymore. There've been too many, and the box office is falling off.'

Sheehan told Tracy there would be more tough-guy parts, but an actor shouldn't let himself be typed. The studio wanted audiences to see him in various roles at the beginning of his movie career.

As soon as *Quick Millions* was completed, Tracy went to work obediently on *A Girl in Every Port*. Midway in the shooting schedule, he was assigned another part in a movie already in production. Tracy exploded. He went storming into Sheehan's office. *A Girl in Every Port* was bad enough, but the lead in something called *Six Cylinder Love* at the same time was just too much. Sheehan was out of town, but his assistant told Tracy that both could be worked into his schedule, and anyway the part in *Six Cylinder Love* wasn't a lead.

There was a frightful scene with much yelling on both sides. The assistant lost his aplomb. He told Tracy his career was as dead as Baby Peggy's, for there had been a sneak preview of *Quick Millions*, and the audience hated the picture.

For Tracy, the honeymoon was over at Fox. He sulked on the sets of his two movie assignments: Edward Everett Horton, who was in the cast of *Six Cylinder Love*, noted that Spencer Tracy was not especially friendly and stalked around like 'a terribly nervous man'.

Winfield Sheehan returned from the East and soothed Tracy. He was being used in *Six Cylinder Love* because the picture needed a 'name' and therefore Tracy would receive first billing even though his role was small. Sheehan told Tracy to be patient, there would be some good roles coming up for his option was to be renewed.

Tracy calmed down, but he felt like something less than the big new star of the year. His disappointment increased when *Quick Millions* was released with a minimum of tub-thumping. He received star billing, all right, but when the box office was less than predicted, the studio decided that Spencer Tracy was not a 'draw'.

Today *Quick Millions* is regarded as a near-classic gangster film, and Tracy's performance was and is the strength of the picture. When it was released in April of 1931 the reviews were favorable, but they were few in number, and unfortunately for Tracy an even better gangster film, Rouben Mamoulian's *City Streets*, was released at the same time.

*   *   *

The studio doubted that Spencer Tracy was big box office, but it had a real winner in platinum blond Jean Harlow. However, no one expected that her popularity would last more than a season or two, for no one thought she was any good as an actress, and her screen personality was a type that didn't wear well. But Fox, who had borrowed her from M-G-M, decided to cash in quickly by changing the title of *A Girl in Every Port* to *Goldie*, for Goldie was the girl in the port where most of the action was, and most of the action was Spencer Tracy and Warren Hymer fighting over Jean Harlow.

Jean Harlow was then twenty, a lively divorcée who was often out of breath from giggling, and who was burning the candle at both ends, in between marriages. She had a finishing school background, but it didn't show. And she had the leggy stride of a much taller girl. Tracy watched carefully during the shooting of *Goldie*. On days they were to work together they would meet on the sound stage before the crew showed up to go over lines, because Harlow did not have Tracy's knack for memorizing lines. She was working out a scene one morning when Tracy stopped her.

'Jean, why are you acting so God-damned phony?' he asked.

Tracy told her how good she really was, that when she was away from the studio or just being herself on the set she had a great laugh, a great way of talking, and a great way of shaking her fanny. But as soon as she started to act, she put on phony diction and a phony walk, as if she was trying to be the Queen of England. Tracy told her what Ethel Barrymore had told him — just be yourself.

She worked on getting rid of her mannerisms in a comedy love scene. Tracy said, 'Now you're really Goldie.' He predicted that by playing it naturally, they could have a hit.

When they played the scene for the cameras, the director, Ben Stoloff, was not happy. He thought Harlow was losing Goldie's character. Harlow looked over at Tracy, who gave her a wink.

Tracy used to say he never gave advice on acting unless an actor asked for it. Harlow gave Tracy the credit for making her a spontaneous performer, and indeed she soon was the darling of film critics.

Goldie was a fair success at the box office, clearly outdrawing *Six Cylinder Love*. As Sheehan promised, Tracy was billed first in *Six Cylinder Love,* as he was in *Goldie,* but he was no longer a star. He was featured beneath the title, and the dispay ads for *Goldie* emphasized Harlow.

Both films were 'programmers,' better than Grade B pictures, but well below the monthly 'specials' in quality. Fox produced forty-eight films annually — four a month, of which one would be a 'special' released with a round of parties and a showy premiere. The 'galas' gave the fans a chance to see the stars in the flesh, and in full dress, and to see who was escorting whom.

Being under a Fox contract, Spencer Tracy was given to understand that he was obliged to dress up and attend premieres of Fox specials. These movies would usually be a Will Rogers yarn, or Janet Gaynor and Charles Farrell in a sugary romance. Spencer and Louise were bored by the galas, and their few dress-up appearances were to keep peace with the studio. The only reason for going is to be seen, Tracy figured, and he preferred being seen on the stage or screen. He wouldn't mind a premiere for a Spencer Tracy picture, but that was a dim possibility indeed; he realized he was a long way from the top in Hollywood.

*   *   *

The studio publicity department was in a quandary. How could they push Spencer Tracy? The fan magazines weren't buying. Tracy wasn't big enough, wasn't hot enough, was a washout as far as looks went, and all things considered, he just wasn't colorful.

But behind the scenes Tracy was colorful, all right. He was becoming more so as he became more dissatisfied at Fox. But the studio didn't relish publicity about his drinking and his erratic behaviour, and did its best to squelch the stories.

A new trade paper, the *Hollywood Reporter*, ran a particularly sly and ungenerous gossip column. Some of the stories skirted libel, and their victims were often enraged. Tracy was one of those whose indiscretions were most frequently hinted at. The *Reporter* caught on in a hurry in the film colony. At the Riviera someone asked, 'What makes people read the *Reporter*?' and one wit pointed to a drowsing Spencer Tracy and said, 'He does.'

In the free-wheeling film world Tracy wasn't really 'doing' anything. He did not 'play around' or gamble or get involved with the underworld as some of the well-heeled Hollywood figures were known to do. On the surface, it looked as if Tracy gave the gossipmongers little to work with. But Tracy had made it plain he was not their kind of boy; he wished to have no truck with *them*.

He drank more than he should — unlike Humphrey Bogart, he couldn't hold his liquor well. But he did not drink so much or as often as the colony was led to believe. Physically he was in good shape, as his polo demonstrated. If he took to carousing in the evening, it didn't show the next day at the studio. He was always on time and usually was early — even for the calls at dawn, and he rarely had a hangover.

But the one thing that got him into trouble was his

temper. He lost control more and more frequently, with less and less provocation — he would blow up if someone took his spot in the studio parking lot. He was a bundle of nerves, so he yelled a great deal, and drank a little, and acted childishly. He missed the stage and the real challenge of acting, and the poor scripts Fox gave him were small satisfaction. He took it out on Louise at home, and she was perhaps less comforting than she had been in earlier times. She had lived with his moods and his depressions a long time. His home was still a retreat, but sometimes there were scenes; and sometimes he didn't come home at all.

*   *   *

Frank Borzage tried to get Tracy for a script he really liked. It was called *Bad Girl*, and it was based on a best-selling novel by Vina Delmar. The heroine had a boy friend whose part was as big as the girl's, Borzage told Tracy. But Tracy didn't need to hear a thing about it, he didn't even need to read the script. If Frank Borzage thought it was a good part and a good picture, he wanted to do it.

But even though Tracy was available, Borzage couldn't clear it with Sheehan. The studio chief, genuinely apologetic, told Tracy he had 'orders' to get someone new for the part. When Tracy asked who was giving the orders, Sheehan shrugged and replied, 'Some bankers in New York.' Fox Films had their problems.

Borzage ended up choosing James Dunn, whom Tracy learned was getting 'the treatment' and was going to be the studio's new top star. *Bad Girl* was a surprise hit with both the press and public, and Borzage won an Oscar for direction. 'Don't worry, we'll get together,' he told Tracy.

But Tracy did worry. The studio might drop him, or the studio might renew his option and continue giving him terrible parts. He didn't know what to think when he was told he was being loaned to Howard Hughes to appear in *Sky Devils*. Pat O'Brien had fared well with Hughes in *The Front Page*, which augered well for Tracy, and his old friend William Boyd was to be in the picture too, which would make

95

the project pleasant. But what of his foothold at Fox? Did this mean he was really on his way out?

Sky Devils was fun to make but a poor picture. Six writers — Robert Benchley among them — shared credit for the screenplay, but nobody could salvage the script.

Tracy's return to Fox was reassuring. He had three pictures waiting for him. The first two weren't much, but the third seemed promising, and Frank Borzage would direct it.

In *She Wanted a Millionaire* Tracy got the girl in the final fadeout for the first time. The girl was Joan Bennett, then a blond, and this picture was designed to push her toward stardom. Tracy told some friends at the commissary that he felt more like an onlooker than an actor as the production crew buzzed around Miss Bennett, who was in virtually every scene. The remark got printed, and Tracy had the worst press possible during *She Wanted a Millionaire*.

The producer, John Considine, was having a romance with Joan Bennett, and a fan magazine made up a story that Tracy was Considine's rival for Miss Bennett's affections. The story enraged Tracy and did not help his already thorny relationship with Considine.

When the film was released, the reviewers didn't find Joan Bennett quite ready for stardom, and as usual, the best notices were Tracy's.

Considine directed Tracy again in *Disorderly Conduct*, but the fact that they patched up their personal grievances didn't salvage the film. The only good thing to come out of the picture was Tracy's friendship with Ralph Bellamy, who was also in the cast.

Tracy tackled Sheehan once again. By now Sheehan was used to Tracy's chronic state of agitation. Tracy angrily suggested a release from contract as the quickest route to their mutual happiness. Sheehan said he couldn't do it.

'Why not? I'm nothing to the studio.'

'Spencer, you're the best actor under contract to Fox Films. If I can believe the writers in New York, you're the only good actor we have.'

'You really mean that?'

'Of course I do,' Sheehan smiled. 'That's why I put up with you.'

The Depression finally hit Hollywood in 1932. Motion picture attendance dipped throughout the country. There was retrenchment at all the film studios, and some folded. Paramount went into receivership, closed its Long Island studio, and lost out to M-G-M as the most powerful film company. Attendance fell off most sharply at the 'programmers', as radio moved into its golden age and attracted an audience with little money to spend on mediocre films.

*　　　*　　　*

Spencer Tracy's shaky emotional state during the first half of 1932 was due in part to his wife's pregnancy. He was terrified that their second child would have a birth defect. He became more considerate, more helpful at home, and very attentive toward Louise. He was working constantly that year, and although none of the movies was particularly good, he threw himself into his work with a new dedication. He did not spend an idle week for a solid year. Seven Tracy films, beginning with *Sky Devils*, were released in 1932.

The fourth was *Young America*, and it did little to add to the reputation of Frank Borzage, the director. It was the last film called for in his Fox contract. He went on to direct *A Farewell to Arms* for Paramount, and promised to make a deal for Tracy's services when the right property turned up.

In what seemed an exceptionally considerate gesture, the studio gave Tracy his choice of two projects about to go into production. Tracy declined *Man About Town* in favor of *Society Girl*, which was about the good old prizefight game. The role of the fighter had solid personality potential, and there was a subordinate role, a fight manager, which Tracy saw as a good opportunity for Lynne Overman to break into pictures. During his first meeting with producer Al Rockett, Tracy said nice things about the script and casually asked if the part of the manager had been cast. Rockett stared at him. Tracy repeated the question. Finally Rockett explained that the fight yarn had been purchased for James Dunn and that he, Tracy, was going to play the manager. After a few moments Tracy sheepishly asked if *Man About Town* was still up for grabs. No, Warner Baxter had inherited it.

Tracy played the manager. He felt he had hit rock bottom. Those who knew Fox Films and those who knew Tracy were often astonished by his ability to apply himself to silly parts in bad films, and to come through consistently with strong performances. There was no better example than *Society Girl*, a run-of-the-mill dud that Tracy's performance almost made a hit. The reviewers began to call attention to the discrepancy between Spencer's fine acting and the films it was wasted on.

Tracy was on location at Catalina Island for *The Painted Woman*, a 'South Seas' picture with nothing to offer except the scenery, when he became a father for the second time. He flew home to be with Louise and their healthy and fat baby girl. They named her Louise.

Tracy's joy in his new daughter lifted his depression completely, and even his problems at the studio became unimportant. Susie, as they nicknamed her, completely beguiled her father, and he started to spend more time at home once again. His relationship with Louise improved, and he found a new companionship with his son. Around the studio he was whimsical and irrepressible, teasing the ladies and holding court with Will Rogers in the studio commissary every lunchtime.

If Tracy ran true to form, this good humor would sooner or later fade into another depression. But for the moment he felt good, and there was more than a hint that his career would take a turn for the better, as well.

Tracy knew his way through the labyrinthine studio. He knew the cameramen, sound men, grips, and costumers, and he began to follow the activities of the story and casting departments, which had a critical bearing on his career. He was friendly with Julian Johnson, the new head of the story department, and he learned about properties being considered for production. He read all the mimeographed scripts, and so was ready to turn down bad ones before he was asked to do them. He was on his toes.

The quality of the scripts at Fox was improving, thanks to Julian Johnson, whose talents would survive many mergers and company upheavals. Tracy read an Arthur Kober story called 'Me and My Gal' that was apparently being fashioned for James Dunn and Sally Eilers. It was not one of Johnson's best finds, but Tracy was enthusiastic and surprised the casting office by asking for the lead. And he even suggested that Joan Bennett would be superb as the girl. He was astonished when both he and Miss Bennett were cast.

Me and My Gal was about an ordinary cop, a 'little guy' whose heroism catapults him into fame, wealth, and the arms of the girl at the fadeout. As usual, Tracy had misjudged the merits of a script, but he and Miss Bennett acted very well together, and the picture did unexpectedly well at the box office. Both principals often looked back on *Me and My Gal* with fondness, but it was still only a 'programmer'.

In later years. Spencer Tracy complained that he didn't like to talk about acting, but all the while he was doing a great deal of it, and enjoying it, for all his crustiness. He had a consuming interest in the work of other actors. At Fox he was acquainted with the work of just about everyone who could be called an actor. He often saw all the studio's new films, either in a Fox screening room or at a private screening. He would not miss a Barrymore film, and he much admired Fredric March, Walter Huston, Paul Muni, and Will Rogers. He thought most people missed seeing what a great actor Will Rogers really was. 'Oh, he's not acting, he's just being Will Rogers,' people would say. Tracy was baffled by the comment. 'What's the difference?' he asked. 'The whole idea is to be natural. Hell, Will *has* to be a great actor, why, he's acting even when the camera's not there. He has to act just to be able to keep talking the way he does, with all that colloquial speech when he knows better, and after all the proper talking he's been exposed to.'

Tracy believed that an actor should use his own personality for the shading of any role. Rogers did this in very

99

different roles, such as *Lightnin'* and *A Connecticut Yankee in King Arthur's Court.*

'I can't do what Will does,' he said. 'I can play a thug or a country boob or a flatfoot cop, but if somebody said, "Now act like Spencer Tracy," I wouldn't know what to do.'

Tracy thought Lionel Barrymore was the best of the lot, and that his role in the famous *Grand Hotel* was the finest thing an actor had accomplished on the screen.

Despite his intuitiveness about male actors, Tracy showed little real interest in screen actresses. His concern for a Jean Harlow or a Joan Bennett was a departure for him. Tracy knew who the important female stars were, and he shared in the general fascination with Greta Garbo. Otherwise, he found most of the movie actresses bland and, except for the color of their hair, interchangeable.

But when Tracy saw a sleazy, independently made picture called *Hell's House*, he was most excited by the vitality of an angular, big-eyed blond girl who was not especially pretty but who had an awkward grace and real talent that even Tracy could see. Then he remembered that her co-star Pat O'Brien had raved about her. Her name was Bette Davis, and it was coincidence that she became Spencer Tracy's leading lady in his next picture.

20,000 Years in Sing Sing promised to be a big winner for Warner Brothers, so the Fox studio was pleased when Michael Curtiz, the director, requested the loan of Spencer Tracy for the leading role. Tracy's pleasure was magnified when he learned that Bette Davis, recently taken on by Warners, was to be the girl — in this case, the moll.

Miss Davis knew something of Spencer Tracy's work, too. They got along well from the start of the four-week shooting schedule. It seemed that Bette was chafing at the bit, for she too felt that she was ready for better parts in better pictures than her employers were giving her.

Tracy told Bette she just might be the most talented woman in pictures.

'Damn right,' she agreed, 'but who are we against so many?'

They joked about their similarities — neither was handsome, and both had fierce tempers. And both missed the stage. They felt such rapport — it might have been that they were both Aries and, in fact, had the same birthday. Someday when they were rich they planned to make more and better pictures together, but for one reason or another, they never did.

20,000 Years in Sing Sing wasn't a big picture after all, but it had some things to recommend it. The picture was shot at the old First National studio in Burbank which had been absorbed by the growing Warner organization. Jack Warner ran the company with brisk efficiency. Tracy was impressed when he saw that his film's executive producer, Hal Wallace, the writer-supervisor, Robert Lord, and Curtiz were forging their own style for the studio. The attitude at Fox didn't compare well with the Warner enthusiasm for the business.

The picture was a box-office hit that clearly advanced Tracy's standing. But upon returning to Fox he learned that he was the cause of a studio quarrel.

While Tracy was at work in Burbank, Jesse L. Lasky brought his own production unit into the Fox organization. He upset a good many people by saying he was going to make better pictures at Fox than had ever been made there before, and after his first picture, *Zoo in Budapest*, it looked as if he was going to succeed. Tension was building over the limitations of Lasky's power and the extent of Sheehan's authority. One of the first Lasky-Sheehan disputes concerned Spencer Tracy.

Lasky wanted Tracy for the lead in what everyone conceded would be Fox's most ambitious production of the year. Sheehan was most concerned with making a profit on Fox pictures; it didn't always happen and, much as he admired Tracy's acting, he doubted that he could ever be big box office. He told Lasky that Tracy was too 'common' and Lasky was delighted.

'It's a picture about a common man,' he said. And it was decided that Tracy would be the hero of *The Power and the Glory*.

Although Preston Sturges wrote the screenplay, *The Power and the Glory* bears Lasky's stamp. It was his brain-child.

Jesse Lasky was a poor boy from San Francisco who hunted for gold in the Klondike, led a Hawaiian dance band in Honolulu, tried vaudeville and nickelodeon movies, and at last was inspired by some of Griffith's earliest work to try to make motion pictures. Lasky was a true Hollywood pioneer, organizing the company that made the first feature-length movie shot in Hollywood. Lasky made and lost a fortune, and the hard days of 1932 almost finished him. He conceived *The Power and the Glory* as his own personal testament.

During a preproduction phase that spanned several weeks, Tracy occupied himself by making *The Face in the Sky*. When work began on *The Power and the Glory*, Tracy once again started to worry. Lasky's project could be ruined if he made a poor showing. He could be solely responsible for a picture's failure. Tracy set about learning his role with almost fierce concentration. He went into seclusion to memorize the longest, as well as the most important part he had yet attempted.

Lasky's director was William K. Howard, who was Tracy's own age but had been well known around Hollywood since his teens. Howard, who had met Tracy earlier on the polo field, left him to his own resources. Howard said, 'When I saw the performance Spence was building all by himself I just gulped and said "roll".'

Colleen Moore, who had had a long career in silent films, took the part of the wife. She was so moved by Tracy's acting after her suicide scene that Howard had to shoot the 'dead' woman with her head turned away because tears were streaming down her cheeks. Word circulated through the studio that something out of the ordinary was going on, and little crowds would gather to watch the filming of Tracy's scenes. Toward the end of the shooting schedule the onlookers often included Lasky and Sheehan, standing side by side.

The Power and the Glory was one of the fine films to come out of Hollywood during the early 1930's. It was also an expensive one. The public did not respond to a new technique — Fox called it 'narratage' — a voice-over commentary tying together scenes that are out of chronological order. It was a brilliant device, and the technique was better received some years later in *Citizen Kane.* (It still works — witness 1967's *Two for the Road.*)

Production was completed in March of 1933 and release was withheld until August; it was a 'major' production with special promotion, and it had a premiere. The critics cheered. Tracy played a penniless young idealist who, aided by the sacrifice and love of his wife, rises to power as a railroad tycoon. He dies broke and tormented by grief and guilt after the destruction of his personal life. For people who knew Spencer Tracy and remembered *The Power and the Glory* the irony was inescapable.

After the critical response was in, Winfield Sheehan tore up Tracy's contract and had another one drawn up with a sizable salary increase and no option clause. It extended Tracy's commitment to Fox until 1937 and called for four films a year, which was standard for those days of mass production. Loan assignments to other studios could be negotiated only with Tracy's consent. There was also a vague understanding that Tracy would not be prevented from doing a Broadway play if he so willed it, but that the additional time would be owed the company. Tracy did not hesitate to sign; he believed his apprenticeship was over at last.

An interesting new project was announced for him, and then cancelled. He was told to take a vacation. Summoned back to the studio, he was told he was to costar with Lilian Harvey in *My Lips Betray.* He read the script and knew he was all wrong — and that even if he was right, it was a terrible script. Leslie Howard, who was filming his stage success *Berkeley Square* for Lasky, encouraged Tracy to refuse the role. Tracy finally took his advice and told Winfield Sheehan that he would not do *My Lips Betray.* Sheehan replied that Tracy was probably right — they had to be careful. Tracy was stunned. Sheehan then asked him if he was interested in doing a picture with Frank Borzage, at Columbia. Tracy said he'd take it, sight unseen. The picture was *Man's Castle*, and it was his first picture as a star. It also confirmed his reputation as the bad boy of Hollywood.

CHAPTER FOUR

TURBULENCE AND TRIUMPH: 1933–1936

WHEN Frank Borzage went independent, he hired a press agent to keep him in the public eye. The film colony knew all about *Man's Castle*. Even after Borzage knew that Spencer Tracy would play the lead, he would see that hints were planted in the trade papers that Gary Cooper might take the part, of James Cagney, or Paul Muni. It would look like hot news when it was announced that Spencer Tracy was signed for a role many big stars had 'sought'.

The name of the leading lady was also hidden behind the mystery Borzage's press agent trumped up. She was to be Loretta Young, just twenty years old. She was one of four sisters, and legend said that during her adolescence she answered a talent call for an older sister and got the part herself. At fifteen she was Lon Chaney's leading lady in *Laugh Clown, Laugh*, and she had made more than forty films before she came to Columbia to begin *Man's Castle*. She even had a 'past': she had married Grant Withers at seventeen, and her annulment trial the same year was well publicized. She was a Roman Catholic, unmarried, and a popular girl about town. It was kindness to say her acting was promising, but her beauty made such matters irrelevant.

When *Man's Castle* was released late in 1933, it was a critical success. Its story was one of true love during the Depression, and its box-office return far surpassed the forecast. There had to be a reason.

Perhaps it was because Loretta Young and Spencer Tracy had hit the gossip columns.

They fell in love when the shooting started. Hollywood

knew about it quickly. Soon the nation knew. And finally, all the good folk in Wichita Falls and Council Bluffs knew who Spencer Tracy was.

The romance affected the production schedule. Actor Walter Connolly said he felt like an intruder. Frank Borzage admitted he was embarrassed as a friend of the Tracy family.

Spencer Tracy moved out of the family home and soon there was a formal announcement to the press, nominally issued by Louise. They were separating, after ten years of marriage, on grounds of incompatibility. Tracy was quoted as saying to reporters that he hoped he and his wife would be able to work out their problems; but everyone knew the problem was Spencer's, and its name was Loretta. Tracy tried to avoid reporters, for he considered the press his natural enemy. During the fall of 1933 he was reported to have chewed out newsmen, kicked one reporter, wrestled with photographers, and smashed a few cameras.

Of course Louella Parsons quoted Tracy's assurance that his friendship with Loretta Young was casual and platonic. Actess Helen Twelvetrees, who was working with Tracy at the time, wanted to know when he was sober enough to say a thing like that.

Smashed cameras notwithstanding, Tracy and Miss Young were photographed together frequently — in restaurants, driving, arriving at places — looking as if they only had eyes for each other.

The affair was caught up by the fan magazines, and running accounts would take the form of monthly serials. In one installment the Tracy–Young romance is over: they say a fervent good-bye — Loretta is in tears — in the garden of a Los Angeles hospital, where Miss Young is recovering from an operation. Next month Spencer Tracy rushes into the Fox commissary to see Loretta Young, and they kiss fondly.

In October of 1934 Loretta Young issued a simple statement to the press saying that as she and Mr. Spencer Tracy could not hope to marry because of their Catholic religion, they had agreed they would no longer see one another.

Tracy characteristically said there was nothing to it. In later years he insisted that the whole affair was blown out of proportion by the press. But there have been responsible accounts of his love for her and his unhappiness at the end of the affair. He had 'gone Hollywood', rented a hotel suite, and bought dinner jackets, top hats, white ties and tails; he had taken Loretta to every nightclub in town, and they did the party circuit. He lost himself in the glitter and romance of Hollywood, and in his own words, 'accepted all the attitudes and philosophies I'd despised for so many years'. The romance affected his work as well as his home life, and the situation rapidly became impossible.

Louise had not exactly been pining. She had her own career now and it meant a lot to her. And she may at last have understood Spencer Tracy. He said, 'Louise knew I was going to come home eventually. She must have known that sooner or later I was going to slip out of the socket and take on a kind of life I'd never known . . . the wonder was that she would take me back at all.'

The Tracys were separated for a year. Then Louise wanted him to come home. Tracy later said: 'When I walked into the house, a door closed over the year that had passed and neither of us will ever open it again. She has never mentioned the affair from that day.'

*   *   *

Tracy seemed to be poised on the threshold of stardom when he completed *The Power and the Glory*. But although his performance in *Man's Castle* showed he could play a romantic hero, when he returned to Fox from Columbia, he hit rock bottom. The studio personnel hadn't seen *Man's Castle*, for Frank Borzage was deferring its release for several months. The fine reviews of *The Power and the Glory* were followed by low receipts at the box office, and they blamed it on Spencer Tracy's lack of drawing power. And on top of that, Spencer Tracy was courting scandal, and coming to the studio drunk!

Over the years Tracy was candid and often whimsical

about his periodic drinking bouts. But he claimed never to have been drunk while acting in a picture. And this was literally true, for there is no evidence he ever was reeling in front of a movie camera. But there were times when he came close. He would sometimes show up for work still wearing his dinner jacket from the night before, and obviously working on a hangover. Fox Films said they were unhappy with Tracy because he drank too much, but Tracy said he drank too much because he wasn't getting anywhere at Fox. Whatever the reason, during the year he was separated from Louise, Tracy drank enough to get him into scrapes and worry his friends. And Sheehan said that Tracy was not to be trusted with a major assignment until he had gotten himself in line. He worked in a couple of mediocre pictures, *Shanghai Madness* and *The Mad Game*, that, ironically, made more money for Fox than *The Power and the Glory*, and then started to rebel at the parts he was offered.

He refused to do *Orient Express*, which he thought didn't compare with Dietrich's *Shanghai Express*. He flatly refused to do *Hold That Girl*, despite a good screenplay, because he had a grudge against the director. He turned down *I Believed in You*. Sheehan, patience wearing thin, asked Tracy what on earth he'd be willing to do, and Tracy replied that, frankly, he'd be willing to work somewhere else.

Tracy had come to regard Winfield Sheehan as his private bête noire, but Sheehan tried harder to please Tracy than Tracy gave him credit for. Sheehan was having his own problems, and it affected the way he coped with his actors.

Sheehan had been the foremost organizer of the Fox Films company and the architect of its growth, although his efforts were less publicized than those of the colourful William Fox. But now the company was in debt, and there was talk of a merger which, if consummated, could hardly benefit Winfield Sheehan. He was a generation removed from the Thalbergs and Selznicks and Bermans who understood the new public and the new times. The company had outgrown Sheehan, and he was caught with too much responsibility and too big a job.

He was not in a position to put up with Tracy's erratic behavior. Two or three times in 1934 Tracy disappeared for two days or a week, and no one, including Louise, could find him. Then he would suddenly appear, bright and cheerful and ready for work, with no explanation. But the most famous incident occurred when Tracy was all alone at the studio.

He had showed up one late afternoon, reeling, and in an ugly mood — a more and more common state. He roared and swore a bit, and finally fell asleep on a sofa that was part of a set. To keep Tracy safe, and also to make sure he would be there the next morning, Sheehan had him locked inside for the night and everyone went home. In the early morning hours there was a terrible racket. The next morning Tracy looked haggard, amazed, and guilty at the same time. The set was a shambles, completely destroyed.

Tracy had said he was willing to work somewhere else, and by now Sheehan was willing, too.

*   *   *

Another Hollywood actor was also named Tracy, and was equally famous for getting into trouble.

Lee Tracy — no relation — was older than Spencer by two years, and thanks to his Broadway appearance in the Hecht-MacArthur *The Front Page*, he was a good deal more successful in Hollywood as well as in New York.

When Spencer Tracy went to Darryl Zanuck's and Joe Schenck's new, independent 20th Century company for a one-picture loan, he hoped to play the lead in the film version of Nathanael West's *Miss Lonelyhearts*, but he ended up in a routinely bad film, *Looking for Trouble*, and Lee Tracy played *Miss Lonelyhearts*. It was Lee who had a contract with Metro-Goldwyn-Mayer and good exposure in big, important pictures like *Dinner at Eight*. He was promoted to leading roles and played opposite Jean Harlow in *Bombshell*. He was on his way. Spencer Tracy couldn't help envying him.

Then an ironic turn of events reversed their fortunes.

Lee Tracy managed to get in a bigger scrape than Spencer had ever dreamed of. He touched off an international incident while acting in *Viva Villa*.

On location in Mexico, Lee Tracy had a little too much to drink, got in a fight, and although no one is sure of the facts, he was thrown in jail and charged with insulting the Mexican Government, its army, its people, and the country itself. He had offended with a 'gesturing' finger.

Louis B. Mayer fumed. Then he issued an eloquent apology to the Mexican Government, and fired Lee Tracy.

Mayer told Hollywood's inner circle that he would keep Lee Tracy out of Hollywood. Although Lee Tracy did pick up some minor picture assignments here and there, Mayer had power throughout the industry. In the end, Lee Tracy returned to New York, never again to succeed as a star in motion pictures.

One of the roles left open by Lee Tracy's abrupt departure from M-G-M was that of Aubrey Piper in Herman Mankiewicz's screenplay of George Kelly's satire, *The Show-Off*. With the aid of his friend Frank Morgan at M-G-M, Tracy was chosen for the part. Tracy agreed to a one-picture loan swamp with M-G-M, Robert Young going to Fox. *The Show-Off* became one of Tracy's happier experiences, for it made money and the reviews were good. Tracy, who was given solo star billing, was not particularly pleased with the end result. 'It ought to be better and so should I,' he said. But he was impressed with the professionalism of M-G-M and he liked working there.

Tracy met Irving Thalberg, M-G-M's legendary young producer, who was most interested in Tracy's work. Thalberg visited Tracy in his dressing room and wanted to know how much time remained on Tracy's Fox contract. Three years was a long time, but perhaps Tracy might be available sooner. Tracy hoped it was possible.

In a way, *The Show-Off* was one of the milestones of Tracy's career. It laid the foundation for everything that came after.

*   *   *

Tracy's last years at Fox were emotionally violent. They were wearing him down physically as well. His once-hard physique now was twenty pounds heavier than when he had arrived in Hollywood.

In June of 1933, while playing in the Brandeis Cup matches on the Riviera polo green, Tracy was involved in a three-horse spill in which he sprained an arm, wrenched his back, and suffered facial cuts. He was between movie assignments, having just completed *The Power and the Glory*, but the studio was now naturally concerned about his interest in the game.

Tracy stopped playing briefly after the accident and soon was out of shape. When he separated from his wife, he gave in to a kind of compulsive eating and drinking. He was also smoking too much and drinking ten to twenty cups of coffee a day.

He resumed polo, but when Fox revised his contract it forbade him to play while making a film. Tracy, like some of his friends at the club, disobeyed by playing under false names. A favorite was Ivan Catchanzoff. Tracy often pulled that trick after he became M-G-M property. Winfield Sheehan was furious when Tracy was hurt in another fall during the shooting period for *Marie Galante* in the summer of 1934.

It was a wonder that Tracy survived at all. He seldom slept. 'I'm the open-up guy!' he said. He was notorious for his early morning studio calls, since he was often up before dawn. He took naps at the studios when not on call for a scene, but regardless of when he went to bed at night, he would be worrying over his part in the morning. He took long morning showers, often prepared his own large breakfast, and arrived at the studio braced by several cups of coffee . . . the open-up guy.

In February of 1934 he was so worried over a kidnapping threat he was 'written out' of some scenes in *Bottoms Up* so he could rest and get hold of himself without delaying the picture. Tracy had received an anonymous letter demanding $8,000, with the threat that if he didn't hand over the money, he or one or both of his children, or, as reported in *The New York Times*, the 'young actress with whom his name has been linked romantically', would be kidnapped. Tracy called in the police, and although the threat turned out to be a bluff, thereafter Tracy was more cynical than he had been, and a good deal less trusting.

*   *   *

After being loaned out for two pictures in a row, Tracy wanted to be released for a third. Frank Borzage wanted him and had a good part in mind. Fox's answer was a flat no.

After all, Tracy had fallen for Loretta Young, and Fox thought that there was a chance he would fall for the brilliant newcomer Margaret Sullavan, who was to play the ingenue lead in Borzage's film. Miss Sullavan, who had once been married to a then unknown actor named Henry Fonda, was not married at the time and was one of the most sought-after ladies in Hollywood. Although she wasn't beautiful she had a certain magnetism.

Fox Films scheduled Tracy for a musical, *Bottoms Up*, which was designed primarily to exploit the talents of the new English actress, Pat Paterson. The picture was entertaining enough and Miss Paterson was a charmer; offscreen she charmed Charles Boyer and retired to become his wife. But Tracy's talents were wasted in the only musical he ever made, and he was angry.

The next picture — *Now I'll Tell*, written by Mrs. Arnold Rothstein, wife of the slain gambler — was better for Tracy, who was suddenly given star billing again. The picture was topical, and people flocked to see it.

Now I'll Tell also profited by the brief appearance of a Fox starlet who had done a specialty bit in *Stand Up and Cheer*. Paramount borrowed her for a film about a race track, called *Little Miss Marker*. The two Fox films and the Paramount film were all May releases in 1934, and when the comet that was Shirley Temple blazed across the sky, Mrs. Rothstein's lurid story was all but eclipsed. Tracy too was upstaged, for no one could compete with Shirley Temple.

In the late summer of 1934 George M. Cohan came west to make a film of one of his comedies, and he soon became a fixture at Will Rogers' table in the Fox commissary. Tracy, who usually lunched with Will, avoided the two men. He was jealous, and hurt that Cohan ignored him, as a rebuke for his recent behavior. The first time they spoke to one another was one day when their car bumpers locked in the Fox lot. After they separated the cars with the aid of a studio policeman, they made small talk for a few moments. Then Cohan's voice began to rise, and Tracy began to give him an argument. But he thought better of it, for Cohan gave him such a tongue-lashing that Tracy could only listen in stunned silence. Cohan finished by saying, 'Spence, you have a responsibility to your talent!' Cohan was no prig, and had had his own lapses now and again. He didn't care how Tracy led his life away from acting, but he did care that Tracy was in Hollywood instead of on Broadway, and that he was muffing even that small challenge. He told Tracy, 'You're still a good actor, Spencer . . . *almost* as good as you were five years ago.' Cohan drove away, and Tracy got into his car. Minutes passed and Tracy just sat there, slouched over the steering wheel, bawling like a baby.

Some time later, during the course of Cohan's film, *Gambling*, Tracy rejoined the Rogers table and was, for a few weeks, a good-humored companion, full of jokes and pranks. Tracy returned to his wife during the period of Cohan's visit, and temporarily seemed to be at peace.

Cohan was again in his glory. Some of his bitterness had been wiped away by the enthusiastic response to his performance as Nat Miller in Eugene O'Neill's *Ah, Wilderness* the year before. Now he was giving Hollywood another chance. But *Gambling* was a disaster.

Hollywood wasn't going to give Cohan another chance, although Warners and James Cagney would pay him the compliment of a splendid musical tribute in *Yankee Doodle Dandy*, released in 1942 just months before his death.

At the time of Tracy's return to his wife, Louise suggested that he go on the wagon. He wasn't the sort of drinker who loved the taste of liquor; when things were going well, he could take it or leave it. But his last three pictures for Fox were mediocre — though *Dante's Inferno* is remembered for a ten-minute depiction of hell, and a spectacular fire touched off by a pair of whirling Spanish dancers, one of whom, Rita Cansino, would change her last name to Hayworth. Tracy, despite his return to his family, his affection for two-year-old Suzy, and the pleasure of teaching John how to play polo, wasn't able to stay away from the bottle. He started missing studio calls and his last Fox picture, *It's a Small World*, ran over its small budget as production dragged into March of 1935. In fact, when the picture was ready to wind up, Tracy was far from Hollywood. He was arrested March 11, in Yuma, Arizona, on charges of being drunk, using excessive profanity, resisting an officer, and destroying private property. The manager of the Yuma hotel where Tracy was staying with his friend Hugh Tully called the police when he heard a terrific ruckus from Tracy's room. The police found Tracy screaming incoherently into the telephone at Louise. The room was a mess and Tracy was smashing dishes against a wall.

When Louise got to Yuma to collect her husband he had been released and was gone. Tracy and Tully had made their way across the Mexican border to Nogales.

The incident made the headlines, but when Tracy returned, it was more or less forgotten. He didn't get in as much trouble as he might have because Sheehan, Sol Wurtzel, and most of the other top men at Fox were in New York, where talks were going on with increasing frequency.

On a Sunday late in March, Tracy went to the races with Will Rogers and sought advice from the only man he ever really confided in. When Will pointed out Louis B. Mayer in his private box, Tracy told Rogers he was trying to work a deal to join the M-G-M company.

'If I can pull it off, you think they'll let me go?'

Rogers knew who *they* were, and he thought Tracy should be patient awhile and see what kind of merger Sidney Kent, the Fox president, was going to work out. Besides, Will said,

Spence was going to be in a big picture at Fox, *The Farmer Takes a Wife*, with Janet Gaynor, then a reigning queen of Hollywood.

But Tracy wasn't going to get the leading role; it would go to a new actor, Henry Fonda. Fonda had a Fox contract and was already at the studio. Tracy's was the supporting role, the 'heavy'. He told Phil Friedman and Ed Butcher, the only studio people of consequence he could find, that he just wouldn't do it. If this was his punishment for his sins, forget it: he'd rather be fired.

So he was fired.

Tracy left the studio. No announcement was made, because nothing was official until Winfield Sheehan returned from New York. *The Farmer Takes a Wife* went into production with Tracy's name on the roster, but he was nowhere in sight. The announcement that Spencer Tracy and the Fox Film Corporation were parting company after an association of almost five years was issued on April 8, 1935.

That same afternoon, Tracy began his twenty-year association with Metro-Goldwyn-Mayer. He didn't lose a day's pay; indeed, he got a raise — only one feature of a contract that contained more than the usual number of conditions and restrictions.

Tracy's departure preceded Sheehan's by three months. In July the Fox empire crumbled. Sidney Kent stayed on, but Joe Schenck became chairman of the board. It was a capitulative merger, Schenck and Darryl F. Zanuck were in, and Zanuck was the new production boss, replacing Sheehan.

Tracy liked Zanuck and had a few qualms at leaving just as Zanuck was getting power in the company. But he didn't worry long.

*   *   *

Louis B. Mayer was not in favor of taking Tracy on. No matter that Spencer Tracy was so good an actor.

'He wrecks sets. Besides, he's a galoot . . . and we already have a galoot in the family.'

The galoot was Wallace Beery. The 'family' was M-G-M: its executives, directors, technical specialists, workmen, clerks and secretaries ... and its actors, among whom were some of the greatest stars in the world.

Mayer really did think of his company as a family, and he was certainly its head. Some close friends teased him about it, others made fun of him behind his back. Mayer was a strange, terrifying, funny man, and probably Hollywood's greatest actor.

And yet somehow he brought it off: Metro-Goldwyn-Mayer *was* a family, and like all fine families it had pride, fierce loyalty, the ability to close ranks in a crisis, and dedication to its tradition.

Because it was so large a family there was a good deal of squabbling, but without a doubt it was the greatest motion picture organization in the world.

If Mayer didn't think Tracy belonged with M-G-M, he was won over by the realization that Tracy would be happy there, and that when Tracy was happy he didn't cause trouble. Mayer loathed the kind of trouble that got in the papers and embarrassed the family.

Actually, the fact that Irving Thalberg had put in a good word for Tracy after *The Show-Off* made it easier for Leo Morrison, an agent whom Tracy had known in New York and contacted during the final days at Fox, to convince Mayer that Tracy would be an asset.

Most of the big men at M-G-M thought Tracy would be a good acquisition because he could act and had a fairly respectable name. Moreover, Mayer did not know just how bad Tracy's behavior had been at Fox.

There was a welcoming ceremony and Tracy was photographed shaking hands with Mayer and various other executives. He talked briefly with Thalberg and learned that his first M-G-M assignment would be opposite Jean Harlow in a picture Thalberg would produce.

Tracy was immediately impressed by the efficiency of the studio operations. The first project was to give him an image and Tracy was photographed, biographed, and made ready

116

for exploitation. He met two men who would be permanent friends: Howard Strickling, the West Coast head of publicity, and Frank Whitbeck, in advertising. Whitbeck told Tracy that Howard Strickling was possibly the only person at the studio who had the confidence of both Mayer and Thalberg.

This was the first inkling Tracy had that Mayer and Thalberg weren't getting along.

*　　　*　　　*

The lion originally was the symbol for the Goldwyn Company. Samuel Goldfish and Edgar Selwyn formed the company in 1917, and Sam liked the name so well he took it for his own. He was no longer involved with the company when it merged with the Metro firm that Mayer had helped organize in 1915. The merger, possibly the most significant in movie history up to that point, was engineered principally by Mayer, who brought his own production unit into the new organization that officially became Metro-Goldwyn-Mayer in 1925.

Mayer's group included Irving Thalberg. In this brand-new industry that featured so many spectacular successes, Thalberg remained the boy wonder. He came to Hollywood at the age of eighteen to take a clerical job with Carl Laemmle at Universal, and through a combination of aggressiveness and extraordinary instinct, he was running production at the studio before he was old enough to vote. Mayer, with some instinct of his own, placed him in charge of production at M-G-M. Thalberg, like Mayer, was vain and proud, money mattered to him and so did power. But unlike Mayer, Thalberg had innate good taste, was something of an intellectual, and wanted to make good films as well as successful ones. Mayer was expert in the business areas that Thalberg found less interesting, so they made a good team.

Mayer once thought of making his executive producer into his son-in-law, but when he learned that Thalberg had a weak heart he changed his mind. Thalberg did marry into 'the family', however, and it was a perfect Hollywood marriage: he chose Norma Shearer, already an M-G-M star before their marriage in 1927, and destined for one of the great screen careers under Thalberg's guidance.

Both Mayer daughters married young film producers not of their father's choosing, and one — David Selznick — was the son of a former Mayer arch enemy. But Mayer was smart enough to overlook old grudges. He was impressed by young Selznick's work, first at Paramount and then at RKO, where he had charge of production at the age of twenty-nine. Mayer brought David Selznick into M-G-M when he needed him.

After building up the company to unprecedented success, Thalberg cracked physically under the strain of his job and went to Europe to recuperate. Mayer took pains to see that nobody, not even Thalberg upon his return, would have so much power again. He hired Selznick to produce the studio's more ambitious films, and upgraded several Thalberg lieutenants — Hunt Stromberg, Bernie Human, and Lawrence Weingarten among them — to full producers. When Thalberg returned, he was pacified by a fair amount of cash, and he became an autonomous producer responsible for six pictures annually. Thalberg and Selznick, although still good friends personally, became jealous rivals at M-G-M.

Rivalry was a healthy spur. At M-G-M, Selznick made *Dinner at Eight* (after Thalberg's *Grand Hotel*), *David Copperfield*, and *Anna Karenina*. Thalberg produced *The Merry Widow* and *The Barretts of Wimpole Street*, and brought the Marx Brothers into the family with *A Night at the Opera*. Obviously M-G-M aimed at, and hit, higher targets than were ever raised at Fox.

Louis B. Mayer now favored Selznick in what he genuinely believed was a battle for his affection. What both Selznick and Thalberg wanted was total artistic independence; neither really needed Mayer, however much Mayer needed them. Selznick decided that getting out was his only solution. Thalberg, convinced that he and not Mayer was responsible for the studio's success and prestige, decided to stay on and fight. After Selznick completed arrangements to leave M-G-M and form his own company Thalberg's rivalry was with Mayer alone. The old rapport was gone; what remained was a bitter alliance, disguised by a mutually artful show of diplomacy.

When Spencer Tracy checked in at the Culver City studio, Selznick was at work on *A Tale of Two Cities*, his final obligation, and Thalberg was producing *Mutiny on the Bounty*. At M-G-M the actual production sometimes took three to five months. Editing was not the hasty mechanical function it was at Fox. M-G-M might be a factory, but it turned out an excellent product — precise, machine-perfect — sometimes handled lovingly but always with efficiency. A major picture completed in the spring might not be released until fall, if it would benefit from a lengthy promotion.

Tracy quickly changed his thinking about the movie business.

*   *   *

'Spencer Tracy will become one of the important M-G-M stars.' So said Thalberg when Tracy started work on *Riffraff*.

Who were the 'important' M-G-M stars?

At the beginning of 1935 the studio roll listed sixteen official 'stars'. (The status had precise definition in the Hollywood of that day, but never so consciously as at M-G-M.) There were eight female stars and an equal number of men (if you counted three Marxes as one star, as M-G-M did).

Three vacancies occurred just before Tracy arrived. Marion Davies, whose fabulous 'bungalow' had been the studio's center of gravity socially, left for Warners and took the bungalow with her, because William Randolph Hearst was miffed that Irving Thalberg wouldn't let her play Marie Antoinette. Helen Hayes, who in three years with the studio made seven moderately successful films and received an Oscar, chose to return to Broadway and not come back. And Ramon Novarro, a silent movie star who couldn't make it in talkies, was let go.

But the stars who stayed on were spectacular, particularly the ladies, M-G-M had the 'biggest' female stars of the day: Greta Garbo, Norma Shearer, Jean Harlow, Joan Crawford, Jeanette MacDonald, and Myrna Loy. Although the studio didn't have many leading men, it had good ones — Clark Gable, Robert Montgomery, William Powell. The others — besides Groucho, Chico, and Harpo — were character actors Wallace Beery and Lionel Barrymore, and the best of the Tarzans, Johnny Weissmuller.

Stardom was determined by the executives at M-G-M, and you had to be good to be chosen. The gaps left by Davies, Hayes, and Novarro were filled by Freddie Bartholomew, a marvelous boy actor; Nelson Eddy, who had wavy blond hair and a pleasant baritone and was well suited to operettas with Miss MacDonald; and the least certain prospect, Spencer Tracy.

Among those who played leading roles and had some national following but were not yet stars, were Franchot Tone, Robert Young, Maureen O'Sullivan, and Rosalind Russell. Others in the background and on their way up were Mickey Rooney and Spangler Arlington Brugh whose name had been changed to Robert Taylor.

Few of the studio executives, except Billy Grady, the talent head, agreed with Thalberg that Tracy was the M-G-M idea of a star. The company, and the moviegoing public, was in for a surprise.

*   *   *

Tracy was to be given feature billing in his first picture, *Riffraff* with Jean Harlow, and was scheduled to be raised to stardom in his second.

Riffraff was postponed because of a conflict in schedule, and rather than have Tracy sit idle, the studio assigned him *The Murder Man*, a quickie shot in three weeks that was not particularly memorable.

For Tracy, the best thing about *The Murder Man* was a

new friendship with a young actor fresh from Broadway.

Playing the role of 'Shorty', the gangling James Stewart gave the film — his very first — a built-in laugh. Throughout his career, Tracy preferred actors trained on the stage, He liked Stewart personally and liked his seriousness about the job of acting.

'I told him to forget the camera was there,' Tracy said. 'That was all he needed; in his very first scene he showed he had all the good things.'

Tracy was at work on *Riffraff* before *The Murder Man* was finished. He had a difficult part to play, for he had to make an unpleasant character sympathetic.

One afternoon during the first days of shooting Tracy was about to go home after a hard session trying to please Robert Z. Leonard, the director, who had ideas about acting. Jean Harlow stopped him.

'Hey, Spence, ain't you gonna look at the rushes?'

The 'rushes' of scenes recently shot were rough, unedited footage without sound, and it was a tradition at M-G-M to review the rushes at the end of a day's work. At Fox, Tracy usually saw his performances only in the finished print. He went into a screening room with Harlow, Leonard, Una Merkel, and assorted crewmen, and watched the grainy takes, fidgeting and grimacing at each scene. When the session was over, he glared at the blond star and said, 'Don't ever ask me to do that again. I couldn't stand it!' And that was the last time he ever watched rushes.

After *Riffraff* 'wound' on a Friday in early October, Tracy went to work the following Monday on *Whipsaw*. Tracy was to receive co-star billing with Myrna Loy in *Whipsaw* — his first chance to share above-the-title billing with a major female star.

After starting in movies in 1925 typed as the Oriental siren — hence the last name of Loy, Myrna Williams had some fifty films to her credit when Thalberg gave her a contract as a supporting player in 1932, on the hunch she could be shaped into a specific kind of star, a 'lady'. She proved him right, and *The Thin Man* established Myrna Loy and

William Powell as the screen's most sophisticated romantic team. The studio used her to good advantage, and after ten pictures in two years, without a proper raise, Myrna Loy felt she was being exploited. She went on a long salary strike and didn't come back until the studio met her demand.

Her absence had the unforeseen effect of further expanding the company's roster of leading ladies; Eddie Mannix once remarked that if M-G-M got a new star every time Myrna Loy didn't make a picture, he hoped she never came back. Two pictures bought for her and Powell were made with other actresses playing opposite Powell, and both women — Rosalind Russell, who had been playing 'other woman' parts, and Luise Rainer — went to the top.

Whipsaw was also purchased for the star team, but when Miss Loy was ready to work at the studio again, William Powell was at work on another picture, and Thalberg suggested to Harry Rapf, the associate producer, that he try Spencer Tracy in the romantic lead. Rapf and the director, Sam Wood, were probably inclined to do anything Irving thought was a good idea. But right away, Tracy and Sam Wood were at one another's throats. Tracy thought Wood wasted a lot of time, and he blew up when, after a long 'take', Wood decided to shoot the scene over because he wasn't sure Myrna Loy had the proper romantic lighting. Thalberg heard of the friction between the two men, and visited the set. He pulled Wood aside.

'Well, Sam, what's your opinion of Tracy?'

Wood glared at Thalberg for a moment, then snapped, 'I think the red-headed bastard is the best actor on the lot!' And, in fact, a friendship eventually developed between Wood and Tracy.

Whipsaw was a routine cops-and-robbers picture, with Tracy cast as a G-man and Miss Loy with the robbers. She switched sides just in time for a clinch before the final fade-out. Tracy was no Bill Powell for urbanity, but it was a good performance that showed he had a style of his own.

By a quirk, *Whipsaw* was released before *Riffraff* because the studio officials thought it wise to get Miss Loy back into circulation as quickly as possible. As a result, Tracy had star billing in the film preceding the one in which he was only featured.

On December 4, 1935, Tracy made the headlines again, when he squared off with William Wellman on the floor of Hollywood's Trocadero nightclub. The fight was kicked off by a remark Wellman had made to Tracy about Loretta Young, and Tracy got the worst of it. Wellman, known as 'Wild Bill', gave Tracy a black eye and suffered what he called 'a slight aggravation of the knuckles'. The fight lasted only a few seconds, but it was long enough. The papers showed a picture of Tracy with the caption, 'Fights over Loretta'.

Louis B. Mayer was furious about the story, but not nearly so angry as Tracy. The story implied he was still carrying on his affair with Loretta Young, which was far from the truth. (Miss Young, in fact, had made *Call of the Wild* with M-G-M's Clark Gable and this combination touched off a new round of stories in the gossip columns, shortly after which Gable's second marriage, to a leading socialite, came to an end.)

Tracy wasn't so concerned about his image, or his pride — he was unhappy about what such rumors might do to his life with Louise. The incident occurred at a time when their relationship, helped out by his new pleasure in his work, had strengthened. Fortunately, it was strong enough to ride over the Wellman fracas, and as matters would have it, that was Tracy's last brush with scandal for almost twenty years.

The Tracys turned their thoughts to buying a house — something they had talked of intermittently since coming to Hollywood. In 1936 they purchased a twelve-acre ranch in Encino that had once belonged to Gary Cooper. The rambling house was like a Mexican ranch house, far from ostentatious, but very comfortable. The place was Tracy's idea of paradise — fifteen miles from the studio, well out in the country.

He had bought his first polo pony in 1932 and had

continued to acquire them, in twos and threes, until he had more than a dozen. The horses were his personal friends, so he would not sell them when they were too old for the game. The Encino ranch became an old folks' home for horses.

Tracy still played polo and Louise also took it up, and became a superb horsewoman. John inherited his father's passion for pool, and also was on his way to becoming a champion swimmer.

The whole family loved ranch life. Tracy enjoyed pitching hay; he liked good hard work. The ranch house was a place where he could really relax, and where he began to do more reading — biography and history.

In time the ranch ground would be inhabited by Shetland ponies, goats, chickens and ducks, turkeys, and dogs — mostly Irish setters. And no cats.

*   *   *

M-G-M publicity men liked to describe Tracy as a 'man's man'. Ed Sullivan had already tagged him the 'actors' actor'. M-G-M housed many men's men — Gable, certainly; directors like Sam Wood, Jack Conway, and Victor Fleming; executives like Eddie Mannix and Billy Grady and Frank Whitbeck. But Tracy pointed out a man whose hobby, according to a studio biography, was work, and whose name was right out of an Oscar Wilde drawing room.

'There,' he said, indicating W. S. Van Dyke II, 'Is a man's man's man.'

Woody Van Dyke who, like Irving Thalberg, would die before his time, is a Hollywood legend, a man dear to all whose lives he touched. He touched Tracy's, and changed his career.

He convinced Tracy that he should take the part of Father Mike, a priest, in *San Francisco*. Clark Gable had the lead, playing opposite Jeanette MacDonald. Van Dyke thought the movie would be a smash hit.

'But there's one important thing it has to have ... and that's *humanity*. Father Mike has to supply it, and so help me, Spencer, you're the only actor I know who can bring humanity into a part. I don't know where you got it, but you have it.'

Tracy was touched. Still, a 'supporting' part ... well, could he see a script?

Van Dyke gave Tracy a script of *San Francisco* and the next day Tracy was worried sick about it. From what Van Dyke had heard that was a good sign. Tracy liked the part, and it wasn't like any supporting role he'd ever seen. It was smaller than the two leads but it was fat enough and had character and was strong ... and yes, it needed humanity. But he was worried about playing a priest, of all things, for fear of sacrilege ... especially considering his rough reputation! Mayer, however, thought it was a great idea. He didn't like Roman Catholics much anyway, and thought it was a good thing that they had an actor who *was* one, so they wouldn't run the risk of seeming prejudiced.

San Francisco went into production early in 1936. Gable and Tracy developed a deep personal friendship at the studio, but contrary to publicity accounts they seldom met socially away from the lot. They were not so much alike as many claimed, but both were masculine by instinct rather than by studied effort. Gable was an extrovert; he started and carried conversations that Tracy ended with a few well-chosen words. Gable's respect for Tracy was unbounded. Although Gable scoffed outwardly at his own acting pretensions, inside he wanted to be a good actor. Tracy was his criterion.

Woody Van Dyke was the fastest director in Hollywood and became a favorite of Mayer's because he always brought his pictures in under the allotted budgets, finishing well ahead of schedule. He filmed *The Thin Man* in seventeen days. *San Francisco* took considerably longer, but Tracy's scenes were almost all accomplished in one take. And from the start it looked as if this would be a Spencer Tracy picture all the way.

*   *   *

Fritz Lang was one of the great German directors, and the

most notable figure of the European cinema to escape to Hollywood during the Hitler regime. Courtly, monocled, and militarily slim, he did not have a studio contract but was looking for a property with as much potential as his silent classic *Metropolis*, or the later film *M*, which made Peter Lorre a household name.

M-G-M had a Norman Krasna story that Lang liked, and although a picture about mob violence and a lynching would not be a money-maker, everyone — except, of course, Mayer himself — was enthusiastic about the project because it was unusual and uncompromisingly bold.

Lang reportedly was given a list of actors who would be made available and was told to take his choice. His choice was Tracy. A one-picture arrangement was made with Silvia Sidney, whose specialty was strong dramatic roles.

It went before the cameras as *Mob Rule* and Tracy reported late, for it overlapped *San Francisco*. Nobody liked the title much, and they were looking for a new one to follow *Reckless*, *Escapade*, *Rendezvous*, *Riffraff*, *Whipsaw*, and *Speed*. Tracy suggested *Fury*; it was perfect, and they got on with the picture.

The shooting schedule was short for the sake of economy, but Lang would have brought the picture in under any circumstances, and *Fury* took only four weeks. Lang came from a movie-making environment that gave the director absolute rule over hours and meals as well as the actors' roles. If Lang didn't want to eat, nobody ate. If he didn't want to go home, he would insist that the crew and the actors work on into the night. No one said much about union regulations because they were all somewhat scared of him. However, Tracy wasn't scared; he was angry. He liked to act but nothing was worth working through lunch, and then staying on the job and working through dinner. He and Lang screamed at one another and almost came to blows. And that was what Lang had in mind.

Lang had a theory that to really do justice to a part, an actor had to take on the character completely. Tracy was playing an emotionally and physically exhausted man, wrung out by his own rage. And by the time Tracy was well into the film, he didn't have to do much acting to get the mood across.

Tracy played Joseph Wheeler, a young man mistakenly arrested as a kidnap-murder suspect, identified as the guilty man, and jailed to await trial. A violent mob burns down the jail after failing to break in to get Wheeler. When the real kidnapper is caught and confesses, the mob leaders go on trial for Wheeler's murder, for Wheeler is presumed dead. But in fact Wheeler has escaped. Now, however, he is a changed man — bitter, violent, intent on revenge. Fritz Lang shot the film in sequence to capture the gradual change in Joe's personality.

Many have said that Spencer Tracy turned in his finest performance as Joe Wheeler. And it would be hard to find a scene to equal his final speech in *Fury* when, after the defendants have been declared guilty, he strides down the aisle of the courtroom, and addresses the judge.

'Your Honor, I'm Joseph Wheeler . . . first of all, I know I arrived just in time to save the lives of twenty-two people. I can't help that, that isn't why I'm here . . .'

*　　　*　　　*

They next asked him if he could do farce. Hell, it was the only thing they thought he could do during his days in stock, he told them.

So he was in *Libeled Lady*, one of the great examples of screwball comedy, a form perfected in the 1930's.

Not since *Dinner at Eight*, three years earlier, had M-G-M made one of its all-star specials, but the press releases indicated that *Libeled Lady* would sport four 'major' stars, including Spencer Tracy. He knew he would be fourth on the list, but he hoped his part and his billing would not be far behind the other three stars. His status seemed to go up and down at M-G-M.

Because *San Francisco* required long editing time and big promotion, *Fury* was released first in New York's Capitol

Theater, and *San Francisco* followed in the same house three weeks later.

Suddenly Spencer Tracy was in. *Fury* was an overwhelming critical success, although it only made money in its Manhattan engagement. Every critic heaped superlatives on Tracy, yet it is possible that his performance was upstaged by Lang's directorial debut in America, which was at a level he never again reached.

San Francisco was not as important a film artistically, but it turned Tracy into a star, at last as popular with the audience as with the critics. The story was corny, but Clark Gable and Jeanette MacDonald were a pleasing pair, and Tracy's performance guaranteed *San Francisco* would be a smash. The film was Tracy's. Coverage didn't stop when the reviews were in — feature stories, character studies, career retrospectives of the new star crowded the newspapers.

In Hollywood the professional community made it official. *Fury* and *San Francisco*, one after the other, earned for Tracy the Screen Writers' Guild award for the most distinguished performance of the month. Tracy was the only actor ever cited in successive months.

His emergence as a true star turned the *Libeled Lady* set into a madhouse. Reporters and photographers overran the set to document Tracy's activities, and the studio's public relations forces were on hand to restrain Tracy's temper when a lady reporter asked him to name his favorite breakfast cereal, or when previously indifferent gossip columnists telephoned the set demanding to talk to him.

When *Libeled Lady* was winding up, Irving Thalberg paid Tracy an unexpected compliment. During a party on the set, at which Jean Harlow and William Powell announced their impending marriage, Tracy received a summons from Irving Thalberg. He hadn't known that Thalberg, who was increasingly occupied with production of *The Good Earth*, was even in town.

Tracy had long ago decided that he and Thalberg were not meant to be friends, for despite Thalberg's initial sponsorship Tracy saw very little of him and he seemed to be rather cool. In any case, Tracy felt they were not the same type. Thalberg usually was pleasant in a dignified way, but he was too reserved for Tracy's taste, and a little prim. Tracy's language offended him, and in some ways he seemed stuffy. But Tracy respected him nonetheless, for these mannerisms fell away when Thalberg was giving orders or chewing someone out. Then he was efficient, and sometimes awe-inspiring.

Thalberg told Tracy he considered him the finest actor in the movies and he took Tracy into his confidence. He told Tracy that his own departure from M-G-M was now assured and would be effective in eighteen months. Then he would form his own company whose films, like M-G-M's, would be distributed through Loew's, Inc. The sensitive part of the arrangement, naturally, was the allotment of the stars. Thalberg would take a small but select group as part of the settlement: Norma Shearer, Jean Harlow, Robert Montgomery, Franchot Tone, the Marx Brothers, and one half of Greta Garbo. Now he was entitled to one additional selection — anyone except Clark Gable — and he wanted Tracy; but he told Tracy that in all cases, the players had to agree to it. Tracy told the producer that he would accept, keep the confidence, and do anything else Thalberg asked. But the project never went through as planned, for three weeks later Thalberg died, at the age of thirty-seven.

Libeled Lady was received enthusiastically, and the money poured in at the box office. Slick and slapstick by turns it belonged to Harlow and Tracy and the audiences almost forgot William Powell and Myrna Loy were in it. Tracy said it was the easiest piece of acting he did in his early days at M-G-M.

The plot was silly but the pace was fast, and the *joie de vivre* the cast brought to it was a treat. Tracy spoke his lines in a lightning-fast staccato, every word coming through clearly.

Before reporting for *Libeled Lady*, Tracy had sought and received permission from M-G-M to make a film for RKO. Not since *Up the River* had he worked with John Ford, and now he was eager for the chance. Ford wanted Tracy to play the leading role in a production of Sean O'Casey's *The Plough and the Stars* opposite Barbara Stanwyck, and Tracy wanted the part so badly he could taste it.

But he was in for a big disappointment. M-G-M didn't want to risk their new star's image in what might be a flop, and so they said no to the deal.

The honeymoon was over. Tracy blew his top. If he was so hot, couldn't he have something to say about what parts he did?

He didn't win his point, but they made it up to him in other ways. They doubled his salary. His old contract was ripped up and a new one put him in the big money: five thousand dollars a week. Good reviews alone couldn't bring it about, but the studio didn't miss the fact that Tracy's fan mail had zoomed from three hundred to three thousand letters a week after *San Francisco*.

CHAPTER FIVE

THE STAR: 1937–1941

TRACY'S new success did not affect him in predictable ways. He seemed neither triumphant nor complacent in the security of his lavish new contract. He felt guilty about it, as if he were 'putting one over' on everybody. His tension did not subside; if anything, it increased. He had a few parts of some substance, and he worked on them obsessively at home. He would pace the floor for hours and grumble like a bear when he was working ... and now he was almost always working. In fairness to his family as well as to himself, he began to spend less time at the ranch during the week, and often slept at Carroll Tracy's home on Beverly Drive.

During this time Tracy was happiest with a group of close friends who spent much of their time together — so much, in fact, that they virtually formed their own club. The group was almost all Irish, and came to be known as the Hollywood Hibernians by most of the film colony, and sometimes as the Irish Mafia by their Jewish employers, with whom many of the actors seemed constantly at odds.

Most of these friends had met in New York in the 1920's, when they were trying to break into the theater. In fact Romanoff's, where they gathered, was known as 'Lamb's West'. Bob Armstrong, Frank Morgan, Frank McHugh, and James Gleason were some of the people in this informal club; Pat O'Brien was the ringleader, and Lynne Overman never missed a gathering of the group. James Cagney became a stalwart member after he and O'Brien worked together on some Warner pictures. And the group sometimes included Ralph Ballamy, George Murphy. William Frawley, Alan Hale, Allen Jenkins, and moon-faced Bert Lahr.

Not all were actors. The group included Billy Grady, the M-G-M casting executive, and Carroll Tracy was also a frequent member of the clique; indeed, dinner on St. Patrick's Day at Carroll's became one of the favorite traditions.

The get-togethers often were at Chasen's, and sometimes at Lucey's or Perino's, and at the Brown Derby after the fights, but the headquarters was Romanoff's. Mike Romanoff was one of the greatest of restaurateurs, and gave the Hibernians a sanctuary; many diners in this establishment never suspected that they were sharing the restaurant with so many celebrities. Photographers were discouraged.

Out of place as it seemed in Hollywood, everyone in the group, being mostly Catholic, was married to his first wife. Possibly because of this they didn't talk much about women; sports and politics were discussed, as was the movie business, but most of all they joked and teased one another.

They met regularly on Wednesday nights. The regular members took turns picking up the tab.

They were all loyal to the group, sometimes at the expense of their employer. The Irish actors felt some resentment at the Hollywood social and economic structure — 'out here the Kellys are working for the Cohens', as Spencer Tracy put it. Lynne Overman claimed it was harder on the Jewish executives, knowing they *had* to hire Irish actors, particularly if your name was Cagney and you were richer than any Warner.

Cagney was the first of the group to become a really big star. He had invested his earnings wisely, and so was able to ride out a two-year Warner suspension until they met his demands. By the time Warners grudgingly acquiesced, Spencer Tracy had just collected his first Oscar and was as big a star as Cagney, but not as wealthy.

Tracy wasn't the greatest talker in the group, but when he spoke he had something to say. As well as being a man of few words, he was also the man least able to cope with liquor. This was a problem only part of the time, for the Hollywood Hibernians would sometimes go on the wagon for months at a time, although at other times they would drink without letup. But whatever they did it was always done in unison.

The stories the group told don't seem as funny in the retelling; perhaps the humor sprang as much from the setting of Hollywood and Romanoff's as from the members of the club. When Bert Lahr told a few anecdotes in New York not even he could bring back their charm. 'It took a special atmosphere,' he sighed.

Many years later, a reporter asked Tracy on the set of *The Old Man and the Sea* if he could recall any great tales from those Wednesday night meetings.

'Yes, a great many,' Tracy said. 'None you could print.'

*　　　*　　　*

Before the first scene had been filmed, Victor Fleming said, 'This is going to be a great picture or I'm in the wrong business.' Kipling's *Captain Courageous* was a perfect movie story, and Tracy was perfect for a part in it. But it was Freddie Bartholomew who was to play the lead; Tracy had to be persuaded to take the part of Manuel.

In the novel the part was minor, a likable Portuguese who met a tragic end. Tracy admired the screenplay, but couldn't see himself in it even though Manuel was built into a major role.

He was worried about the accent the script called for, and he certainly didn't have Manuel's thick, curly hair. Moreover he swore he would not sing or play the vielle.

He asked his wife to read the script — Louise had been quoted as saying she had taken to reading the trade papers to see what Spencer was doing since he said so little at home — and he was hoping she wouldn't like it. But Louise told him to do it by all means.

He took the part. He learned to play the vielle. He learned to sing. It was a struggle, but he got some sense of tune, and Victor Fleming said, 'Don't get any better, Spence, then you'd be awful.' And they curled his hair.

Shooting began in the fall of 1936 after lengthy preparations. As Manuel, a Grand Banks fisherman, Tracy learned how to row, fish, trawl, chop bait, dress down cod and herring, and steer. The crew spent months on the water — mostly the Pacific in an authentic Gloucester schooner purchased, refitted, and christened the *We're Here*. Production was winding up in January but Fleming took advantage of unexpected interruptions: the cameras caught a violent storm that blew up one day, and another time the crew had to work in the coldest temperature ever recorded in California waters, which added an extra touch of realism to the film, and to the expressions on the faces of the hard-pressed actors. Tracy went so far as to catch pneumonia. While the picture was being edited, Fleming kept going back for more, yanking Tracy from the set of his next picture, *They Gave Him a Gun*, with Franchot Tone and Gladys George. Tone was a seasoned stage actor whose stay at M-G-M resembled Tracy's unhappy trial at Fox. A rumor circulating was that being married to Joan Crawford prevented Tone from getting the full studio buildup but also assured his permanent employment.

In *Captains Courageous*, which was released two months after *They Gave Him a Gun*, Tracy had the pleasure of working in a picture with two of his favorite actors; Lionel Barrymore, his longtime idol, and Freddie Bartholomew. Tracy said many years later, 'Freddie was different, he was the only child actor I ever saw who was trying to be real instead of cute, and it's harder to be real. Freddie was both. He was like a good hitter trying to slap out an honest single, but he got home runs instead because his swing was so sweet.'

M-G-M tailored Freddie's part four years younger to suit him — as M-G-M's child star. Kipling's character was already past adolescence. Freddie hit this stage during the filming, and was a good deal taller toward the end of the picture than at the beginning.

Tracy never shook his embarrassment over his studio-curled hair. Joan Crawford took one look at him, and cried, 'My God, it's Harpo Marx!' Tracy saw himself in a mirror and said, 'If my father had lived to see it, *this* would have killed him!'

He complained he was not able to do an authentic accent — indeed he wasn't, nor was it consistent, but it was curiously provocative — and he grumbled that he operated a dory like a washerwoman. He never did think his performance was very good, and at the premiere he said, 'This is Freddie's night and that's the way it should be.' But the vitality that *Captains Courageous* has retained over three decades is largely in Tracy's touching and human Manuel.

The *Captains Courageous* experience convinced Tracy it was time to get a boat. He purchased a forty-foot ketch and renamed it the *Carrie B.*, for his mother. For a time it was his passion, and all the Tracys cruised up and down the coast. Tracy loved sailing, but he was always restless and would drop a hobby he once loved when some other interest caught his fancy.

The Tracys were briefly in the horse business, buying several Thoroughbreds and racing them out of Bay Meadows, without much success. Tracy wasn't the sort to stick with any amusement for long. It even worried him that now that he finally had money for all the things he had always wanted, he still had money left over after getting them.

Many screen actors who had been in the big money longer than Tracy had little to show for it beyond debts and memories of high living. Tracy gave all the credit for his solvency to his brother. 'I could never have made it in this business, I'd have been sunk in a month. I'm impractical but Carroll is level-headed and smart. He keeps my contracts straight, takes care of the money, he even gives me an allowance.'

Although Tracy became a client of the William Morris agency, his association with Carroll was a permanent one that was not confined to business. Tracy liked to have his brother near him, and this became a real need as his stock soared at M-G-M. Many high-powered stars had their own entourages, but Spencer Tracy had only Carroll and rated him first as friend, confidant, and adviser. His brother became a familiar figure on the set, and served as a buffer, taking phone calls and managing to keep Tracy's life as uncomplicated as possible.

Horses were becoming one of the few interests that Spencer and Louise Tracy had in common. At the ranch Frank Borzage noted that Louise had her things, and Spence had his things, and not much was *theirs*. The Borzages were among the Tracys' few close friends from the film colony, along with the Victor Flemings and Joe Mankiewicz.

Louise had her own circle of people, and a growing list of friends from her work with deaf children. Tracy was proud of her skill and her talent, but could not himself become completely absorbed in the educational theories Louise thrived on.

A detractor of Tracy's once said, 'Spence and Louise had one real common interest and that was himself, so when she found other interests he took a powder.' Certainly Louise gave him helpful advice on his career more than once. Still, he confided in her less as time passed, and also knew less of what she was doing from day to day. Once he returned home from the studio and decided to try out a new sprinkling system and soaked twenty guests at a garden party he didn't know Louise was giving.

He was playing polo less, but he kept a room at the Riviera Country Club. He was spending less time at home.

*   *   *

Frank Borzage's reputation declined after *Man's Castle* and *Little Man, What Now?*, so in 1937 he gave up his independent status to sign a fat contract as a regular director at M-G-M. He directed Spencer Tracy in the first two films of his contract, *The Big City* and *Mannequin*. Neither was particularly well received, although people were saying that after *San Francisco*, *Fury*, and *Libeled Lady*, Tracy was ready for an Oscar.

But *Big City's* only significance for Tracy was lead billing over his co-star; even in *Captains Courageous* he was listed second to Freddie Bartholomew.

Mannequin was a Joan Crawford soap opera, about which the best that can be said is that it was good Crawford. Miss Crawford mentions *Mannequin* with some affection in her autobiography and comments on her relationship with Tracy.

It was inspiring to play opposite Tracy. His is such simplicity of performance, such naturalness and humor. He walks through a scene just as he walks through life. He makes it seem so easy, and working with him I had to learn to underplay. We worked together as a unit, as if we'd worked together for years, yet there was also the extra little fillip of working with a new co-star, a powerful one. No matter how often you rehearse a scene, when the camera starts turning he surprises you with some intonation or timing so that your response is new and immediate.

Slug I called him, from the day he was clowning around and took the stance of a boxer. In the most serious scene, Slug could break me up. As Jessie, I was supposed to be so serious about my life, my job; and as I spoke my lines, he'd watch me slyly, give that half grin of his, and rub his finger along his nose. I'd have to laugh. Take after take. But I learned. From Slug I learned to keep my own identity in a scene, not to be distracted by anything, including Tracy. Columnists insisted we were feuding. We never had a moment's disharmony. He was most considerate of me on the set.

When Tracy and Miss Crawford's doctor got her to take up polo during her recuperation from the pneumonia that hit her midway through the shooting, fan magazines showed them on horseback; photographers went wherever Miss Crawford went. But Tracy's polo days were just about over. Shortly after *Mannequin* he took another spill, and although he was not hurt, the studio persuaded him to abandon the sport; he was too valuable for the risk. And besides, the first white hairs were beginning to show around his temples.

Mannequin was a money-maker, and it profited from the presence of an Academy Award-winning star.

*　　　*　　　*

In 1937 just to be nominated was an honor. There were too many good male performances to give credit to all — Ronald Colman's *Lost Horizon* had to be ignored, as did *The Awful Truth* with Cary Grant, who had displaced M-G-M's Robert Montgomery as the screen's first master of drawing-room comedy.

Montgomery was nominated for *Night Must Fall*, and Tracy's other competition included the two actors in Hollywood whom, besides Lionel Barrymore, he most admired: Frederic March in *A Star Is Born*; and Paul Muni, for his portrayal of *Emile Zola*. The other nominee was Charles Boyer for *Conquest*. Everyone told Tracy he would be nominated but he was surprised, even apologetic, when it happened. He still considered his Manuel a poor showing, and felt Lionel Barrymore should have been recognized instead.

'Lionel doesn't care,' Bud Lighton, the producer of *Captains Courageous*, told Tracy. 'He has one of those crummy little statues already, and now he wants you to have one. And you will, Spence, you're going to get it. Everyone is town is going to vote for you.'

Tracy heard that Robert Montgomery was hearing similar words. Tracy had squirmed with discomfort and embarrassment during the previous banquet — the awards were still given out at a dinner sponsored by the industry — and he dreaded going through it again. Instead he went into the hospital for a hernia operation which was where he was on February 8, 1938.

Louise attended the ceremony at the Biltmore Bowl unescorted; she wanted to be there 'just in case'. She arrived early, the first invited guest there, and lingered alone and unrecognized until the crowd began to gather.

When Spencer Tracy was announced as the winner, Louise received the statuette, and with great poise she delivered the shortest speech of the evening.

'I accept this award on behalf of Spencer, Susie, Johnny, and myself.'

There was the briefest silence, then a deafening roar from

the crowd, most of whom were getting their first look at Mrs. Spencer Tracy. Ed Sullivan suggested that the film industry was endorsing Louise's denial of rumors that the Tracys were about to separate.

People clustered around Louise to congratulate her, but she pushed her way to a telephone to notify the winner. 'Darling,' she said, 'you won it.'

A group of doctors and nurses were in Tracy's room with M-G-M's Frank Whitbeck when Louise called. Tracy burst into tears. The new Oscar winner later told reporters it was only right that Louise had accepted the award, for he would have given up acting if she hadn't prevented him.

Traditionally at Academy banquets a co-worker said a few words, and Lionel Barrymore, on crutches because of arthritis, spoke briefly and simply of Tracy's total dedication to his craft. Then Louis B. Mayer, unannounced, took the floor, doubtless feeling that as the Academy's founding father, he was entitled.

'I'd like to praise Spencer Tracy's sense of discipline. Tracy is a fine actor, but he is most important because he understands why it is necessary to take orders from the front office . . . because he understands why it is wise to obey directors . . . because he understands that when the publicity department asks him to cater to certain visitors, it is a necessary inconvenience.'

When Tracy heard what the studio chief had said, he asked if it was meant as a compliment or a threat.

*   *   *

The hernia was only one of Tracy's ailments. Although Tracy continued to be punctual when he showed up at the studio, he was not always there. Louis B. Mayer claimed that the studio tolerated more 'sick time' from Spencer Tracy than all the other leading men combined.

Tracy was plagued by a thyroid ailment, and had a tonsillectomy on his thirty-seventh birthday. One of his most frequent companions was his physician, Howard Dennis.

No doubt the years of physical rigor and hard living were

beginning to wear him down, and were certainly aggravated by his insomnia, and by eight years of steady work before the cameras. Whether at Fox or M-G-M or on loan, Tracy was one of the hardest working men in filmland. *Test Pilot*, which followed *Mannequin*, was his thirty-fifth picture. Hollywood was mass-producing its product as never before to meet a growing demand, and a 'hot' actor was necessarily a busy one. Tracy's vacations had been few and brief, and he was tired. His worries now centered on his physical condition. He worked out at a private health club, lifted weights, took steam baths, rode an exercise bicycle, and had massages. The massage became an obsession; he insisted on one daily.

The deaths of others touched Tracy very deeply. Although they had not been close, Irving Thalberg's death bothered him, as did Monroe Owsley's premature demise — also in 1936. Tracy was stunned and bewildered, as was the rest of the film colony, by Jean Harlow's death at the age of twenty-six in June of 1937. He was genuinely fond of her, a 'square shooter if there ever was one'. It was Harlow, on the set of *Riffraff*, who had broken the news of Will Rogers' death to Tracy. Will and the noted aviator Wiley Post crashed in Alaska on August 15, 1935'. Tracy said, 'Will was a lot of people's best friend, but he was mine, too.'

Amateur psychologists could have a field day interpreting Spencer Tracy's analysis of Will Rogers while the Oklahoman was still the homespun prince of Fox Films; it is not unlike other people's later recollections of Spencer Tracy.

'The longer and more intimately I know Will Rogers the more I admire him — the more I am convinced that much of his charm lies in his boyishness. In spite of his wide contacts with world affairs and with the men who bring them about, Will has never grown up ... a strange paradox ... he is, at the same time, one of the best known and one of the least known men in the world, by inclination a great mixer, by instinct a hermit; when he talks about someone else, he's brilliant, but about himself he's shy, ill-at-ease, embarrassed.'

When Will Rogers died, Spencer Tracy attended the

Forest Lawn memorial service. Death was becoming more and more an everpresent thought.

*   *   *

He had not been entirely happy about making *Test Pilot*. Although he certainly didn't mind working for Victor Fleming again, it was a 'Gable picture' ... Gable and Loy. Tracy's nose was out of joint, for once again he would play a good-natured simple fellow while Gable got the girl.

Jean Harlow's death was a further complication. Tracy was making *The Big City*, with Louise Rainer, while Gable and Jean Harlow were working on *Saratoga*. After Jean's death — she never completed *Saratoga*, but it was artfully put together with long-shot use of a stand-in, and released — the search was all over Hollywood for 'another Harlow' and M-G-M decided to shelve a project that had been planned for Tracy and Harlow until they found one. Tracy did *Mannequin* instead, and then along came *Test Pilot*.

Shortly after *Test Pilot* went before the cameras the studio decided that it was not after all the best possible use of a star like Tracy. His part was beefed up. The advertising posters showed Gable, Loy, and Tracy blown up big, and a routine formula picture was made to look like the big event of the year. After seeing it, many still thought so — it certainly did no harm to Tracy's prestige.

Spence liked to tease, and took every chance he got. He had a death scene — in the film it is quite moving — that took a full day and part of another to shoot. Gable might have had the fatter part but Tracy died the 'slowest, most lingering death in history' according to Gable. Time after time he seemed to have finally expired, only to weakly open an eye, manage a wan smile, and go on living for another few seconds. He was in Gable's arms for the duration, and Clark was hard put to react believably. During one memorable take when Tracy was finding it particularly hard to give up the ghost, Gable dropped Tracy's head on the canvas with a hard thud.

'Die, God damn it, Spence! I wish to Christ you would!'

Gable's admiration for Tracy was limitless. He mentioned a shot in *Test Pilot* that he claimed was stolen by Tracy who was 'not doing a damn thing except driving the car and chewing a piece of gum' while he and Loy were doing all the talking. Gable said, 'The guy's good and there's nobody in this business who can touch him, so you're a fool to try. And don't fall for that humble stuff, either; the bastard knows it!'

*   *   *

Tracy might have known he was good, but he wasn't convinced he had any business — or any right — to play Father Flanagan. The priest in *San Francisco* was one thing; impersonating on the screen a well-known figure and one Tracy himself idolized was another matter entirely.

Tracy had met Father Edward J. Flanagan previously. Now they met again, became close friends, and spent much time discussing *Boys Town* and the approach to the movie before the first scene was shot. Tracy felt that Father Flanagan's statement that 'there are no bad boys' was a thoughtful and constructive approach; it probably made Tracy feel better about his own wild childhood.

Much of the picture was photographed at the actual Boys Town in Nebraska, and the young townspeople acted in the background with a supply of M-G-M child actors in the major roles: Bobs Watson, Sidney Miller, and the new box-office winner, Mickey Rooney, who was all of seventeen but looked about twelve. He had been in many pictures, but he was new to being a money-maker. Mickey played Whitey Marsh, the pool-hall delinquent who was reclaimed by Father Flanagan. The director was Norman Taurog, a specialist at the direction of children.

If Tracy had picked up a 'bag of tricks' as a screen actor, he decided none would help him play the founder of Boys Town. He quietly studied Father Flanagan and found him a modest but open man, without mannerisms or idiosyncrasies, devout but not sanctimonious, a man of great physical as well as emotional strength. And he was attractive, extremely masculine. Tracy didn't usually model a characterization after a real person, but in *Boys Town* he patterned his portrayal on Father Flanagan himself. The result was a performance of quiet conviction, dignity and strength.

Just before *Boys Town* went into production a poll conducted nationally by Ed Sullivan revealed that the four most popular male stars in the nation were Clark Gable, Robert Taylor, William Powell, and the Oscar winner, Spencer Tracy. It surprised even M-G-M: they accepted Tracy as a major star and treated him accordingly. Before the year was out, Tracy would clearly be ahead of both Taylor and Powell in popularity, with help from Mickey Rooney, whose role had made him, for the moment, more popular than *anybody*. The combination of Tracy and Rooney helped make *Boys Town* a blockbuster. M-G-M hadn't counted on it; it wasn't that 'big' a project; the budget was small and the shooting schedule was short enough. It became one of Louis B. Mayer's favorites — his admiration for 'family' pictures overrode whatever feelings he may have had against the Catholic faith, and he thought it was just about the greatest movie ever made.

The 1938 Oscar competition narrowed to a battle between Tracy for *Boys Town* and James Cagney for *Angels with Dirty Faces*; Cagney had won the New York Film Critics' award and was a slight favorite. But it was Tracy who won, with Bette Davis, each winning for the second time (in *The New York Times* that week they were called the king and queen of American films).

Upon accepting his second Oscar, Tracy said that it really belonged to Father Flanagan. So he gave it to him, shortly afterward, with the inscription:

> To Father Edward J. Flanagan, whose great human qualities, timely simplicity, and inspiring courage were strong enough to shine through my humble effort.

*   *   *

In the summers of 1937 and 1938 the Tracys vacationed in New York, going once by boat through the Panama Canal and once by train. The first vacation interrupted a shooting schedule as a special accommodation, for Tracy had worked without letup for two years; the second was during one of the Tracy recuperations, and Dr. Howard Dennis was along. Selena Royle remembered that on the first occasion she 'saw a figure coming down the street, all hunched over and with a hat over to one side in that way of his, and I knew it had to be Spence ... so I went up to him and threw my arms around him and said, "Well, you always said you wanted to be as good as Lionel Barrymore, and now you are ... and better." '

Both times he was the toast of the town. He avoided crowds, made no public appearances, and slipped quietly into theaters to see the new plays, although someone usually spotted him, and a crowd would gather. He gave few interviews, but a few of the more established columnists were able to get through, and filled the papers with their comments on the now well-established actor whose strongest characteristic, they decided, was his humility.

Each visit to New York brought speculation that Tracy would return to the stage. He kept that thought alive by announcing every now and again his desire to get back into a play, and even suggested that he preferred the theater and wanted to act in films only as a sideline.

But for one reason or another, Tracy was not to appear on Broadway in the 1930's, and his time in New York was spent mostly at the Lambs Club. There he staged a succession of drunken sprees that New York reporters either knew nothing about or decided against reporting. The situation became critical when Tracy was scheduled to fly back to Los Angeles. At the Lambs Club, Tracy and another actor had been put to bed upstairs after passing out. The Club did not tolerate intoxication, but wouldn't be harsh with so famous a member. Attempts were made to contact Mrs. Tracy at her hotel, and the first report was that she was in; then, after word had been given that it was the club calling about Mr. Tracy's condition, Mrs. Tracy was 'out'. According to one of the observers, what she should not see, she would not see.

The Tracy family (*left*)
in Milwaukee, about 1910.
The freckled smaller boy
is Spencer.
Mrs. Spencer Tracy

An overgrown 12-year-old
(*below left*) shows off
his first long pants.
*Academy of Motion Picture
Arts and Sciences.*

A patriot of 1918
(*below right*).
Mrs. Spencer Tracy

Northwestern
Military Academy
portrait

On the steps of Ripon's West Hall, 19:
Tracy's arm is draped over a likel
matinee idol, Ken Edgers. *Academy
Motion Picture Arts and Sciences*

Carrie Tracy and her b
about 1920. *Mrs. Spencer T*

1922 portrait.
Barrymore
shouldn't worry.
Mrs. Spencer Tracy

Louise Treadwell,
about 1921.
Edwin F. Townsend photo

THE WOOD PLAYERS
In

"Getting Gertie's Garter"

A Farce in Three Acts

By Avery Hopwood and Wilson Collinson

Produced under the immediate Stage Direction
of Raymond Capp

CAST
(as you meet them)

atty Walrick	Dolores Graves
ily Felton	George Simpson
anette	Millie Beland
ertie	Louise Treadwell
len	Thomas Williams
en Walrick	Jack W. Cowell
eddy Darling	William Williams
arbara Felton	Helen Edwards
gy Briggs	Spencer Tracy

SYNOPSIS

The Action of the play takes place on a night in June,
a Bungalow on an estate in the Westchester Hills.

Act 1—The Lounging Room.
Act 2—The Barn.
Act 3—Same as Act 1.

Scenic Artist—G. V. Fisher
Stage Manager—Russell Rhodes

Spencer supporting Louise
in stock, 1923.

Louise presents Spencer with his first Oscar (*above left*); she accepted it
banquet while he was hospitalized. *Wide World Photos*. The Tracys (*above
right*) return home after the tumultuous trip to Europe, 1939. *Wide Wor
Photos*. (*Below*) Spencer, Carroll and Lee Tracy convene at the Brow
Derby after watching a 1935 boxing card at Hollywood Legion. *Len Weissme
photo*

With 11-year-old John, 1935.
Metro-Goldwyn-Mayer

With 8-year-old Susie, 1940.
Metro-Goldwyn-Mayer

With his mother in Hollywood. *Mrs. Spencer Tracy*

Ingrid Bergman visits Tracy and director George Cukor during the filming of *Edward, My Son* in 1948. *Pictorial Parade, Inc.*

What every man wanted in 1954: a date with Grace Kelly. *Pictorial Parade, Inc.*

Stanley Kramer, at far left, celebrates completion of *Judgment at Nuremberg* with Judy Garland, Spencer Tracy, Richard Widmark, Maximilian Schell and (*rear*) Burt Lancaster. *Academy of Motion Picture Arts and Sciences*

Two studies of the American screen's greatest star team on the set of their
final film together, Stanley Kramer's *Guess Who's Coming to Dinner. Columbia
Pictures*

Test Pilot (M-G-M, 1938). This famous publicity still of Gable, Myrna Lo and Tracy represents the heyday of M-G-M's star-accented omnipotenc *Ernest D. Burns, Cinemabilia*

Boys Town (M-G-M, 1938 With Mickey Rooney. Po trayal of Father Flanaga earns Tracy his secon Academy Award. *Academy of Motion Picture Arts and Sciences*

Dr. Jekyll and Mr. Hyde (M-G-M, 1941). Ingrid Bergman as Ivy opposite Tracy's Hyde. He called her the best actress he ever worked with "except one". *Ernest D. Burns, Cinemabilia*

Woman of the Year (M-G-M, 1942). The first Hepburn-Tracy film, a classic romantic comedy directed by George Stevens. *Ernest D. Burns, Cinemabilia*

Cass Timberlane (M-G-M, 1947). Zachary Scott, Lana Turner, and graying Tracy in a Sinclair Lewis story.
Theatre Collection of The New York Public Library

Adam's Rib (M-G-M, 1949). With Katharine Hepburn in a brilliant comed directed by George Cukor and written by the Kanins. *Academy of Moti Picture Arts and Sciences*

...ther of the Bride (M-G-M, 1950). The altar-bound daughter is Elizabeth
...ylor, and Joan Bennett is the mother.
...eatre Collection of The New York Public Library

...and Mike (M-G-M, 1952).
...s Hepburn as a multisport
...z and Tracy as her manager.
...orial Parade, Inc.

The Actress (M-G-M, 1953). An endearing Cukor film, with Jean Simmons as Tracy's stage-struck daughter and Teresa Wright as the mother.
Theatre Collection of The New York Public Library

Bad Day at Black Rock (M-G-M, 1955). With Lee Marvin. Melodrama in the desert.
Theatre Collection of The New York Public Library

e Desk Set (20th Century-Fox, 1957). The penultimate Tracy-Hepburn ture, with Joan Blondell and Gig Young.
torial Parade, Inc.

e Last Hurrah (Columbia, 1958). Tracy as an old-style politico and frey Hunter as his newsman nephew, under John Ford's direction.
torial Parade, Inc.

The Old Man and the Sea (Warner Brothers, 1958). Tracy said filming t[...]
Hemingway story was "becoming my life's work".
Warner Brothers

erit the Wind (United Artists, 1960). The screen's two finest actors square in court: Tracy and Frederic March in the first of Tracy's four films Stanley Kramer. The judge is Harry Morgan.
est D. Burns, Cinemabilia

Judgment at Nuremburg (United Artists, 1961). In Tracy's own opinion, the best film he made. A Kramer production. *Pictorial Parade, Inc.*

It's a Mad, Mad, Mad, Mad World (United Artists, 1963). America's greatest comics supported Tracy; here he's chased by Sid Caesar.
Theatre Collection of The New York Public Library

Guess Who's Coming to Dinner (Columbia, 1967). The Tracy valedictor with Katharine Hepburn and Sidney Poitier.
Columbia

It took some effort, but the Lambs managed to get Tracy on the plane, to make his shooting schedule.

*   *   *

During a five-year period beginning with 1938, more than three dozen novels, plays, and other story properties were purchased by M-G-M as possible Tracy vehicles. Of that number only one — *Tortilla Flat* — would come to the screen with Spencer Tracy in it, although he did appear in a story developed inside the company — *Edison, the Man*. Some of the stories gathered dust on the shelves and others became films starring lesser screen actors. Obviously Mr. Tracy's sudden rise in stature was a problem that kept M-G-M awake nights.

In 1937 the studio had purchased, at an undisclosed 'record' expenditure, the screen rights to Kenneth Roberts' historical novel, *Northwest Passage*. It was an epic, sprawling and complicated, and it was a literary event as well as a best-seller. M-G-M planned to make *Northwest Passage* a mammoth project that would not be obscured by David Selznick's independent *Gone with the Wind*. Spencer Tracy was just the man to play Major Rogers, the principal character in the historical drama.

Tracy, who was reading a good deal of history and historical fiction in those days, read the novel and told Victor Fleming he liked it.

It would be a super-production. It would be in Technicolor and the cast would have three male stars besides Tracy — Robert Taylor, Wallace Beery, and Franchot Tone. There were no large female roles, but the part of Taylor's girl friend in England would be a good chance to try out Greer Garson, a new actress personally discovered by Louis B. Mayer in London, where she was performing in a minor music hall, a complete unknown.

Tracy had hoped to follow *Boys Town* with the colossal *Northwest Passage*. But the project bogged down early. Writers got to work on it, but had not produced a satisfactory outline, and when Tracy was ready to get back to work, the estimate was that it would take another six months to have *Northwest Passage* ready for production. Louise B. Mayer said he'd think of something to keep Tracy busy. And he came up with two ideas.

First, he decided that perhaps it would be wise to let Darryl Zanuck and 20th Century-Fox borrow Tracy to play in *Stanley and Livingstone*. Zanuck, whose company had been prospering and who had occasionally turned out some fine pictures, wanted Tracy for the role of Henry Stanley. Mayer realized he could make a good trade. Zanuck lent Mayer his handsome new star, Tyrone Power, for *Marie Antoinette*, which Norma Shearer was finally emerging from mourning to make. The price for Power was Tracy as Stanley.

Tracy read Stanley's journals and was almost as enthusiastic as he was for *Northwest Passage*. He also felt a certain exultation at returning to his old company in triumph. There was a difficulty: *Stanley and Livingstone* would not be ready for filming for three months.

So Mayer thought of *I Take This Woman*.

When Mayer was in London discovering Greer Garson, he also found an astonishingly beautiful Viennese girl, Hedwig Kiesler, in the same city. Both girls arrived in Hollywood early in 1937 and waited for a part, reporting to collect their salaries, and occasionally tossing out the first baseball or christening a boat. They were 'the old man's follies' and the old man had to be catered to; no one around the studio thought either girl would amount to anything, certainly not the red-haired English girl; and the other, for all her beauty, seemed at best a candidate to become another Anna Sten or Ketti Gallian. Even Miss Kiesler's sensational appearance in the European film *Ecstasy* was something the studio did not choose to publicize. So the only thing to do was to change Hedwig Kiesler's name and wait. Mayer recalled that the most beautiful woman he had ever seen, until this girl, was a silent star who had died young, named Barbara LaMarr. So Hedwig Kiesler became Hedy Lamarr.

Miss Lamarr's wait finally ended. Early in 1938 Walter

Wanger wanted to borrow her for *Algiers*. The studio was delighted to oblige Wanger, and was startled when the film became a smash hit. Miss Lamarr was a terrible actress, but she was the beauty sensation of the age, and possibly of all time in films. (*Algiers* was also responsible for all the imitations of Charles Boyer which began, 'Come wiz me to zee Casbah,' although no such line was used in the film.)

With *Algiers* in orbit, Louis B. Mayer determined to make Hedy Lamarr the greatest motion picture star of all time. Forget about Greta Garbo; she was beginning to give him a pain with her moodiness. If Hedy was not actress enough to be a second Garbo, she could certainly be a bigger star than Dietrich. He would get Josef von Sternberg, director of Dietrich's big American hits, to direct Hedy Lamarr in a prestige picture. And he needed a big name for the leading man — Spencer Tracy. So Mayer hired Charles MacArthur to write an original story that would serve as a vehicle for Hedy Lamarr and Spencer Tracy. He gave in and reversed that billing, but he continued to think of it as 'my Hedy Lamarr picture'.

Charles MacArthur, who had written some excellent screen material in earlier years, including scripts for Metro, had shown little enthusiasm for Culver City since Irving Thalberg died. He said that going to M-G-M after that was like going to the Automat. MacArthur and his wife, Helen Hayes, were close friends of the Thalbergs. But MacArthur managed to come up with a story about a doctor who marries a beautiful European without the assurance she loves him, decides she doesn't, and then is convinced that she does. That was it, and Mayer read it and thought it was a monumental drama that would make *Algiers* look like a small picture. Furthermore, it adhered to his guideline that the girl's part should be slightly larger than the man's.

Josef von Sternberg was engaged to direct, and Spencer Tracy did consent to play the doctor. If Tracy had any objections at the time, no one seemed to know of them. Mayer had managed to sell everyone in sight that *I Take This*

Woman was going to be an important picture. Certainly he convinced Miss Lamarr.

Perhaps Tracy saw that the screenplay from the MacArthur story was bad, and perhaps Mayer again convinced him he had to be wrong. But Josef von Sternberg took one look at it and started demanding changes. Soon he realized he was not dealing with writers, he was dealing with Mayer. *I Take This Woman* was probably the only picture Mayer ever 'produced' personally. He was not credited, of course, and during its history several people had been officially called the producer, but on the final print there was no producer credit at all. *I Take This Woman* was Mayer's obsession. He spent his time on the set, taking charge of photography, direction, and anything that concerned Miss Lamarr. On at least two occasions he tried to tell Spencer Tracy how to act a scene. The crew stood and stared in disbelief and so did Tracy. Among themselves they agreed they were probably hatching a monster, and Hedy Lamarr, who was no idiot, was soon feeling uncomfortable.

Sternberg took two weeks of it, most of the time screaming. Then he left. He said he quit. Mayer said he fired him. Mayer personally went through all of the footage and scrapped everything except a few well-photographed studies of Miss Lamarr. He said it was all lousy, and Sternberg would probably have agreed.

Mayer assigned Frank Borzage to take over the direction, not so much to placate the obviously unhappy Spencer Tracy, but because Borzage was riding high after his *Three Comrades* and *The Shining Hour*, both displaying brilliant performances by his discovery, Margaret Sullavan, who came to work in 1937 on an M-G-M star contract. Borzage looked like a whipped dog when he reported to work; the picture was the talk of the studio.

Borzage tried to get hold of the project but Mayer wouldn't let go. The squabbling went on for weeks. Then the word came: Spencer Tracy was expected at 20th Century-Fox to go to work in *Stanley and Livingstone*. Mayer shrugged and told everyone it was all for the best: the picture wasn't ready, and it was going to take a while to get it in shape. It would take about as long to get it in shape as it would take Spencer Tracy to make *Stanley and Livingstone*, and in the meantime Hedy Lamarr could go right ahead and make her next picture, since *Lady of the Tropics* was ready and waiting, and so was Robert Taylor.

The gossip went that *I Take This Woman* would hit the ashcan and stay there, and that was the hope of many, including Walter Pidgeon who had been assigned the second male lead. Pidgeon and all the other actors were spared when Mayer threw out all their footage — all except Tracy and Lamarr, two of whose scenes directed by Borzage won Mayer's endorsement. Apparently he was dead serious about resurrecting the project, although Tracy told intimates he had no intention of returning to work on it, especially after he learned that Frank Borzage was officially fired.

I Take This Woman was in the works again in mid-1939, and Spencer Tracy was in it despite himself, after finishing the film at 20th Century-Fox. He was not happy to be back. He and Hedy Lamarr were the only survivors from the original cast. The new lineup featured a promising starlet named Laraine Day.

Everything about the production was different. For one thing, Mayer was hardly around. In the interim the picture called *Lady of the Tropics* had been completed, and although not yet released, it had been screened at the studio and everyone, including Mayer, had heard the unmistakable gobble of the turkey. Thereupon Mayer became disenchanted with the 'new Dietrich'; in time Hedy proved that she had something that was marketable, and possibly a little talent, but she would make it mainly on her own, with little help from Louis B. Mayer.

Woody Van Dyke was brought in to direct because he was a quick worker. Throughout the film colony the project was dubbed as *I Re-Take This Woman*. Van Dyke, Tracy, Lamarr, and company worked twenty-three days and wrapped up the picture. They all worked very hard to put some life into it, but the set never lost its gloom. When someone asked Van Dyke how things were coming, the director said, 'This is the funniest thing in Hollywood since Jean Harlow died.' When a commissary greeter said, 'What's new, Spence?' the actor said, 'Well, I'm not going to send Charles MacArthur a Christmas card. That's new.'

I Take This Woman competed with Gable's *Parnell*, Ramon Novarro's *The Night Is Young* and Luise Rainer's *Dramatic School* for the honor of being the worst movie M-G-M produced in the thirties. Actually it was not released until early in 1940; it took that long to decide what to do with it. Later Louis B. Mayer was heard to remark, 'I told them they were making a lousy picture, but they wouldn't listen to me!'

Spencer Tracy decided that he wouldn't ever again. He said he was 'on to the old man' after *I Take This Woman*, and that Mayer knew it. After that the two men, who had seldom been together before, hardly met at all, and almost never spoke.

*   *   *

When Tracy completed *Stanley and Livingstone*, he had some time to kill. Hedy's *Lady of the Tropics* was still shooting, so the Tracys took off on another vacation, this time not stopping in New York. They sailed for Europe, and Tracy told Victor Fleming he spent a lot of time on deck, alone at night, watching the water and hoping that the *Northwest Passage* script would hurry up so he wouldn't have to return to *I Take This Woman*. It was also during the voyage, coming and going, that he read several novels M-G-M had purchased with him in mind. He was apprehensive about *National Velvet*, and of the talk that Shirley Temple would be borrowed to star in it with him; he was interested in Conrad Richter's *The Sea of Grass*, a western romance; and he knew he wanted to do *The Yearling*.

The European tour was notable for Tracy's conquest of the London press, usually critical of visiting American screen stars. To this day some Englishmen say there has not been another demonstration to equal Tracy's arrival in London. It was April 27, 1939, and they called it the Battle of Waterloo Station. Word had spread that Spencer Tracy would be arriving at the station by train. So he would have, had word not reached Tracy that a huge mob was collecting in the station. He arranged to be transferred to another train, and was not aboard the one that pulled into Waterloo Station and was assaulted by eight thousand Spencer Tracy fans. It was bedlam. One of those leaving the train — the famous old actor and early Oscar winner, George Arliss — was jostled about in the melee, and Arturo Toscanini was knocked to the ground and trampled. Tracy felt terrible about the whole thing and made personal apologies to the maestro. Louise wondered what would happen if Robert Taylor were to come to London.

When the messy doings of *I Take This Woman* resumed, Tracy at least had the satisfaction of knowing that *Stanley and Livingstone* was a hit.

An exceptional lineup of character actors surrounded Tracy — Charles Coburn, Walter Brennan, Henry Hull, Henry Travers, and Sir Cedric Hardwicke who made a stirring Livingstone.

There was much buzzing over how the 'Doctor Livingstone, I presume?' scene would be handled. The scene was shot over and over; Tracy would break up just before he delivered the critical line. But he was game. In the release print, Stanley's meeting with Livingstone was simple and eloquent. In the film, Tracy had given one long speech — 640 words in a single take — that showed he was about the only actor around who could and would memorize long speeches, and do them brilliantly.

From the time of its release there was some speculation that Tracy might win a third successive Academy Award. The surprise came when he was not nominated. It was the first evidence he was now merely doing what was expected of him. It would be ten years before he would register another Oscar bid.

Stanley and Livingstone was the only Tracy film released in 1939, in contrast to seven in 1932, and an overall average of four a year up to that time. M-G-M squandered a lot of revenue by committing so much of Tracy's time to 'taking' poor Hedwig Kiesler.

* * *

'Mr. Tracy, what are your favorite pastimes in your private life?'

Again, the Tracy glare.

'Private life? Now you're kidding me. There's no such thing as a private life in this town. It isn't allowed. The only person who has a private life is Fatty Arbuckle.'

Spencer Tracy's relations with the press were not all bad. In his own words, he didn't hate all newspapermen, just the reporters. He didn't even hate all reporters, once he was assured they weren't going to pry into his private life.

Throughout his career he never had his own press agent or a public relations firm tie-in. After he earned his big stardom he didn't need one; in earlier days, though, he could have used some promotion. The movie fan magazines of the early thirties showed few pictures or stories of Spencer Tracy. The same magazines are full of the activities of Arline Judge, David Manners, Richard Cromwell, Rosemary Ames, Roger Pryor — none, even briefly, the equal of Tracy at his lowest moments of popularity.

He asked, 'Why should the magazines matter?' And he decided they didn't matter at all. All you owed the public was a good performance.

Most young actors relish being in the public eye and many go to desperate lengths to be there; some, like Jean Arthur, cooperate during their apprenticeship and are recluses when famous. Tracy was always indifferent; he didn't want to be bothered.

His image was that of a stay-at-home who never went out to a nightclub, seldom took his wife to a premiere or any other function, and generally avoided social life away from the studio, especially after he quit polo and sold his boat and his horses. In truth he was often out somewhere and sometimes had Louise with him, but only after he was assured there were no photographers or reporters near the place.

The kidnap threat in 1934 and the Bill Wellman scuffle the following year were but two incidents that prompted Tracy to avoid the press. Frequently he was infuriated by reporters' attempts to revive the Loretta Young affair. In 1936 Miss Young reported to M-G-M to play opposite Robert Taylor in *Private Number* and Tracy invited her to lunch in the commissary. A photographer not only wanted to take their picture but wanted another of Miss Young's headline romances, Clark Gable — who was seated at another table — in the shot, too. It was embarrassing for both M-G-M stars and especially for Miss Young, who was about to make headlines with her romance with Tyrone Power. Tracy blasted the photographer and made certain he didn't get his picture.

He agreed to see newspaper and magazine feature writers because the studio insisted, but he was rude and impatient with many of them.

'Write anything you want to about me,' he told one reporter. 'Make up something. Hell, I don't care.'

He did care, more than he let on. Once he gave Gladys Hall, a prolific free-lance writer for the fan magazines, a particularly difficult time. But he was impressed by her story, which accurately recorded the interview and his own impatience. Thereafter he always made himself available to Miss Hall, and she could get a personal interview with him at times when no other writers could. But Tracy still gave her a hard time.

He liked Adela Rogers St. Johns, who was 'strong without being pushy', and possibly no other magazine writers. The syndicated columnists, especially the men, were anathema to him unless they were friends like Sidney Skolsky.

The bane of his existence, predictably, were the female gossip columnists, but oddly enough, Tracy never waged a vendetta against any of them. He refused to speak ill of Louella Parsons, and on one occasion when the Irish Mafia was maligning her, Tracy said, 'Listen, you've got to be careful when you talk about *anybody* in this town, but especially someone with a little power.' He may not have been chummy with Hedda Hopper — he certainly despised her political views — but he respected her because 'Nothing is phony about Hopper, and she has guts.' Tracy was genuinely fond of Sheilah Graham, and called her a 'good broad'.

Photographers were particularly unwelcome at the Encino ranch, especially if they wanted pictures of the Tracy children. He relented just once, in 1939, and posed with four-teen-year-old John and six-year-old Susie.

*   *   *

Finally, in the late summer of 1939, *Northwest Passage* was ready to roll. Or was it? Locations had been chosen and a shooting schedule confirmed, but the script was still up in the air. The first part was in fairly good shape, but the major part of the novel proved too unwieldy to condense suc-cessfully. It defeated even such pros at Talbot Jennings and Laurence Stallings. But M-G-M decided to go ahead with the picture anyway. It may have reminded Tracy of the *Up the River* experience.

The studio obviously had less faith in *Northwest Passage* this time around. The new cast showed it. Gone were Taylor, Beery, and Tone, and Greer Garson was a new star in the just-released *Good-bye, Mr. Chips.* The only holdover was Tracy. Robert Young and Walter Brennan were now in the cast, and Ruth Hussey was the girl. The director was not Fleming, who had suffered a physical collapse directing *Gone with the Wind*, but King Vidor, who had made the silent *The Big Parade*, the first great M-G-M picture.

Tracy had once said, 'The physical labor actors have to do wouldn't tax an embryo.' Working for King Vidor he changed his mind. Vidor tackled *Northwest Passage* as one inspired and he put his actors through a physical ordeal in the rugged American Northwest, driving them until they were ready to drop. In two hectic days of shooting a river-crossing scene without the use of doubles — for Vidor wouldn't allow it — Tracy wore out a pair of leather pants. He assured Robert Young it was worth it, it was for art; Young later claimed he came out of *Northwest Passage* in top physical condition. Looking back, Tracy said that the whole experience was almost uplifting: for the first time he felt he was earning his money.

The location shooting — about ninety percent of the picture — was free-wheeling and boisterous, for the company was made up only of men. Sometimes Tracy joined in, but most of his free time was spent in his cabin where he read everything Agatha Christie ever wrote.

In Oregon, Vidor tried to hire some native Indians as extras for five dollars a day, apiece. The Indians held a council and decided to ask for ten. Tracy told Vidor to tell them the parts were only half-breeds. They worked for five.

Vidor kept the production on schedule, but no additional script arrived. Finally the company was on the hot line with the studio; there was nothing left to shoot. The studio told them to wind it up.

We will never know what *Northwest Passage* might have been. The picture that was released was entertaining but looked like a prologue for a story that never was told. The studio heads chose to abandon the balance of the screenplay ('We can make the rest of it some other time') and go in with what they had. Some introductory material was put together to make sense of the fragmentary story, but it ended up sounding like an apology. The story that emerged on the screen had nothing to do with the quest for the Northwest Passage, for that was to be the second half. Instead, it was based on one of Rogers' rangers missions to wipe out some hostile Indians.

The critics were disappointed, but *Northwest Passage*, with a title and a star that were pre-sold, became one of 1940's biggest money-makers.

*   *   *

If *Northwest Passage* proved a major physical challenge, playing Thomas Alva Edison was the greatest challenge yet to Tracy's acting ability. He had never prepared for a role so diligently. He read books about Edison, pored over the inventor's own papers, and went to Menlo Park to soak up the background of the man's life. In the course of this study, Edison became one of Tracy's heroes.

'Edison and I had at least one thing in common,' Tracy said. 'We both had it pretty rough for awhile. There were times my pants were so thin I could sit on a dime and tell if it was heads or tails, but for Edison there wasn't even a dime to sit on.'

Tracy said he wanted to give a performance that would reflect Edison's greatness of character, and the nub of that character was simplicity itself.

There was universal agreement that Tracy did a fine job in *Edison, the Man. Young Tom Edison*, released two months earlier, also in the spring of 1940, was the first half of M-G-M's Edison festival. When that picture laid an egg at the box office — Mickey Rooney's first failure as a star — there was some concern over how the Tracy picture would do. However, the public turned out in good numbers to see *Edison, the Man*, in which Tracy's old pal, Lynne Overman, had a supporting role.

Neither the gossip columnists nor the community at large knew what to make of Tracy in late 1940 and early 1941 when he became, briefly, a black-tie regular at Ciro's. Sometimes he brought Louise and sometimes he came alone, but usually he brought some young starlet, and rarely the same one twice.

Tracy was photographed one evening at the club with Olivia de Havilland, who was then the most eligible single girl in Hollywood if not the prettiest, and was James Stewart's frequent date. It may have been a one-shot meeting at the table, but the fan magazines made copy out of it for months. He was also seen with eighteen-year-old Judy Garland. People started talking, and the gossip columns started to ask if the Tracys were breaking up, or if they had broken up already. Was there a new romance, or was he looking for one? The speculation stopped abruptly. M-G-M and its public relations department denied any possibility of a Tracy separation.

In truth, the Tracys never did separate. In a certain sense, he never left home. Instead, the marriage simply eroded. Tracy rented a suite in the Beverly Wilshire Hotel where he stayed while he was making a movie in town; the ranch was where he lived the rest of the time, where he would go on weekends while a picture was being shot. Tracy's marriage improved as less strain was put on it — since they weren't together all the time, the time they did have together meant more. It was turning into a different sort of marriage; they were better friends.

*   *   *

Boom Town was the last of Tracy's 'Gable pictures' and this time his part was as big as Gable's. That was its only distinction for Tracy. It was about oil drillers and it made money.

*   *   *

On June 10, 1940, Tracy returned to Ripon College to receive the honorary degree of Doctor of Dramatic Art. The event touched him profoundly, and he said many years later that 'I had, in one moment at Ripon, real pride in the motion picture business.'

He had notified the college several months earlier that he would come to Wisconsin to receive the award. He knew he would be expected to say something, and he wrestled with the speech for weeks.

What could he say that would be meaningful to a bunch of college kids?

'You could put it this way, Spence,' someone suggested. 'You could say, "Well, boys and girls, I don't know what you're staying in college for; I didn't graduate and look at me!"'

Tracy went to Ripon with Frank Whitbeck. The studio's advertising director had become probably Tracy's closest friend in Culver City, and he was along to make sure the college wouldn't erupt into another Waterloo Station scene.

As they drove into the little college town, which was all spruced up for his arrival, Tracy felt a touch of guilt at upstaging the college's seventy-fourth commencement and the elderly construction engineer who was also to receive an honorary doctorate.

Most of central Wisconsin was there, and it did look the way Tracy imagined Waterloo Station must have, except that the crowd was orderly. He donned a doctor's gown and mortarboard, and joined the procession. Frank Whitbeck noted that the first sight of his old college professors knocked Tracy out with emotion for the rest of the day.

H. P. Boody and J. Clark Graham — the latter now a dean — introduced Tracy in turn, and the college president conferred the degree. Tracy said, 'There are some things I had intended to say. I wanted to thank Dean Graham and Professor Boody in particular for the great confidence they displayed in me and for their help. If through their work I have done some small justice to them, I am happy indeed. I do want to say that I owe whatever success I had to the start I got at Ripon College, to Professor Boody and Dean Graham. I shall always be grateful. I had intended to say something to the graduating class. Please bear with me, because when you come back you'll feel this, too. I'd like you to accept from me a "God bless you all and give you strength to carry on".'

Tracy gave the rest of the day to Ripon and its people, slightly embarrassed but enjoying himself. He joked with old friends from the West Hall dormitory, including his friend from college plays, Jack Davies. Professor Boody reunited his debating team of Bumby, MacDougall, and Tracy. Harold Bumby had become a successful businessman and had been mayor of Ripon, and Curtis MacDougall was a journalism professor at Northwestern University.

That evening Tracy was the guest of honor at a large dinner party hosted by Bumby, who had stayed in contact with the actor through the years. Lola Schultz, one of Tracy's Ripon girl friends, was seated next to him. Later on Tracy put in personal appearances at Ripon's two movie houses, where, by no stray chance, *Edison, the Man* was playing. He spent the night at Harold Bumby's Green Lake Cottage, near Ripon, and Bumby recalls that the next morning Tracy and Frank Whitbeck sat gravely over cups of coffee, their attention on the radio. Paris had fallen to the Germans.

*   *   *

Tracy was unhappy while working in *Boom Town*. He was beginning to feel exploited.

Gable, Crawford, MacDonald, Montgomery, Shearer, Powell — most of the vintage M-G-M stars — now were working on contracts calling for only two pictures annually, at no loss of salary. Greta Garbo was doing just one picture a year. Only the newer big names like James Stewart and Judy Garland were working as frequently as Tracy. And Gable's films were doing better than ever, because what few he made were more carefully done.

A new rider in Gable's pact stipulated that he was guaranteed first billing in all his pictures, which meant no more Gable-Crawford pictures or Gable-Shearer pictures, because those ladies had always been billed first. (Joan waived the right once because she wanted to do the hussy in *The Women*, which already had Miss Shearer.) What Tracy requested, in effect, was that there would be no more Gable-Tracy pictures or Crawford-Tracy pictures, either. It was a matter of professional pride.

Northwest Passage raked in good cash but Tracy was bitter about what he considered a failure. The Edison picture was more gratifying, but there was still the specter of *I Take This Woman*. He wanted pictures as good as *Fury* and *Captains Courageous*, and he didn't want *Boom Town* or the warmed-over *Smilin' Through*.

He got the works. Two pictures a year. Guaranteed top billing. The studio wanted a happy Spencer Tracy, and they would even have made a sequel to *Captains Courageous*, had not Manuel been killed off already. So they started off the new Tracy deal with *Men of Boys Town*.

The sequel turned out to be the 'little' picture the original *Boys Town* wasn't. Hollywood has a way with sequels. Furthermore, the public reacted as if they had seen the picture already.

* * *

In 1940 two-time winner Tracy had been master of ceremonies at the Academy Awards. It was the last time he would attend. When he did not show up in 1941 it was rumored that he was miffed that *Edison, the Man* wasn't in the competition.

In April of 1941 Broadway columnist Danton Walker reported that Spencer Tracy, briefly in town before going down south to start a movie, was hitting the bottle again.

* * *

Tracy was so good an actor he had hardly had a bad review. Even in *I Take This Woman* critics gave him credit for trying to make the cadaver walk. But there was no mistaking their response to *Dr. Jekyll and Mr. Hyde*. The picture was a slick, typical M-G-M success but for the playing of the title role, and the consensus was that Spencer Tracy was a flop. However, the film did give a boost to the American career of a Swedish import whose talent was the equal of her beauty — Ingrid Bergman.

Miss Bergman won an uphill battle to play poor Ivy, the girl tormented and finally defeated by Mr. Hyde. Tracy tried and failed to get out of the Jekyll-Hyde assignment. He said candidly that he had no business doing it, but the studio worked on his vanity. They wouldn't make the picture without him, he was the only reason they were making it, he was the only actor they had who could play the double role.

When Tracy suggested Fredric March for it, they laughed. If Fredric March could get an Oscar for a Jekyll-Hyde stunt, Tracy should too. He began to consider it.

Lana Turner, the well-publicized 'sweater girl' Mervyn LeRoy had discovered a few years earlier, was originally assigned the part of Ivy. Playing opposite Tracy's Hyde was to be the next step in a carefully built career. Ingrid Bergman wanted the part too. She had been introduced successfully in Selznick's *Intermezzo: A Love Story*, had been in *Rage in Heaven* at Metro, and had also done *Adam Had Four Sons* at Columbia with Warner Baxter and Susan Hayward.

'In my first three pictures,' Miss Bergman recalled, 'I was always the nice little virgin, all sweetness, and they wanted me to do it again. Of course, they thought I was wrong for Lana Turner's part. Tracy said to the director, Victor Fleming, that I was entitled to the courtesy of a test. He played Hyde in the test.'

Fleming and Tracy were both startled. Tracy said, 'Vic, you don't even have to process it. Now you've got to give it to her.' Possibly he would have quit then and there if they hadn't.

A rumor that Tracy had fallen for Miss Bergman made the rounds of the studio, and was confirmed many years later by Billy Grady, one of Tracy's close friends at the time. 'But Spence was too discreet,' Grady said, 'and he knew this was one girl he couldn't have, so they settled for a nice professional friendship.'

Miss Bergman remembers only that 'I was thrilled to be working with Spencer Tracy because he was respected in my own country and at the Royal Academy in Stockholm, where I had been. He was helpful to me, and friendly, and we both talked about making other pictures together, which we never made. He was not at all happy about doing the picture.'

Tracy and Miss Bergman went every day to Simon's Drive-In in Beverly Hills for hamburgers and milk shakes and they talked only about acting. The relationship ended with the picture.

Tracy's unhappiness was as obvious to others as it was to Miss Bergman, but by now it looked like a good sign when Tracy was miserable about a part. Victor Fleming thought the picture was terrific when it was finally put together and so did most of the studio powers. They hadn't counted on the critics going after Tracy.

The trouble was Fredric March's artistic success as Hyde in a 1932 Paramount version. March's was a far more in-human monster than Tracy's characterization, and at the same time, since Fredric March was a very handsome fellow, he made a much more debonair Dr. Harry Jekyll. Some people felt the critics didn't review the picture at all, but merely compared Tracy with March, and Tracy lost.

He lost on the set, too, when George Cukor brought the visiting Somerset Maugham around for a look at Spencer Tracy in action. Tracy was looking dapper and elegant as Dr. Jekyll when Maugham pointed to him and asked, 'Which is he now?'

When *Dr. Jekyll and Mr. Hyde* opened in August of 1941, the ranking members of Mayer's vast family shook their heads and thought, 'This will kill Spence!' It didn't, and people were surprised over his gracious acceptance of the pasting. Perhaps he didn't mind the novelty of bad personal notices. He always liked to quote the most devastating New York review, the one that began, 'Abbot and Costello opened last night at the Astor...'

Not all of Hollywood could be persuaded that Tracy had given a bad performance. One of those who thought Tracy had turned in quite a good account was none other than Mr. Fredric March.

'I thought Spence did a fine job, as he always does,' March recalled. 'His Jekyll and Hyde weren't anything like mine, but why should they be? After all, we're two different actors, aren't we? I'm sure Spence would never look at a performance and try to copy it.'

When Fredric March telephoned Tracy to tell him what he thought, Tracy laughed and said, 'Why, Fred, you son of a bitch, I've just done you the biggest professional favor you'll ever have!'

*   *   *

With *Dr. Jekyll and Mr. Hyde* safely in the can, Tracy left for Florida in May in a state of excitement over *The Year-ling*, which began shooting on location in the Everglade country. He was pleased with the strong script and with the cast, whose other principals were newcomers he had helped select: Anne Revere, who would play his wife, and the adolescent Gene Eckman, cast as their son.

Trouble again. Partly it was the setting. Insects in the swamps not only bothered the cast and crew, but even worse, swarms of them would cluster on the camera lens, making photography very difficult. There was also trouble between studio and director. After a month on location, with very little usable footage shot, Victor Fleming replaced King Vidor. Two weeks later the studio decided to shelve the project indefinitely.

Tracy was disappointed, but he had the consolation of knowing that by canceling *The Yearling*, the studio was making it possible for him to make the other picture he'd wanted to, the one with Katharine Hepburn.

He was forty-one; she was not yet thirty-two.

CHAPTER SIX

THE SUPER STAR: 1942-1949

In The Warrior's Husband her entrance was a spectacular fifteen-foot leap to the stage, and Broadway had not seen her like before. When she spoke in that chiseled way of hers, it was clear she was one of a kind and also, perhaps, a capital talent.

The films beckoned. She wasn't interested, so she named an impossible price . . . and RKO met it. She was twenty-two when she arrived in Hollywood. Her first picture, in the fall of 1932, was *A Bill of Divorcement*. The director, George Cukor, thought her the oddest girl he'd ever met. She did not get on well with John Barrymore, who had the starring role of her father; toward the end of shooting she told him she'd never act with him again, and Barrymore asked, '*Have you?*'

But she was a sensation. Hollywood, too, admitted they had an original. She strode through town in slacks, sassed the press and the movieland Establishment, slouched in a chauffeur-driven Rolls, demanding attention and getting star billing in her second picture; she was a new style in movie stars.

She kept them off balance. She denied having married, but when asked about children, said, 'Yes, I have five. Three of them are colored.' But the well-born Miss Hepburn, whose unique beauty began with her elegant cheekbones, her freckles, and her vagrant red hair, was wed to a young broker whose name had been Ogden Ludlow Smith until she made him shorten it; they had seemed happy enough, and Ogden Ludlow wanted to get her back . . . but she wanted to act.

She earned an Oscar for her third film, *Morning Glory,* in which she played a young actress with dedication much like her own. She was a magnificent Jo March in *Little Women,* and then her fortunes turned. Back on Broadway in *The Lake,* she provoked Dorothy Parker's remark that the Hepburn girl ran the gamut of emotions from A to B. She returned to Hollywood to make extraordinary pictures like *Alice Adams* and *Stage Door* and *Bringing Up Baby* and *Holiday.* She took her triumphs in her stride, but couldn't cope with defeat; after some poor films the Hepburn fans were few. She was enraged in 1938 by a major exhibitor's report that labeled her 'box-office poison' and she made such a fuss about it that people forgot that Marlene Dietrich, Fred Astaire, and Joan Crawford were also on the list. She bought her way out of the RKO contract that no longer suited her, and left Hollywood vowing not to return except in a golden chariot.

Broadway again was at her feet. She mixed tenderness and sophistication in *The Philadelphia Story,* and got herself involved in the film rights. When M-G-M wanted to make the movie, they had to take her in the package, so they gave her Cary Grant and James Stewart as leading men to make sure that audiences would want to see the picture. *The Philadelphia Story* was one of those rare, nearly perfect films; it was directed by George Cukor, who had shaped four of Miss Hepburn's earlier exercises.

But it did not accomplish for her what she wanted. The picture was a one-shot agreement, and she wanted an M-G-M star contract. She read dozens of novels and plays, searching for the right property. She suggested Eugene O'Neill's *Mourning Becomes Electra,* thinking it had parts for both Greta Garbo and herself, but Louis B. Mayer wasn't interested. She also thought she would like to do a picture with Spencer Tracy.

Garson Kanin had the idea first. In 1937 Kanin had come to Hollywood to work for Samuel Goldwyn, but he soon gained attention on his own as a writer, director, and producer at RKO. He became one of Miss Hepburn's confidants, and also managed the difficult feat of maintaining a friendship with Tracy. Since they were the two film stars he most admired, Kanin suggested the idea to both of them. Tracy was apprehensive. He had not met the lady, but knew he did not approve of the way she dressed. (Asked what he was most afraid of — Tracy once replied, 'Greta Garbo' — he was just as wary of the Hepburn woman who was Garbo's good friend, and played tennis with her.)

In the spring of 1941 a young writer of *Doctor Christian* screenplays, Ring Lardner, Jr. — the son of Tracy's friend at the Lambs Club — brought Garson Kanin a story outline he had conceived with Miss Hepburn in mind. Kanin liked the sound of it but since he was going into the army, he put Lardner in touch with his brother, Michael, who also had a few minor writing credits. Lardner and Michael Kanin completed the screenplay in a hurry. The lead male role had more than a casual resemblance to Spencer Tracy. They delivered the work to Miss Hepburn, whose good instinct upon reading it told her that this at last was the right property.

Convincing M-G-M wouldn't be easy, and Miss Hepburn went about that task with extraordinary consideration for the young authors. To guard against the customary studio distrust of young writers (and to assure them a decent amount of money when the story was sold), she removed the title page with their names on it and declined to say who had written 'This wonderful story'.

Her first ally was Joe Mankiewicz, her *Philadelphia Story* producer who was, besides, a Tracy friend and a major writing talent who could recognize a good script. He saw the merit of *Woman of the Year*, and that it was right for both Tracy and Hepburn. Mankiewicz helped Miss Hepburn put the pressure on Mayer and his staff, and she called all the shots. The studio yielded to her hard bargain. The price tag was $211,000 — astronomic in that day. Miss Hepburn got a flat $100,000, and the two writers got $50,000 each. When she explained that $10,000 was the fee for her agent, someone asked what the extra thousand was for. She said,

'It's for my having taken all this trouble to find M-G-M a good story.'

Later there was considerable publicity about Miss Hepburn's smart business maneuver, and it infuriated Louis B. Mayer, who didn't like to look as if he had been taken. But Mayer, too, was somewhat in awe of the strong-willed aristocrat so full of Yankee spirit. She could get her way with him, and over the long haul they always got along.

There was one loophole in the *Woman of the Year* deal, and that was Tracy. Billing was not the problem. Miss Hepburn was ready to relinquish her customary top billing to Tracy if that would win him over to making the film. But Tracy had just started work on *The Yearling*. It had an unusually long schedule, and once M-G-M decided to do the *Woman of the Year* they didn't want to wait around. There was talk of Clark Gable getting the part, or perhaps Walter Pidgeon.

Just at this point, *The Yearling* was postponed indefinitely. Tracy's assignment to *Woman of the Year* was immediate. It made news, for all Hollywood thought it the season's oddest casting.

Miss Hepburn made an additional demand that was even bolder than her request for Tracy. She announced that none of M-G-M's directors would be suitable; she wanted George Stevens. Hepburn's memorable *Alice Adams* had launched George Stevens as a major director, and there were few directors now who had as fine a reputation. (No doubt she would have accepted Cukor, but he was still occupied with the unfortunate *Two-Faced Woman*, which would be Garbo's last picture.) Hepburn got her way: Columbia loaned Stevens to M-G-M.

Tracy's customary way of getting into a new picture was to isolate himself, memorize his lines, and work out characterization. Not this time. In an M-G-M screening room he had a projectionist run off Miss Hepburn's RKO pictures. The lady had already seen every Tracy picture, and had seen *Captains Courageous* over and over. (Some years later she estimated having seen it thirty times in all.) Before their first meeting, each had a healthy respect for the other's talent.

They met like two heads of state who had just established diplomatic relations. It was a tense but also an exciting day all over the studio. Everyone was talking about the new project.

The famous account of their first meeting may be apocryphal, but one can't help hoping the story is true. They say that when Miss Hepburn, five feet seven in her bare feet, greeted her new co-star, she observed, 'I fear I may be too tall for you, Mr. Tracy.' He answered, 'Don't worry, Miss Hepburn, 'I'll cut you down to my size.' Miss Hepburn said, 'I hope my being in the picture won't keep all your fans away, Mr. Tracy.' 'Don't worry, Miss Hepburn,' he said. 'Boys Town has pledged to see all my pictures.'

After a day or two of formality, Miss Hepburn and Mr. Tracy were calling each other Spence and Kate, and the relationship was a comfortable one by the time they finally got around to shooting the first scene.

She wanted a closed set, and that was approximately what they had. Reporters kept their distance and tried to get their stories from the amiable Stevens. The director said, 'They're imitating each other.' They were hitting it off just fine.

The picture went before the cameras late in July and was completed in October. During that time accounts of an on-the-set romance touched off some sly gossip, but was hardly acknowledged in the newspapers. There were plenty of stories, some rather arch, describing how well they were getting along together. It stopped there because no one really knew much about Spencer Tracy's private life; but more important, for once people seemed willing to try to do the decent thing.

Tracy gave one interview during the shooting period.

'I was impressed with the legitimacy and honesty of the story. It's about understandable people and their problems, particularly the readjustment of a man and a woman genuinely in love but poles apart in their outlook on life and marriage. Kate and I both tried to play our comedy scenes as simply as possible, and we had fun with them.'

When *Woman of the Year* was previewed at the studio in November, everyone, from Mayer down, was ecstatic. Because of the fine acting and the intelligent Stevens direction, every minute seemed credible. M-G-M was in the unusual dilemma of not having a serious contender for the 1941 Academy Awards, and some wanted to rush *Woman of the Year* into late December release. The idea finally was vetoed because of Frank Whitbeck's excellent advertising campaign. When the picture premiered in February of 1942, it was something for critics to admire and for audiences — vast audiences, at every level of sophistication — to love.

The story focuses on Tess Harding, a famous columnist — a kind of amalgam of Dorothy Thompson and Claire Boothe Luce, who falls in love with Sam Craig, a sports editor. It is a comedy of mutual readjustment, and it required not just acting, but acting together.

When the Tracy-Hepburn relationship didn't end when the picture was completed, the columnists' hints grew louder. Sheilah Graham set the tone. 'For your information, Spencer Tracy and Katharine Hepburn got on like a house afire during the making of the film. The love scenes in the picture are extremely convincing!'

Katharine Hepburn, with a new M-G-M star contract, wanted Spencer Tracy in her next picture.

*   *   *

Practical jokes abounded at M-G-M in the heydey of Jack Conway, Woody Van Dyke, and Victor Fleming. The directors set the standard that the Gables and Stewarts tried to match. But Tracy became famous throughout Hollywood as a practical joker and only Humphrey Bogart could top him.

On the afternoon preceding a Memorial Day holiday, Tracy asked Billy Grady to take a sail with him on Errol Flynn's boat, which Tracy said he had borrowed for the day. That boat was huge, and legends had sprung up about it. Grady came to Tracy's suite at the Beverly Wilshire all decked out for the sail. Tracy wasn't nearly ready. In fact, he kept stalling and finding distractions until Grady was fit to be tied. It seemed they might never get off. When Tracy was ready at last, he suggested to Grady that perhaps they should eat something before they left. While they were arguing the point, the telephone rang.

It was Frank Whitbeck. He needed Tracy's help, and wouldn't be put off. Within a few minutes Whitbeck had arrived, dressed for an evening on the town.

'Spence, you've got to stay here today. I've tried Taylor, Gable, everybody, and they're all out of town already. I have to have a top male star for a promotion job, or I'm in trouble.'

Tracy looked quizzical. Grady started to swear.

'It's this group of exhibitors, Spence. They're very power-ful, and now they've sent these two dames on a Hollywood tour and L. B. promised they'd be escorted by one of our top guys.'

'What kind of dames?' Billy Grady asked.

'Oh, they're . . . nice young kids. They look all right. You could come along, Billy.'

Grady was still trying to get Tracy out the door, but Tracy felt he owed Frank Whitbeck a favor.

'Thanks, Spence. The girls are on their way now.'

'They're *what*?'

'I knew you'd go along with it. You know, they want to see where a movie star lives. So we'll go to dinner from here.'

Grady was disgusted by the change of plans. He said he'd go along, but first he'd like to see what the girls looked like.

When the guests arrived on the street below, the men peered out the window. There were two little girls, probably in their late teens, wearing white sailor dresses with blue collars, and each had blond ringlets.

Grady headed for the door, 'They're cute,' he said, 'but too young for me. Why, a guy can get in trouble!'

He got as far as the hallway. The girls were getting out of the elevator and he was trapped. They started to giggle when they saw Tracy bringing up the rear, and Whitbeck didn't help at all.

'Mr. Grady runs the studio casting office. He might get both of you some parts in M-G-M movies.'

On that thought the girls giggled shyly at meeting Mr. Grady, too.

At last the five of them made it to a restaurant; Grady was seated with a girl on each side of him. The girls were cute, all right, but they weren't strong on conversation. They spent most of the time staring at Tracy, with large moist eyes filled with love. What a thrill it was to be having dinner with Mr. Spencer Tracy, and they couldn't wait to tell the folks back home. The young ladies weren't used to having a drink, but as the evening wore on the men were feeling no pain.

Suddenly a strange gleam came into Tracy's eye, and then he began to chuckle. At the same moment Grady realized he was being assaulted. The girls had worked his trousers loose, and now they were going after the rest of him. The sweet young things were hookers hired for the occasion! Tracy and Whitbeck roared, and Grady had to fight hard to keep the ladies from stripping him on the spot.

*   *   *

The threat of world war hovered over America through most of 1941, and in the film colony the awareness of gathering turmoil was most acute at M-G-M. Woody Van Dyke was the first major director to depart for military service, and the first stars to leave were from M-G-M: James Stewart and Robert Montgomery.

The attack on Pearl Harbor came in the middle of the shooting schedule of *Tortilla Flat*. Despite the grim times, and Tracy's own depression at the gloomy headlines, filming the Steinbeck story was an enjoyable experience.

The remarkable set covered three acres teeming with ducks and chickens and turkeys, goats and pigs, and more than a dozen hound dogs. Hedy Lamarr and John Garfield (borrowed from Warners) supplied the romance. They were somewhat miscast as Mexican half-breeds in California.

Tracy and Garfield formed a strong friendship during the filming, and Tracy was impressed by the younger star's hard work. Tracy began to appreciate Miss Lamarr's flair for the medium, too, certainly not apparent in *I Take This Woman*. In the character part of Pilon, Tracy recalled his fine work in *Captains Courageous*.

The studio announcement that Tracy and Hepburn would be reunited in their next picture was supposedly called forth 'by popular demand!' But the studio knew it had to find another strong property for Tracy and Hepburn well before the public really asked for it.

When the pair hit their stride filming *Woman of the Year*, Miss Hepburn began to introduce Tracy into her own circle of friends, among whose members George Cukor was perhaps most prominent. Although the director came to M-G-M before Tracy did, they had until then hardly known one another. When it came out that Cukor would direct *Keeper of the Flame*, it seemed unlikely that the two men would get along.

Cukor was urbane and intellectual; as a director, he was noted for fussing over details and would film a number of takes to get something just right. This did not augur well for a healthy relationship with Tracy, who still was impatient while a picture was in production. Cukor also was known as a 'woman's director', with a sure hand for shaping a feminine 'vehicle'.

But *Keeper of the Flame* was not a film that catered to the ladies. *Keeper of the Flame* definitely was Tracy's picture, in both the size and strength of his role. He played a journalist looking into the accidental death of a national hero, suspicious of misdoing and wary of the man's strange widow — Miss Hepburn's role. After falling in love with the woman who keeps the flame of her husband's greatness, he learns that she had uncovered a fantastic plot to gain control of the U.S. Government and set up her husband as a dictator. The mood of the film was dark; in places, it came close to real tragedy.

As it turned out, Tracy and Cukor got along amicably and

came to have an uncommon respect for one another. They worked together at great length over the motivation and character of the newsman. In this picture Tracy showed how much intense feeling could be conveyed by his eyes alone, in an otherwise impassive face. From Cukor as well as from Miss Hepburn, Tracy reaped the benefit of modern psychological insight. He also found that Cukor helped keep Miss Hepburn from over-intellectualizing. Sometimes she almost took over the directing, but Cukor knew when to give her free rein, and when and how to check her. During the filming of a fire scene, she told Cukor, 'I don't think the people would have to be told about the fire. They would smell the smoke.' Cukor sighed. 'It must be wonderful to know all about acting and all about fires.' Tracy burst out laughing. He admired Cukor's witty handling of Miss Hepburn, and because George Cukor was never dull, he and Tracy would always get along.

*   *   *

In 1942 the John Tracy Clinic was established in a wooden bungalow at the University of Southern California. It was the beginning of the fulfillment of Louise Tracy's dream. Several years later a $500,000 building at U.S.C. would house the clinic, the world's finest education center for deaf children. Louise supervised the staff from the beginning. She was a gifted teacher, the best evidence of which was eighteen-year-old John. Despite his permanent deafness and the complication of an attack of polio, he was a vigorous, athletic boy who liked to learn. He performed as a 'normal' person because Louise had convinced him that he was one. He understood spoken words he couldn't hear, and he himself spoke intelligibly but with some difficulty. Adept in schoolwork, he had a distinct artistic bent.

Louise's first forays in teaching were with a hundred-dollar correspondence course from the Wright Oral School in New York City, designed for the mothers of deaf children. She learned the Wright method, combined it with other approaches, and consulted with education specialists everywhere. The only special requirement for the deaf child, she maintained, is more attention, more consideration, and more love.

'The child's progress depends largely on the mother,' Louise Tracy explained. 'The mother is like a god to a little deaf child. She must make the child as attractive and likeable as possible, and teach him good habits.'

Louise's work in California began in group study. She brought together parents of deaf children, and taught them what she knew. She personally trained many instructors, and was as efficient in the classroom as she was in an administrative office. She learned about various types of deafness and their causes, and offered family counseling.

Tracy gave his wife all the credit for the creation and development of the John Tracy Clinic and for its notable success. Similarly, Louise Tracy maintained that her husband was the first and most frequent benefactor of the clinic, which is supported entirely by voluntary contributions and provides free assistance to parents and children of all economic livels. Although he never was able to talk easily about his son's deafness, Tracy often mentioned the clinic and its accomplishments with pride. He frequently addressed social groups on the clinic's behalf.

Tracy often told friends that he was grateful that his mother had lived to know that the John Tracy Clinic would be a reality. Carrie Brown Tracy died in 1942, by then a special favorite at M-G-M, particularly with the publicity department which often had the benefit of her graciousness.

Louise Tracy and Carroll Tracy attest that Spencer never asked anybody in the film colony, or out of it, for contributions to the John Tracy Clinic. But the contributions came in, nonetheless. People followed Tracy's example, and the clinic became one of the favorite Hollywood charities.

'Everyone in our business,' says Mervyn LeRoy, 'is proud of Louise Tracy, and proud of Spence. We're grateful to know that we've been of some help in the John Tracy Clinic's wonderful contribution to the world.'

*   *   *

In the fall of 1942 Tracy disappeared from the Hollywood scene, making Romanoff's and Chasen's less interesting on Wednesday nights. Some of the spark was gone from the Irish Mafia.

Tracy went to New York for a vacation that stretched into months. He rented a suite in the Waldorf Towers and set about making good on an old promise made to his late mother at least once, and to himself perennially. He wanted to get back on the stage. He spent most of his time indoors, where he wouldn't be recognized, and where he could read new scripts.

His desire to return to Broadway could only have been intensified by his association with Katharine Hepburn. She was making one of her periodic returns to the theater, and again was the toast of the town and of its box office. Philip Barry, who had written *The Philadelphia Story* especially for Miss Hepburn, gave her a new comedy-drama entitled *Without Love*, which she took on after completing *Keeper of the Flame*. The new play was brittle and slick, but not successful. The playwright put into it his concern for war and its causes, and the reviewers found it muddled. However, the public's response was such that Miss Hepburn could have kept the play running for years had she been so inclined. She wasn't, but M-G-M, with an eye to the future, bought up the rights.

Tracy could not find a play that suited him, but eventually he read a screenplay that he liked. (The studio was finding it difficult to please him; he vetoed most of their suggestions.) *A Guy Named Joe* was a fantasy about a dead pilot whose spirit — visible and audible, and played by Tracey — remained on the scene to affect the lives of those he left behind. Once Victor Fleming was confirmed as the director, Tracy returned to California; it would be the last film Fleming would make starring Tracy.

Whitey Hendry, the head of M-G-M's police guard, warned the returning Tracy that things weren't going to seem the same around Culver City. Because of the war, just about everybody was gone. Tracy was not only the biggest star in sight, he was almost the only one.

Men from all departments in the studio had entered military service and were not being replaced. The studio's production log had been reduced to twenty-eight pictures annually, and it was still hard to find enough stars to appear in them.

Clark Gable and Robert Taylor had joined Stewart and Montgomery in uniform, and William Powell was cutting down on the work he was doing. The old guard was almost gone. Norma Shearer and Greta Garbo had retired, and neither Myrna Loy nor Jeanette MacDonald was working at all. Joan Crawford and M-G-M had parted company.

The only stars who had been at the studio longer than Tracy were Wallace Beery and Mickey Rooney. With the exception of Tracy, the only major leading man was Walter Pidgeon. The female stars were Greer Garson, Judy Garland, Hedy Lamarr, and Lana Turner. A new contingent included Gene Kelly, Lucille Ball, Donna Reed, Red Skelton, and a remarkable child, Margaret O'Brien. It was quite a list, but still nothing to match the glitter of the 1930's. Tracy was no longer a star at M-G-M; almost by default, he was a superstar.

A Guy Named Joe posed a problem. It needed a leading lady who was a good actress, one old enough to make her long involvement with Tracy plausible, but young enough to end up in the arms of a younger (and living) flyer, in a romance arranged by the dead pilot's spirit.

M-G-M had no such leading lady, and after a long and well-publicized search, in which most of the stars in Hollywood hoped to be chosen to play opposite Tracy, Everett Riskin, the producer, suggested Irene Dunne. Earlier, at Columbia, Riskin had produced two of Miss Dunne's more successful comedies.

Irene Dunne was also a superstar. In 1943 her prestige

probably was exceeded only by that of Bette Davis. She had been around since the early talkies, a musical star when musicals were in style, a soap opera heroine when that was the fad, and when called for, a screwball comedienne as well. In *Guy Named Joe* she could show off her virtuosity. She didn't mind taking second billing for the first time in a decade, for it would be worth it to work with Spencer Tracy.

Or so she thought. Making the picture became something of a trial for Miss Dunne, who for all her experience and charm wasn't tough enough to bear up under Tracy's merciless teasing. Both Tracy and Victor Fleming had a good deal of fun at her expense during the making of the picture.

Tracy was going through one of his bad times, possibly because of his disappointment at not finding a stage property, and he drank heavily during the production schedule for *A Guy Named Joe*. As always, he reported to the set on time, but during working hours he would be cutting and wry; he played tricks and made fun of Irene Dunne. When she twice threatened to quit the picture if Tracy and Fleming didn't stop, the matter became the personal concern of Louis B. Mayer. It was finally solved peaceably by some reciprocal blackmail.

Late in 1942 Billy Grady had signed Van Johnson, formerly a Broadway dancer, after Warners had dropped him. Nobody thought much of the boy, who was worked into half a dozen minor M-G-M assignments. Tracy hardly knew Van Johnson, but he knew he was good, and he got him the part of the young flyer in *A Guy Named Joe*.

After the shooting schedule was well under way, Van Johnson was almost killed in a motorcycle accident. He pulled through, but he had a fractured skull and would take a long time to recover. Only a few of Johnson's scenes were in the can. Mayer started looking for a replacement and John Hodiak and Peter Lawford were considered. When Tracy heard that Johnson was being dumped, he let loose his temper.

Tracy announced that if Van Johnson didn't keep the part in *A Guy Named Joe*, Spencer Tracy would not appear in one more scene. Studio officials protested that although they could 'shoot around' Johnson for a while, waiting much longer would cost a lot of money. Tracy wouldn't budge. Soon Mayer, who tried to avoid Tracy, sent an emissary to make a bargain: *A Guy Named Joe* could keep Van Johnson if Spencer Tracy would start behaving like a gentleman toward Irene Dunne.

Tracy settled down. He concentrated on acting movingly and well in his scenes with Irene Dunne. When the frail Van Johnson reported back to work, Fleming looked at Tracy and said, 'Now the yellow-haired punk had better be good.' He was. Louis B. Mayer persuaded Irene Dunne to star in M-G-M's *White Cliffs of Dover*, and Miss Dunne recommended Johnson for a part in it. After that he made *Two Girls and a Sailor*, the first of many M-G-M Technicolor musicals, and Van Johnson became the idol of high school girls all over America.

Van Johnson has always insisted that he would not have had a screen career at all had it not been for the stubborn efforts of Spencer Tracy.

*   *   *

Tracy was not one of those Hollywood parents who give their children a large allowance and ignore them, nor was he the sort to make sure they got into publicity photographs with him. Tracy, who had appreciated having a good father, wanted his own children to have the same.

In the early 1940's his practice as to spend every Friday evening with John and Susie, no matter what.

Tracy liked to be outdoors with his children. John and Susie hiked, rode, and swam. In their lives, the foaling of a colt was much more important than, say, a visit to the M-G-M studio where the only star who really impressed them was Tarzan.

Tracy taught his son to play polo. It was a shame, Tracy often told friends at the Riviera and Bel-Air clubs, that polo had begun to go out of fashion in the movie colony, for John was so good at it that he could have become a really great player. But polo in Hollywood was not the same after Will Rogers died. Movie personnel grew more interested in golf, and finally the Riviera polo matches were discontinued.

Despite the wide difference in their ages, John and Susie Tracy were very close. Susie treated her brother as any sister would treat a normal brother, thereby strengthening the bond. Susie was precocious, and was always outspoken. She did not see her father on the screen until *Boys Town,* but she had heard the talk about *Captains Couragious* and *Test Pilot,* and she knew what was going on. When she was six she was introduced to Victor Fleming. She told the director, 'I don't like you because you're so mean to my daddy. You've killed him twice.'

* * *

Once in 1943 when Tracy went to the Hollywood Legion Stadium fights he was heckled by some young sailors. They called Tracy, whose dark hair was now shot with gray and whose face was heavily lined, a draft-dodger who was too chicken to fight. Tracy ignored them, and the stadium police finally took them away.

But the incident left Tracy in a gloomy mood, and he left before the main event. He was upset. He had already been feeling guilty for some time — being a World War I veteran wasn't enough, it didn't justify his staying out of World War II.

Tracy had done a little, of course. He went on the radio to push the sale of bonds during the second and third War Loan drives, and also filmed a brief pitch that would precede plate-passing in the theaters during intermission. But he wasn't satisfied with himself, he wanted to do more. Pat O'Brien suggested a U.S.O. tour — O'Brien was one of many Hollywood stars making personal appearances at camps — but Tracy felt he couldn't do anything that would interest the G.I.'s, and he could not be comfortable in just being seen. When John Garfield persuaded him to go to the Hollywood Canteen to shake hands and joke with servicemen, Tracy found he was ill at ease in the crowd.

Lionel Barrymore asked Tracy what was wrong with singing for troops. When Tracy said that he couldn't sing a note, Barrymore answered, 'That's why I'd pay money to hear you try.'

So Tracy became a camp entertainer, first at the California bases, then in Hawaii and Alaska. He told Adela Rogers St. Johns that some of the happiest moments of his life occurred in Hawaii when he realized that the servicemen didn't mind that he wasn't Betty Grable. He had a musical repertoire that included a hammed-up rendition of 'Pistol Packin' Mamma'. The G.I.'s loved him. Tracy liked to tell of a young Marine who, with great politeness, said, 'Gee, Mr. Tracy, I'll bet you could really *act* if you tried. Have you ever thought about going on the stage?'

Tracy was booked for a return tour of the Alaska bases in 1944, and was stuck in Seattle for several days when fog grounded all planes. Tracy had a reunion with Kenny Edgers, his college roommate, who was a dentist in Seattle. One morning, at 4.30 A.M., a day or so after their meeting, Edgers was awakened by a telephone call from Tracy, who as usual was having trouble sleeping, and who wanted Edgers to come down to his hotel.

Tracy told Edgers he had been 'directed' too long. He didn't have to make choices in spending his money, for he could have anything he wanted. He had had five Cadillacs; it wasn't fun to acquire anything anymore because it was too easy. The one real worry he had was his public image. He felt now that he was wasting time in Seattle; the weather in Alaska was terrible, the boys up there could get along without him, he wanted to get back home . . . but what would his fans think?

Tracy returned to Los Angeles, and called Dr. Edgers daily to see if there had been any bad publicity in the Seattle papers because he had given up the trip. Not a word had been written about it. Tracy's career as a camp entertainer ended without controversy.

*   *   *

Tracy had expected to follow *A Guy Named Joe* with the film version of *Without Love*. When that venture did not materialize immediately, rumor circulated that Tracy and Hepburn were feuding. The daily *Variety* said as much, and at about the same time Hedda Hopper reported that 'Katharine Hepburn's romance with a famous star is a thing of the past, though she won't admit it.' Apparently it was safe to mention a romance that had not been acknowledged publicly in the first place, as long as it was a thing of the past.

Miss Hepburn, though, had become involved in a major studio undertaking that Louis B. Mayer said would be a 'wartime *Good Earth*'. The long production schedule for *Dragon Seed* preempted *Without Love*, so the studio looked for another picture to occupy Tracy. They came up with *The Seventh Cross*, a story set in Hitler's Germany about a man who escaped from a concentration camp. It was the first major project directed by Fred Zinnemann.

Tracy's absorption in *The Seventh Cross* was total. His role was extremely arduous, requiring his presence before the camera almost constantly, but with very little dialogue. The performance illustrated Tracy's sure footing on what Garson Kanin called his plateau beyond greatness, when 'the audience is made aware of what a character is thinking and feeling no matter what he is doing or saying.' M-G-M's Emily Torchia remembers that Tracy surprised the publicity department by announcing he wanted to give interviews, to let people know what a fine director Zinnemann was; thus he helped Zinnemann to get a major reputation in a hurry.

During the filming Tracy was emotionally in a shambles, shaken by the deaths of several people he cared about. First it had been the brilliant Carole Lombard, Gable's wife; then Tracy's mother; then George M. Cohan; and finally, Lynne Overman. One afternoon on *The Seventh Cross* set Ray Collins asked a contemplative Tracy what he was thinking about, and Tracy said, 'Dying'. He had received a War Department telegram notifying him that Eddie Carr had been killed in action. Eddie was one of the young friends Tracy made at Boys Town; he had listed Tracy as next of kin.

When Miss Hepburn was ready to pursue *Without Love*, Tracy wasn't. Mervyn LeRoy thought Tracy should play General Doolittle in *Thirty Seconds over Tokyo*, the film he was planning from Captain Ted W. Lawson's best-seller about the celebrated Tokyo bombing mission. It was not a large part in the screenplay — Van Johnson and Robert Walker had the leading roles— but it was an important one, and on the basis of Doolittle's fame it could justify a special appearance by Tracy. *Thirty Seconds over Tokyo* became one of the most popular and well-received war pictures. After its completion in the fall of 1944, Tracy and Hepburn turned their attentions to *Without Love*.

* * *

Hollywood in the mid-1940's didn't have the glamour of the prewar period, nor did peacetime restore the old atmosphere. But Spencer Tracy changed before his studio did. The change was not attributed to war or economics or advancing age, but to Katharine Hepburn.

Tracy was known to have had his 'affairs of the moment' at the studio, but after Katharine Hepburn came to Culver City no other person at the studio had real meaning for him.

'It was all different,' Billy Grady said. 'We had all been Tracy's pals — the executives, the directors, everybody — and he had been our favorite guy. I suppose he still was, but we weren't close anymore. We didn't do things together anymore. You saw Spence only at the studio, and now you were just casual friends.'

Tracy rarely had lunch in the studio commissary now. He usually ate in his dressing room, or somewhere else with Katharine Hepburn. He had only one confidant other than Miss Hepburn and that was his brother. Carroll Tracy was more in evidence in Spencer's working life, and Tracy needed to keep his older brother near him. Carroll also got along well with Miss Hepburn.

Without Love was not one of the more memorable Tracy-Hepburn films. It held no surprises, except possibly for Philip Barry, who could hardly recognize his original play in what appeared on film. Donald Ogden Stewart, who adapted both *The Philadelphia Story* and *Without Love* to the screen, had almost rewritten what he considered an inferior script, and he wanted to build up Tracy's part. But it still was a Hepburn film from beginning to end, although some said that Lucille Ball, in the top supporting role, had stolen every scene she was in.

Without Love was directed by Harold Bucquet, who told what it was like to direct the two stars. 'Directing Mr. Tracy amounts to telling him when you're ready to start the scene. He hasn't let me down yet, and if he does, perhaps we'll get acquainted. Miss Hepburn requires direction, for she tends to act too much. Her acting is much less economical than Mr. Tracy's, but his style is rubbing off on her. The important thing is that I don't coach them on their scenes together. No one should do that, for they do a thorough job by themselves, and know exactly what they want to accomplish when we begin a scene.'

The stars' friendship was based first on a love of acting and an intense professional admiration of each other. One of their friends suggested that Miss Hepburn arrived in Tracy's life at a moment when he needed faith in himself as an actor. The frustration of *I Take This Woman* and the Jekyll-Hyde film were still with him, and Miss Hepburn helped him discover again how stimulating acting could be.

Gradually he stopped meeting his old friends on Wednesday nights, as Miss Hepburn introduced him to a new society that stimulated him in new ways.

Katharine Hepburn took exceptional care to protect the privacy of her personal life, often failing to cooperate with her Hollywood employers. But a private life Miss Hepburn certainly did have, with people who were several cuts above the filmland aristocracy intellectually, and who were involved in the affairs of the nation and the world. Katharine Hepburn was a Connecticut girl from an outstanding family.

Her father was a leading Hartford physician, and her mother had worked with Margaret Sanger in the nation's first meaningful birth control movement. There were six Hepburn children, and the parents encouraged strong individual will and purpose. Katharine was the one with a theatrical destiny, and even her parents were a little surprised by her dedication.

Tracy was taken into the Hepburn family group. Miss Hepburn knew many writers — novelists and poets and particularly playwrights; she knew the most interesting people on Broadway; and her own circle of friends included the President of the United States.

*   *   *

Robert Emmet Sherwood stood a gaunt six feet, eight inches. He was one of Katharine Hepburn's friends, and one of the more interesting men in American letters.

His first love had been the movies. At the age of twenty-one, he began a ten-year stint as motion picture reviewer for the old *Life* magazine. It was his own idea, and Robert Benchley sponsored it. Benchley was the magazine's drama critic, and he developed a paternal feeling for the boy, who quickly became the first important motion picture critic anywhere. Sherwood's skill in the art of good conversation was almost as famous as Benchley's. Then Sherwood wrote some plays: *The Road to Rome, Waterloo Bridge, Reunion in Vienna, The Petrified Forest, Idiot's Delight, Abe Lincoln in Illinois,* and *There Shall Be No Night.* And he collected Pulitzer Prizes. During the war he gave up playwrighting to become an adviser and speechwriter for President Roosevelt. He stayed at the White House, but left upon Roosevelt's death, for Harry Truman's style in speech-making was not Robert Sherwood's.

Sherwood again set his sights on the theater. His years in the White House led him to think of writing a play about individual conscience. Spencer Tracy was the ideal actor to play the lead. On that premise he conceived *The Rugged Path.*

After a dozen years of deliberation and false starts, Tracy's return to the theater was negotiated quickly and painlessly. Sherwood met with Tracy in May of 1945 with an outline. It combined two separate play ideas he had toyed with, one concerning an influential journalist, the other dealing with a philosophical cook on a destroyer. Sherwood now created the character Morey Vinion, a man who would be both a journalist and a navy cook. Tracy was interested, and so was the Playwrights' Company. In June Sherwood submitted a first draft to Tracy and the actor was enthusiastic. 'It has things to say that you can't say in a picture,' he said. He signed the contract.

It was the fall theater season's biggest news. Spencer Tracy was returning to Broadway after fifteen years, in the first new Robert Sherwood play in five seasons. The end of the war in August saw Sherwood rewriting, and also released Garson Kanin from the army to direct the play.

Before leaving for the East, Tracy admitted he was scared silly to face a live audience again. Since *The Last Mile* he had been on the stage only once, as narrator for Aaron Copland's 'Lincoln Portrait' in 1944, with Alfred Wallenstein conducting the Los Angeles Philharmonic Orchestra, and even that experience had unnerved him.

Spencer and Carroll Tracy left Los Angeles by automobile in August. They drove two hundred miles, developed car trouble in the California desert, had repairs and then returned to Los Angeles and took the train to New York.

The play gave its first public performance in Providence on September 28. The rehearsals had progressed satisfactorily, but with each passing day Tracy's stage fright mounted until it became a major emotional problem. The producing playwrights were not apprehensive about Tracy, and they knew on opening night that he was ready. S. N. Behrman says, 'I'll never forget the first reading of the play, how marvelous Spencer was; and then the opening in Providence . . . I have never forgotten that performance.'

The Providence reviews about the play were inconclusive, so carried away were the critics by the fact that Spencer

Tracy was on stage. *Variety* said Tracy made it a hit, and the play really didn't matter.

It mattered to Sherwood and to Tracy. After the curtain was down on the first performance, Sherwood praised Tracy's acting and said, 'Now I've got to get to work and make it deserving of you.'

Katharine Hepburn was among those giving first-night congratulations to Tracy in Providence, and she also went to Washington for the two-week engagement there. She boosted Tracy's morale behind the scenes when he fell into a deep depression over the harsh Washington notices. Robert Sherwood wrote frantically to prepare for Boston, the last out-of-town tryout. Tracy's powers of concentration and memory were a blessing, for his role was longer than Hamlet's.

Boston was not kind to the play, and was polite but not ecstatic about Tracy. Elliot Norton, the most respected Boston critic, found the second act a shambles after a good beginning, and said that Tracy was 'engaging and attractive, never so much as a hairline away from complete credibility'.

After the second Boston performance Tracy stunned the company by announcing that he was pulling out. A clause in his contract entitled him to leave the production on two weeks' notice, an unusually generous concession to a star, and he was taking advantage of it.

Tracy was irreplaceable. If he left, the show would close. Sherwood, Kanin, and others pleaded with Tracy but steered clear of pressuring him with his moral obligation to the cast and company. The next day, after thinking it over, he was back in the show for an 'indefinite' time. The Playwrights' Company announced that the play would close for a week of alterations following the Boston engagement and and would open on Broadway on November 10.

Katharine Hepburn had been in Boston, and there were reports that Miss Hepburn was Spencer Tracy's behind-the-scenes adviser. The Boston *Globe* snidely reported that she was giving the producers fits and was the reason for Tracy's on-again, off-again attitude. Dorothy Kilgallen, however, said that the Playwrights' Company owed Miss Hepburn a debt of thanks. In a cover story on Tracy and *The Rugged Path*, *Life* said that Miss Hepburn alone had talked Tracy out of quitting the show. Pulling out, she told him, would be far worse for his career than an appearance in a failure.

But three days after the resumption of his marathon role, Tracy failed to make a performance. Nearly 1,800 annoyed patrons received ticket refunds when it was announced that Tracy had been rushed to a Boston hospital with a cold and a sinus infection.

He missed three more performances. During the final Boston performances Tracy's health and Sherwood's play both were looking up, and the company was buoyant when it left Massachusetts. Louise Tracy came to Boston for one of the final performances and said she liked the play immensely.

The Broadway proving ground was the handsome Plymouth Theatre where, twenty-two years earlier almost to the day, Tracy had been in a play with Ethel Barrymore. Tracy paced the floor in his dressing room, wading through piles of crumpled telegrams, so tense he was almost in a trance. The ovation on his entrance stopped the show. When the din finally subsided, Tracy had relaxed. Soon the play was over and the audience was cheering with the nervous enthusiasm unique to first-night crowds.

'Great, isn't it?' Tracy was exuberant backstage. 'I agree with Jack Barrymore, opening night is the real fun of this business.' It was over and done with. He'd made it back.

The Sherwoods gave a small dinner party to wait for reviews: Spencer Tracy, Katharine Hepburn, Garson Kanin and Ruth Gordon, Carroll Tracy, and a few others. Tracy wore a tiny carnation in his lapel. 'You know who sent me this? Laurette Taylor!' He was in high spirits for almost the first time during the history of *The Rugged Path*, and also for the last time. When the reviews came in, his concern was for Robert E. Sherwood.

The play was mauled by the reviewers, who without exception were delighted with Tracy's performance. Even George Jean Nathan, who often disparaged screen actors tackling Broadway, praised Tracy, as did Brooks Atkinson, Howard Barnes, and Ward Morehouse. Wolcott Gibbs said in the *New Yorker*: 'Mr. Tracy has a winning modesty of bearing, almost as if he were uncomfortably denying some foolish charge of being an actor. It is hard to imagine what the play would have done without him.'

If Tracy was gratified by the personal tributes, he did not show it. After the first night he seldom received visitors in his dressing room following a performance and doggedly refused newspaper interviews. He took the play's defeat as his own and looked glumly on the audiences filling the Plymouth nightly, disdainful of the play but wanting their look at Tracy in person.

He avoided the public. He spent most of his time in the Waldorf Towers suite he shared with his brother. They did a lot of walking in Central Park, unrecognized, and avoided more popular haunts. Tracy's social life was limited to a few small gatherings at Miss Hepburn's Manhattan apartment.

His fellow actors were disturbed by their star's solitary ways. The thought that he might close the show hovered over the company through the Christmas holidays and into the new year. On Tracy's conscience was the knowledge that he represented job security for fully fifty people connected in some way with the production. He definitely planned to stay in the play until his son John, who had never seen him act on the stage, had flown in from the coast for a performance.

'I can't say I'm enjoying myself,' he said. 'The reviews weren't mixed, they were bad. But I think there's some of the finest writing in the play I've ever seen. I was amazed to find Bob was not treated with more respect by the critics. It's damned unfortunate.'

After John Tracy saw *The Rugged Path*, the play's closing was confirmed. Tracy refused to be considered the villain the rest of the cast thought he was. Tracy said, 'Hell, they'd be sore if the play had been running three years. Ethel Merman has proved that.'

Robert Sherwood thought Tracy's final appearance as Morey Vinion was the best he had ever given. The tumult was rising before the curtain was down on the finale, and one curtain call followed another as the audience cheered Tracy and the other actors applauded him. A speech was demanded but Tracy continued to bow, embarrassed and choked with emotion. In his dressing room he broke down.

'I'd like to come back in another play,' he said. 'You can say I'd like to do another play by Robert E. Sherwood.' But the people who knew Spencer Tracy sensed that he had been on the stage for the last time; and he must have sensed it, too.

He left the play, but he couldn't leave behind his disappointment. When *The Rugged Path* was selected as one of the 1945–1946 season's ten best plays in the annual volume compiled by Burns Mantle, Tracy wrote a personal letter to Mantle, expressing his appreciation. Although the experience was emotionally disastrous for him, he was glad in later years that he had gone through with it. Bill Fields, the press representative for the Playwrights' Company, declared there was no animosity toward Tracy for putting the play in mothballs. 'We were grateful to have had him,' Fields said, 'and to have had the privilege of sponsoring one of the great theatrical performances of all time.'

*   *   *

It was now 1946. Tracy was back from Broadway, Gable was back — and Garson was getting him — from the armed services, as were many male stars, and directors such as Frank Capra, George Stevens, John Ford, and William Wyler as well.

It was quite a homecoming, but things had changed. At M-G-M Gable and Tracy were now the grand old men, surrounded by busier, younger stars such as Gene Kelly, Van Johnson, Frank Sinatra, and Peter Lawford; and on the distaff side, June Allyson, Jane Powell, Ava Gardner, and Kathryn Grayson.

M-G-M was glad to have Tracy back, but not sure what to

do with him. Tracy's wavy mane was now gray, and he refused to dye it. The once-plain Tracy was a handsome man in middle age. After a delay of years, *The Yearling* was rolling in earnest, but Tracy was too old to appear in it, and Gregory Peck got the role. During his New York hiatus Tracy read the rejected several scripts from M-G-M, and made it very clear he would make only movies he liked.

He wanted *The Sea of Grass*. The story had been kicked around the studio for years, and once had been shelved for lack of a leading lady. Tracy wanted Katharine Hepburn, and that settled it. First, though, Miss Hepburn was committed to *Undercurrent* for Vincente Minnelli.

Rather than relaxing at home, Tracy reported to the studio daily. He put the veteran Vincent Lawrence through the wringer over fine points in *The Sea of Grass* script, and vetoed a John O'Hara version of *Cass Timberlane*, which he was to do after *The Sea of Grass*. Perhaps with some tutoring from Miss Hepburn, he was getting tough. He wanted *good* pictures.

A picture that once would have been shot in six weeks now required three to four months, and twice as many crewmen were involved. And Vincente Minnelli was a new kind of director, more like the painstaking Cukor than the more slaphappy but inspired Van Dyke. Minnelli, still fairly new to films, had married Judy Garland, who had become a special friend to Tracy and Miss Hepburn.

Directors were assigned to Tracy films only with his approval, and it was given with enthusiasm to Elia Kazan, the young Broadway director whose only released film was the admirable *A Tree Grows in Brooklyn*. But Kazan was an odd choice to direct the sprawling Western and he was also capable of the kind of fussing that would tax Tracy's patience.

Tracy found that knowing his lines and saying them with meaning and conviction was not enough for Kazan. Kazan wanted to know *why*. Only Katharine Hepburn's tact and ingenuity prevented a real clash between the two men.

The Sea of Grass was a handsome, somber film, with

Tracy and Miss Hepburn giving strong performances, but the picture had little lasting importance.

Tracy took a fatherly interest in Robert Walker, whose marriage to Jennifer Jones had ended two years before. Walker was uncommonly gifted but not stable emotionally, and he had started to drink heavily. Tracy was back on the wagon, and Walker took offense when Tracy wouldn't drink with him. It was one of several discordant notes of *The Sea of Grass* production.

The production of *Cass Timberlane* was also filled with friction. It took two writers after John O'Hara to come up with a script that no one was very happy with, neither Tracy nor Sinclair Lewis, who had written the novel.

Cass Timberlane reunited Tracy with Selena Royle, who had helped him at the beginning of his career. Selena Royle came to Hollywood in 1943 and was under an M-G-M contract soon afterward, becoming one of the studio's fine character actresses. On the *Cass Timberlane* set Tracy would joke amiably with her, saying, 'Selena, if it hadn't been for you I would probably be driving a truck, and happy.'

'I was quite hurt at first,' Selena Royle recalls, 'for I had expected Spence and Louise to ask me to dinner, and of course they never did. I realized eventually that it wasn't anything about *me*, it was just the way things were, with everybody.'

At first, Tracy had been genuinely excited by *Cass Timberlane,* which M-G-M had purchased at a premium because it was tailor-made for Tracy and Lana Turner. In it Tracy played a wealthy widower judge who marries a poor young girl. Tracy thought Cukor or Minnelli should direct, and he accepted George Sidney with some reluctance. *Cass Timberlane* emerged as a money-maker, but something of a loss dramatically. The 1947 Christmas release made Tracy once again one of the nation's top ten money-making stars.

However, Tracy was not mollified. It had been four years since *The Seventh Cross*, and he wanted and needed a really strong picture.

After the war, directors Capra, Stevens, and Wyler formed a Hollywood version of the Playwrights' Company, calling their own enterprise Liberty Pictures. They would group-sponsor their individually directed pictures and the first two productions were Capra's. Although the Liberty entries were released through RKO, M-G-M was happy to loan Spencer Tracy to Capra, for the property was *State of the Union*, from the Pulitzer Prize play by Lindsay and Crouse, about a man, somewhat like Wendell Willkie, who almost becomes a Presidential candidate. The material was updated for election year 1948, and Claudette Colbert played the part of Tracy's wife.

The first Liberty picture, *It's a Wonderful Life*, with James Stewart, was a movie to be proud of, but it was an unexpected failure at the box office, and it put the under-capitalized Liberty organization out of business. Consequently, Louis B. Mayer arranged to have *State of the Union* shot at M-G-M and he subsidized it, tossing in Angela Lansbury and Van Johnson to support Tracy and Colbert.

The night before shooting started, Miss Colbert broke an ankle. Miss Hepburn reported to work immediately.

Capra and his star team finished the picture almost two full weeks under schedule, and $400,000 below the budget allowance. Mayer was impressed. Capra, who probably had been warned about Tracy's growing troublesomeness and Miss Hepburn's reputation for meddling, said he had never worked with actors so cooperative or so dedicated.

Four years earlier Katharine Hepburn had met the teen-age Angela Lansbury when the British girl was acting brilliantly for George Cukor in *Gaslight,* her first American film. In *State of the Union* she was a powerful lady publisher in love with Tracy, whose candidacy she pushes.

'They helped me enormously,' Miss Lansbury recalls, 'and especially Mr. Tracy, because most of my scenes were with him. He was patient, and very earnest, and quite comforting.

'What was exciting about Spencer Tracy and Katharine Hepburn was their presence. Each, of course, has fantastic individual presence, but I mean collectively. Their personalities as well as their talents were orchestrated so marvelously. I began to think of them as one person, really; I suppose most people did.'

Howard Smith, who played a supporting role in *State of the Union*, told of going to the studio regularly, even if he was not involved in the day's shooting, because watching the superstars at work was so fascinating.

'Katharine didn't want a lot of people around, and they tried to have a closed set. But word got around when Spence and Katharine were about to act for the camera, and a crowd would gather, first watching, then applauding.'

On the set there were hints of a drama developing in real life. The role of a political boss was played by Adolphe Menjou, who had recently cooperated fully with the House Committee on Un-American Activities in its Hollywood witch-hunt. Miss Hepburn particularly was scornful of Menjou's action, and refused to speak to him on the set except when they had scenes together. Senator Joseph McCarthy was gaining power, and many artists in Hollywood were blacklisted for alleged Communist activities, among them Dalton Trumbo, Donald Ogden Stewart, Ring Lardner, Jr., and John Howard Lawson, all writers.

State of the Union was a successful film on all counts. Yet it had the ironic effect of convincing Spencer Tracy that he and his career were in a rut. It was his third straight box-office success since returning to films, but Tracy was not exactly warming the hearts of America with his old sureness. James Agee, one of the first Tracy boosters, thought that in *State of the Union* he 'lacked fire'.

The picture clearly belonged to Katharine Hepburn. In writing about a White House prospect, Lindsay and Crouse provided a far more interesting character in the man's wife. Lionel Barrymore saw a screening at the studio before Tracy did, and told him Miss Hepburn had stolen the picture completely; the very idea, he thought, pleased Tracy most highly.

Scripts were being sent regularly to Tracy. He rejected

them all, including some that were made with other actors, including *The Key to the City* (Clark Gable) and *Angels in the Outfield* (Paul Douglas).

Tracy's next film, *Edward, My Son*, started serious talk that Tracy was slipping. M-G-M had purchased the play in 1947 shortly after it opened in London starring its playwright, Robert Morley. It was reportedly bought for Tracy, with Katharine Hepburn presumably scheduled to play the alcoholic wife.

Then England's young Deborah Kerr, whose American career had bogged down after two films, fought for and won the wife's part in *Edward, My Son*.

Most of the filming was completed in England in the summer and fall of 1948. Tracy and George Cukor, who directed the film, were houseguests of Laurence Olivier and Vivien Leigh, and for part of the time Miss Hepburn was also on the scene. The film was a triumph for Deborah Kerr, and for the second time in his career, Tracy was panned by the critics.

A good part of the difficulty was Tracy's American accent and American style. He did not try to assume a British accent, feeling, probably correctly, that it would be ludicrous. But *Edward, My Son* was based on the English social order, particularly the privileged class. Miss Kerr, of course, was a natural. Tracy struck the only wrong note. Moreover, timing was against him; Robert Morley's devastating performance was fresh in American playgoers' memories when the Tracy-Kerr film was released, for by chance, the movie was made before the play was presented on Broadway in the fall of 1948.

Edward, My Son was drama with a satirical edge, so that Tracy's performance missed completely. *Theater Arts Monthly* said that 'in Mr. Tracy's straightforward performance there is barely a chuckle'. But, for Deborah Kerr, the picture delivered the first of six Academy Award nominations.

While *Edward, My Son* was in production in England, two major events imperiled M-G-M. In July of 1948 the first in a long and continuing series of administrative upheavals occurred. Dore Schary, a former M-G-M writer who spent three years at RKO as production chief, returned to M-G-M in that capacity.

The other bombshell was the industry-wide panic of '48. In the first year of mass-marketed home television sets the regular moviegoing audience dwindled.

The Supreme Court also played a hand in the panic of 1948 by handing down its first decision against the 'Big Five' theater-owning companies: Loew's (M-G-M), 20th Century-Fox, Warner Brothers, RKO, and Paramount. An antitrust suit had dragged on in the courts since 1937, and movie tycoons had seen that sooner or later production and distribution companies would not be allowed to own theaters. They had adjusted their budgets accordingly, but hadn't counted on such small audiences. So now payrolls were cut back, and productions were given stringent new budget ceilings. No one knew what effect the new order would have on the supposedly indestructible top stars. Many films released in the first half of 1949 fell far below box-office expectation, and among those was *Edward, My Son*.

Some observers linked Dore Schary's arrival at M-G-M with the mounting panic. Some, too, interpreted his arrival as the beginning of a gradual easing-out of Louis B. Mayer. While outwardly all was serene, Mayer was known to be unhappy about the move. Although Mayer was still the 'executive in charge', Schary was known as the 'executive in charge of production'.

Tracy liked Dore Schary. At RKO he had pioneered such idealistic and liberal films as *Crossfire* and *The Boy with Green Hair* and had supervised *The Spiral Staircase*, *The Farmer's Daughter*, and several Cary Grant comedies, including *Mr. Blandings Builds His Dream House*, the kind of picture Tracy hoped to make for Schary. The political sympathies of Dore Schary were such that his M-G-M regime was known as the New Deal. Louise B. Mayer was a Republican.

Possibly such people as Spencer Tracy, James Stewart,

Lionel Barrymore, Sydney Greenstreet, John Hodiak, and Gilbert Roland all believed that Schary's New Deal would bring a miracle. In any event, all of those actors found themselves involved in *Operation Malaya*, later shortened to just plain *Malaya*. The first picture Tracy did under the Schary setup was a routine adventure set in Hollywood's idea of Southeast Asia. It was such a poor film from the beginning that it was shelved for a time.

The next logical move was to get Tracy and Katharine Hepburn back in another comedy in a hurry. Miss Hepburn, who was more stubborn than Tracy about not making pictures that didn't suit her, had not worked since *State of the Union*.

Garson Kanin and his wife, Ruth Gordon, were back in Hollywood writing screenplays. They had given Ronald Colman *A Double Life* and Colman, under Cukor's direction, finally won an Oscar. Now the Kanins had a script that eventually would be known as *Adam's Rib*. It was the first project since *Woman of the Year* to draw on Tracy and Hepburn for its initial inspiration. In the screenplay two disarming and intelligent lawyers happen to be happily married to one another until they meet in court as opponents arguing a woman's right to shoot her unfaithful husband. *Adam's Rib* seemed to make a comment on the two stars' private relationship, and since it was well written as well, it made for a fine picture.

Adam's Rib had Cukor as director. Judy Holliday played the endearing but dumb young wife, who has badly bungled her attempt at murder. Shortly afterward Judy Holliday was given the part of Billie in the film version of *Born Yesterday*, the part she had immortalized on Broadway, and she was headed for an Oscar.

Adam's Rib, which was M-G-M's 1949 Christmas release, turned out to be a classic. Never had Tracy and Hepburn been better. Robert Garland, a Broadway drama critic who rarely had kind words about movie actors, saw *Adam's Rib* and declared that 'Miss Hepburn and Mr. Tracy indubitably represent Hollywood's equivalent to the Lunts'.

The box-office slump did not affect *Adam's Rib*. Indeed, it brought big audiences back to the movie theater.

1950 ushered in a period of upheaval in the movie business. The Associated Press conducted a midcentury poll to determine the best movie actor and actress in silent and talking films. Charles Chaplin, without contest, was voted the best actor of the silent screen. Greta Garbo was voted best actress for both silent and talking films. And the best actor in the more recent days of film-making, far ahead of Ronald Colman and Fredric March, was fifty-year-old Spencer Tracy.

CHAPTER SEVEN

THE FATHER IMAGE: 1950–1959

He said chocolate candy broadened him into a character actor. He topped 190 pounds and wasn't getting much exercise except for a little tennis, although he was no match for Katharine Hepburn on the court. He absolutely refused to wear a corset, as many of his contemporaries were doing. He said he'd play characters who looked and felt as old as he did. At fifty he was completely gray.

He changed. He spent more time alone, reading, listening to music, sitting and thinking, smoking cigars, cigarettes, pipes, drinking a lot of coffee, but not much of anything stronger than beer. He still slept only fitfully but thrived on cold showers and a lot of swimming.

For years he had only glanced at the newspapers; now he read the editorial pages carefully. Wherever he went, he took books with him. He saw fewer movies, and said he preferred reading a good book that would make a better movie.

He listened to classical music constantly, particular to Brahms's four symphonies. Brahms's personality interested him, and he thought he would enjoy doing a film biography of the composer if he could grow his own beard. When Robert Walker played the young Brahms in *Song of Love* — Katharine Hepburn was Clara Schumann — Tracy gave Walker advice on the character.

When a coed journalist got into the studio to ask the identity of his favorite composer, Tracy said it was Alex Konikowski. When the girl said she hadn't heard of him, Tracy expressed surprise; why, he was one of the giants . . . and there were only about twenty-five of those. It turned out that Alex Konikowski was a relief pitcher for the New York Giants.

The people at M-G-M saw very little of him now. He had fewer and fewer close friends: the Garson Kanins, the Jean Negulescos, the Collier Youngs, the Chester Erskines, George Cukor; among actors, David Niven and James Stewart. He always liked to hear Niven talk.

Most of his friends were Miss Hepburn's as well. They made up a Hollywood set that avoided nightclubs and was hardly noticed by the newspapers and fan magazines. In this group was Greta Garbo, whose beauty was still legendary; Tracy was now no longer afraid of her.

The Hollywood Hibernians had not disbanded, but times had changed. It became hard to find six Irishmen in Hollywood at the same time. Frank Morgan's death in 1949 removed some of the best permanently. James Cagney worked only irregularly in pictures and spent most of his time out of town. Frank McHugh and James Gleason were seldom there, and Ralph Ballamy's attentions were mostly on Broadway. Pat O'Brien remained, but his career had bogged down.

Tracy took up painting: oils, tempera, watercolor. He painted solely for his own enjoyment. He wouldn't let people see what he painted, and he wouldn't give any of his work away. Lionel Barrymore was an exception. When the aged Barrymore requested a Tracy landscape, the man who still worshiped Barrymore as an actor was grateful to oblige.

*   *   *

There were more awards. In 1950, the Women's Research Guild of America designated Tracy as 'the man who most strongly influences American women emotionally'. Tracy had the certificate framed and presented it to Clark Gable as a gift, with the inscription, 'Lest You Forget'.

That same year he became the first American to be awarded the Catholic Stage Guild of Ireland's annual award, in the Guild's centennial season.

He was hardly a movie star anymore; instead he was the

distinguished American actor, Mr. Spencer Tracy. Louis B. Mayer liked the sound of that. Mayer, receiving high-level guests in his office in the Irving Thalberg Memorial Building at M-G-M, once was thrown for a loss when asked to name the greatest actress and actor in films. He did not want to offend any of his stars personally, so he turned it over to his talent executive, Billy Grady. Greer Garson and Spencer Tracy were the names Grady knew Mayer would expect from him, but he thought Judy Garland was the greatest and said so. He also named the French star, Pierre Fresnay. When Mayer heard of it he fired Grady. Grady said he was really worried this time; he didn't get his job back for three days. The person who most appreciated Grady's humor was Spencer Tracy, whom Grady rated only the world's second greatest movie actor.

In his solitude Tracy read story outlines, screenplays, and other ideas sent by the studio. Tracy was 'announced' for Albert Camus' *The Plague*; for a new version of *Robinson Crusoe*; and for *Jealousy*. None of these projects materialized, sometimes because Tracy was not excited by them but more often because of the uncertainties of the movie business in the early 1950's. Today's idea was dead tomorrow.

Then Dore Schary obtained a comedy project that was, indeed, as good as his Cary Grant entries at RKO, and perhaps better. *Father of the Bride* was a best-selling short novel that Frances Goodrich and Albert Hackett made into a fine screenplay. Married and working together much as Kanin and Gordon, the Hacketts eventually would adapt the Anne Frank diary into a prize-winning drama. They kept the comic crises of Edward Streeter's *Father* intact, but made the principal character unmistakably like Spencer Tracy. The part of the daughter was written for the young Elizabeth Taylor, who was not yet eighteen when the picture went before the cameras.

The third starring part of the mother might have interested Katharine Hepburn had she not been in New York as Rosalind in *As You Like It*, proving that Shakespeare was box office and that she had the prettiest long legs on

Broadway. The role went to Joan Bennett, and Tracy was delighted to have one of the favorite targets for his teasing restored to his company after all of eighteen years. He remembered that *Me and My Gal* had ended with their wedding; Tracy thought that *Father of the Bride* indicated the marriage had turned out successfully on all counts, and for Joan Bennett's benefit he pointed to Elizabeth Taylor and said, 'And look what came of it!'

Tracy confessed that it always gave him a start, when beginning the day's shooting, to see the fresh and incredible beauty of the young Elizabeth Taylor. That she could be his daughter was, Tracy believed, the picture's only implausibility. However, Miss Taylor did bear a strong resemblance to Joan Bennett, whose own beauty was ageless.

Elizabeth Taylor had arrived at M-G-M in 1943, an eleven-year-old girl from war-torn England. After three small parts she was given the title role in *National Velvet*, the novel originally bought with the idea that Tracy would play Velvet's father. Elizabeth was not a typical child star, phased out of pictures during an awkward adolescence. In fact those were the years when she was given extraordinary exposure.

Her first attempts at 'adult' romance in *The Big Hangover* and *Conspirator* were inconclusive, and the latter was so bad the studio was afraid to release it. Both pictures were in the can when she reported to *Father of the Bride*, the project that would secure her place as an adult actress.

For perhaps the first time since Clarence Brown directed her in *National Velvet*, she had the benefit of a sensitive and inventive director. Vincente Minnelli's record was strong enough now so that he was no longer thought of as Judy Garland's husband; and, in point of fact, he no longer was. In addition to Minelli's help (and his direction was superb), Miss Taylor also had many scenes with Tracy that were meaningful for her. She later told reporters that they made her aware of communication between actors.

Father of the Bride was a comedy every step of the way, and Miss Taylor's success didn't keep it from being Tracy's picture. He was the central character, he expressed its point of view, and was occasionally the narrator. If Tracy was consciously changing into a character actor it was an impressive trial run. In the mounting pandemonium of his daughter's approaching wedding, Tracy played the forgotten man who pays the bills. He managed to squeeze all the humor from the situation without being a ham.

Released in the spring of 1950, *Father of the Bride* was a bull's-eye, and Tracy was declared the front-runner for the Oscar (the other nominated performances were yet to come). The Spencer Tracy 'comeback' was the talk of the working press, rather shocking to both the actor and his studio, for he had hardly been 'away'. The equally delightful *Adam's Rib*, for that matter, was not yet out of general distribution. But no insult to Tracy was implied: the screen had found a father image at last.

The best of Hollywood's traditional father figures were Walter Huston, Claude Rains, Charles Coburn, Lionel Barrymore, Thomas Mitchell, Edmund Gwenn, Walter Brennan, and Donald Crisp. Each usually played the father of the star, or otherwise lent support to the box-office 'names'. Not since Will Rogers had there been a popular character star, except perhaps Wallace Beery, who like Rogers, was a type first and an actor second. But Beery had died in 1949. Thus, Tracy was, in effect, the first important leading man to move gracefully into the older generation.

*　　*　　*

Tracy's friendship with Humphrey Bogart spanned almost thirty years, from the time they met during Tracy's reading for *Ned McCobb's Daughter* in early 1928 until Bogie's death in 1957. They met daily for several months while both were new at Fox, and raised some hell together after hours; but after Fox dropped Bogart they went for years without seeing one another.

Hollywood had its own class structure, and when Bogart became a superstar in the mid-1940's, he and Tracy were thrown together more often. Bogart was not one of the

Wednesday nighters, but was often at Romanoff's anyway. Nor did Tracy move among Bogie's Homby Hills 'rat pack', but he was revered by them, championed particularly by Frank Sinatra.

The sardonic Bogart liked good conversation, and talked easily and well, while Tracy grew more taciturn as the years passed. They were an ideal pair. Yet the bond during the last half-dozen years of Bogart's life was the jealous pride both had in their profession. Tracy often tried to hide this pride behind self-depreciation and a disdain for acting, but he didn't mean it. Bogart knew he was good and was proud of it, but he also knew Tracy was better. Bogart said, 'Spence is the best we have, because you don't see the mechanism at work. He covers up, never overacts, gives the impression he isn't acting at all. I try to do it, and I succeed, but not the way Spence does. He has direct contact with an audience he never sees.'

Tracy's favorite actors were Paul Muni, Fredric March, and Laurence Olivier, and of course Lionel Barrymore. But he genuinely admired Bogart.

Bogart and Miss Hepburn became friends through Tracy, and later Bogie claimed that it was his own idea that the missionary spinster heroine of *The African Queen* should be Miss Hepburn. No actor was as proud of his Oscar as Bogart, and he said he couldn't have won it without Kate to act with.

The shooting of *The African Queen* was long and arduous, on location deep in Africa. While Miss Hepburn was away, Tracy went back to drinking. Now that Frank Morgan and Lynne Overman were gone, he did most of his drinking alone, and people knew of it only because the papers reported Tracy careening wildly around town in his car.

Some observers linked Tracy's despair with Miss Hepburn's absence, but there were other reasons. Tracy was depressed by the 'Red scare' that gripped the film colony in 1951, with countless investigations and testimonies, and scores of notable motion picture contributors, blacklisted. Careers were ruined overnight. Many said that Joseph

McCarthy really ended the good life of Hollywood. Certainly it had ended at M-G-M. In 1951 Louis B. Mayer lost his job. He was finally fired by Nicholas Schenk, chairman of the Loew's board. Dore Schary stayed on, but no one knew what other changes were imminent. The atmosphere couldn't have been worse.

1951 was not a good year for Tracy's career. Even before editing of *Father of the Bride* was completed, M-G-M was at work on a sequel. In *Father's Little Dividend* Tracy played a grandfather. Tracy remembered *Men of Boys Town*, and wasn't interested in the sequel. Eddie Mannix reminded Tracy that the second *Thin Man* picture had outgrossed the first, and then there were the modest little *Doctor Kildare* and *Andy Hardy* projects, 'sleepers' that began series. (H. Allen Smith once wrote of a brainstorm to bring the two series together in a movie to be called *Andy Hardy Gets the Clap and Dr. Kildare Cures it.*) But *Father's Little Dividend* did not outgross *Father of the Bride*, or come anywhere near its own box-office expectation.

However, it was better, on every count, than the courtroom drama of *The People Against O'Hara*. Possibly the least interesting film of Tracy's postwar career, it was distinguished only for the combined talents of Tracy and Pat O'Brien, acting together in the same picture for the first time. O'Brien's career had faltered since leaving Warners in 1940 and he was having trouble getting work in good films. Tracy had refused to do the picture unless Pat was in it. As it turned out, O'Brien came off better with the critics than did Tracy, for he had a more colorful role. The O'Hara of the film's title was played by James Arness, later to star in *Gunsmoke*. *The People Against O'Hara* was the first Tracy film under the Mayer-less Schary regime, and the first under a revised contract calling for ten pictures in five years. M-G-M was to pay him something like three million dollars.

Now that Mayer was gone, everyone seemed to miss him. The films that the studio put out were no better after his departure. Schary's efforts were a source of embarrassment to many studio veterans. Besides serving as superintendent of all production, Schary was officially the producer of *Battle-ground* and *The Next Voice You Hear*. The former was a fairly standard war picture with all the right platitudes and clichés; the advertising was a mistake, though, claiming that '*Battleground* is the greatest picture since the coming of sound.' 1950 was not the moment for *The Next Voice You Hear*; the voice was God's, and most people were nonplussed and embarrassed rather than awestruck. Nonetheless Schary liked the screenplay so much that he wrote a book about the project, *The Story of a Film*. 1951 brought *It's a Big Country*, surely the worst all-star episode picture ever made, with Fredric March, Gary Cooper, Gene Kelly, William Powell, June Allyson, and a score of others.

Also under Schary's aegis was *Mr. Imperium*, which brought Ezio Pinza to Hollywood from his Broadway success in *South Pacific*. His screen career never had a chance. Pier Angeli, the freshest young hope in the movie world when Fred Zinnemann introduced her in the splendid *Teresa*, also never really made it. Thalberg's and Mayer's knowledge of star-making was now a lost art, and Miss Angeli faded away in a string of inept pictures.

M-G-M was not the only studio in trouble in 1951 and 1952. It wss apparent throughout the industry that film-makers no longer knew what the audiences wanted. M-G-M had been the giant yet now it was making the worst pictures in the world. Typical of the quality were such remarkable efforts as *Never Let Me Go* (Clark Gable and Gene Tierney), *Soldiers Three* (Stewart Granger), *Love Is Better Than Ever* (Elizabeth Taylor and Larry Parks), *The Light Touch* (Stewart Granger and Pier Angeli), *The Devil Makes Three* (Gene Kelly and Pier Angeli), and *Remains to Be Seen* (June Allyson and Van Johnson). Attempts to recapture the old grandeur — *Quo Vadis*, *Across the Wide Missouri* — were disappointing.

During this period Greer Garson's career was wasted, and Judy Garland walked out for good.

A few good pictures surfaced. There was *The Magnificent*

Yankee and the Oscar-winning *An American in Paris*, and exceptionally popular *The Great Caruso* with Mario Lanza. And in early 1952, there was *Pat and Mike*.

Again the Kanins wrote a fine screenplay for Tracy and Miss Hepburn. Work on the comedy was begun shortly after Miss Hepburn's return from Africa. Tracy's Mike is a Runyanesque small-time sports promoter who runs across a prim widow who has incredible talent as an athlete. Once again Cukor directed — it was an unbeatable combination.

Rarely was Tracy's enjoyment of a role so apparent. It was his first opportunity since *Libeled Lady* in 1936 to play such a broadly comic character, and his crude but innocent mien was at once endearing, and the work of an obviously resourceful actor.

Garson Kanin recalls Tracy and Miss Hepburn reading the *Pat and Mike* screenplay: 'Spencer sat in a corner of the room, his eyeglasses perched upon his nose. He began to read, to act, to *be*. The man with whom we had dined a few minutes earlier was no longer there. Instead, we were confronted by Mike — a personality far more real and complex than the one we had imagined — with a way of breathing, thinking, smoking, coughing, speaking, and munching peanuts. For two hours and more, Spencer stayed in character. I saw the art of acting that night, plain.'

Pat and Mike was a hit. Tracy's next picture was a flop: *The Plymouth Adventure*, an ambitious epic about the Mayflower voyage. It was Tracy's first Technicolor film since *Northwest Passage*, and it was a similar failure. The script was terrible, and not even Tracy could make the character of the ship's captain interesting or likable. The film was Tracy's last with Van Johnson, once his protégé, and it marked an unfortunate ending for Clarence Brown, the M-G-M director who had been 'Garbo's Man Friday'. Brown retired after *The Plymouth Adventure*, perhaps feeling he no longer belonged at M-G-M. Most of the directors from the studio's Golden Age were dead or had moved elsewhere, and of the best only George Cukor remained. Fred

Zinneman, too, left the studio to make pictures like *High Noon* and *From Here to Eternity*.

Schary and his story executive, Kenneth MacKenna, struggled vainly to divine the changing public taste. Tracy was handed so many trivial and flat stories to consider that he took it on himself to do his own looking. He read voraciously. He thought he had found a good story at last, a novel called *The Mountain* by Henri Troyat, about an aging mountaineer who leads a rescue party to a crashed plane. He took it to M-G-M and asked them to buy it. When M-G-M decided it was too expensive to make as a movie, Tracy was angry. For the first time he began to think of working for other studios. Only once had he made a picture away from M-G-M — *Stanley and Livingstone* at 20th Century-Fox. He had had all the security he could want at the greatest film company in the world, but it was time for some changes.

In 1950 James Stewart had made a Western called *Winchester 73* at Universal-International, taking a large percentage of the profit in lieu of a salary. That picture and the others that followed made a multimillionaire of Stewart, and other stars began to enter into similar arrangements. It was a risk: one had to have faith in one's own drawing power and in the script, and not all deals worked out as well as Stewarts. But now the star began to wield some power in the economics of independent production. Many were going free-lance, for a single picture could bring as much as a studio contract guaranteed annually. Tracy was not a gambler, but some invitations from outside M-G-M offered a guaranteed salary in six figures as well as a small percentage of the profits, and Tracy was interested.

More than money, though, was the incentive of good pictures. In 1951 Paramount was making some brilliant films, both directed and produced by three men Tracy admired — George Stevens, Billy Wilder, and William Wyler. They made what they wanted to make and didn't have to depend on a story department. Wilder even wrote his own screenplays. He had done *Sunset Boulevard* and *Ace in the Hole*, and would make *Stalag 17*. Stevens had made *A Place in the Sun* and was preparing *Shane*. Wyler's recent credits had been *The Heiress*, *Detective Story*, and *Carrie*, and he would soon make *Roman Holiday*.

Spencer Tracy in fact tutored one of the actors in the film adaptation of Theodore Dreiser's *Sister Carrie*. It was perhaps the only time Laurence Olivier required an acting coach, for he had never played an American. Tracy helped him with his accent and his style, and Olivier turned in a fine performance. The experience helped convince Tracy that Paramount was where the real action was in the 1950's.

He went with Bert Allenberg of the William Morris Agency to see Eddie Mannix who had survived all the upheavals. They asked for a contract change that would enable Tracy to do occasional pictures outside the studio. Allenberg worked out a 'concession that would cost Tracy about a million dollars over a four-year-period. He would be required to make only one M-G-M picture annually, not two.

'The company doesn't make two good pictures a year anymore,' Tracy told Mannix. 'I only want to be in the good one.'

His total obligation was for four films, and he was allowed to consider projects at other studios.

Tracy never regretted the action that cut almost in half his annual salary guarantee. It was the beginning of the end for Tracy at Metro-Goldwyn-Mayer.

*   *   *

Louise Tracy liked to discuss their son's deafness, but Spencer hated to think about it, much less talk about it. John was in fact leading a normal life. He went to college, was popular with his classmates, was a good dancer, and dated the prettiest girls. And he was an honor student.

The Hollywood premiere of *Cass Timberlane* was a benefit for the John Tracy Clinic, and on that occasion Tracy rose from his seat to deliver a gruff but warm expression of thanks to those who had contributed to the clinic.

Afterward he was photographed with his twenty-three-year-old son.

Emily Torchia at M-G-M quickly wrote a story on the event which was read by a good many people. Miss Torchia remembers it as the only time Tracy was genuinely angry at her. It took a long time for him to forgive her.

After college, John worked as an artist with the Walt Disney studios. He was married and in 1952 Spencer became a grandfather. John's son, normal in all respects, was named Joseph Spencer Tracy.

*   *   *

Years Ago was a play by Ruth Gordon that ran on Broadway in 1946, the same year as her husband's *Born Yesterday*. It starred Fredric March and Florence Eldridge, playing the parents of a girl determined to be an actress.

Half a dozen years later the Kanins adapted *Years Ago* into a screenplay called *The Actress*, with March's stage role for Tracy.

Jean Simmons, the English girl whose new American career to this point had consisted of inferior material, played the ingenue heroine.

Cukor did for Jean Simmons what Vincente Minnelli had done for Elizabeth Taylor, but again the result was a strong Tracy picture. His cantankerous but gentle and very warm father was one of the finest performances of his career. Since Katharine Hepburn was traveling about the world as Bernard Shaw's *Millionairess*, Teresa Wright was cast to play the mother in *The Actress*. Making his first appearance on the screen was young Anthony Perkins, playing Miss Simmons' suitor.

In the first days of production of *The Actress* Jean Simmons was a little uneasy with Tracy. He was brusque, and by now had a reputation for being difficult. He didn't like dogs on the set, and Miss Simmons had a dog.

'Get this damn dog off the set,' Tracy commanded. It was a neatly trimmed and manicured poodle, a breed he particularly despised. The dog just shouldn't be there. He said that since Joan Crawford had left the studio the only dog welcome on a set had been Lassie. Miss Simmons woudn't be parted from the animal, but she worried about what Tracy would do next. He did nothing but mutter under his breath and scowl. One day the poodle was missing. After a frantic search he was located in Tracy's dressing room, dining in private with the actor. Thereafter Tracy regularly brought bones to the studio for the poodle, who never left his side during the balance of the shooting schedule.

As a film *The Actress* was a small gem. But by the fall of 1953 when it was released, a picture with its special and elusive quality no longer had an audience, so *The Actress* was a financial failure.

After finishing *The Actress* more than a year passed without Tracy setting foot on the studio grounds. He needed a rest and a chance to think about some of the possibilities with other producers. He still wanted to do *The Mountain*, but he was intrigued by Hemingway's *The Old Man and the Sea*, the novel that had come out in 1952 and won the Pulitzer Prize the next year.

The studios ignored the short novel, but Leland Hayward wanted to make a film of it. Hayward, a leading talent who was once in love with Katharine Hepburn, had become perhaps the most important Broadway producer of the post-war years, and he now wanted to try movies. He and Ernest Hemingway wanted to film *The Old Man and the Sea*, and they wanted Spencer Tracy as the fisherman. When Tracy agreed to it, the Hollywood trade papers conjectured that M-G-M might distribute the picture for Hayward, who, in any case, was determined to retain independent control. Hayward and Hemingway invited Tracy into their partnership, and he accepted. Once the agreement was made, there was no reason to hurry into production, and Tracy was free to relax and travel.

He became something of a Hollywood expatriate, returning to the film colony only rarely for a film commitment. Because he had stayed away from the more popular Hollywood haunts for years, few people realized that he was out of town so much. He had gotten over his dislike for air travel and he spent time in New York, in Mexico and the Bahamas, and in Europe.

He traveled to England, Scandinavia, and the middle European countries, usually with Katharine Hepburn. He was part of a new international set of screen personages, and he could run into Humphrey Bogart in Rome or Laurence Olivier in London, or see Clark Gable by accident in Amsterdam. For the most part he traveled off the beaten path, often icognito. Paris, with its little side streets and small cafés and art galleries, was his and Katharine Hepburn's favorite.

Sometimes he traveled with the Kanins, and Garson Kanin recalled an almost comical moment at the Louvre: Spencer Tracy staring transfixed at the Venus de Milo, and a hushed crowd of perhaps fifty people staring at Spencer Tracy.

In early 1953 American newspapers picked up a wire service story from Stockholm. Tracy had announced that upon completion of the three pictures remaining under his M-G-M contract he would retire from the screen. The truth was that he had been misquoted, he had only said he *might* retire. But Tracy was amused by the resulting clamor. He said if he had known people cared, he'd have talked of retiring sooner.

A rumor followed that Tracy was in poor health. He did have a history of aches and pains, and his stamina was not what it once was. When shooting he was permitted a full hour's rest after lunch, nor was he asked to work overtime. Nothing was wrong with him except that his heart wasn't very strong; he was fifty-three years old and slowing down. He was indeed hard-pressed to keep up with Katharine Hepburn.

In 1954 Tracy agreed to a colorful Western, *Broken Lance*, for 20th Century-Fox. Under the arrangement worked out by Bert Allenberg, Tracy collected payment of $165,000 plus a percentage of the profit the film eventually made.

Broken Lance was a remake of a film called *House of Strangers*, which the studio had made a few years before with Edward G. Robinson as the tyrannical patriarch. Philip Yordan's story was set in the old West, and 20th Century-Fox's new discovery, CinemaScope, made the most of the spectacular scenery. Tracy was rather pleased with *Broken Lance*. M-G-M was less happy, for the first picture Tracy had made outside the studio strongly resembled a Western spectacular they had written for him called *Jeremy Rodock*.

Clark Gable told Hedda Hopper that Tracy's acting was not as effortless as it looked; in *Broken Lance* Tracy had reached a point of not having to act at all.

'Spence *is* the part. The old rancher is mean, unreasonable, and vain. All he has to do is show up and be photographed.'

Gable had just finished *Betrayed* at M-G-M and did not renew his contract. He too wanted to work with the independents. While Tracy was at 20th Century-Fox, Gable was also there working out a deal for *Soldier of Fortune* and *The Tall Men*. Every studio was losing its old stars. Gary Cooper was gone from Paramount; Humphrey Bogart and Joan Crawford had left Warners after Bette Davis; Betty Grable and Tyrone Power were finishing up at Fox. Only Robert Taylor now had been at M-G-M longer than Tracy.

M-G-M shelved *Jeremy Rodock* temporarily and Tracy agreed to do *Bad Day at Black Rock*.

The shooting location for *Bad Day at Black Rock* was Lone Pine, a desolate tank town on the western rim of Death Valley, California, just east of Mount Whitney. It was early summer, 1954, and Lone Pine was sweltering. The camp built by M-G-M was less than luxurious. Tracy didn't complain throughout the shooting, and he developed a strong liking for John Sturges, who earlier had directed his lackluster *The People Against O'Hara*. Tracy said he had a feeling about *Bad Day at Black Rock* much like the one he'd had with *Fury*, and that knowing you were making a good picture made the physical punishment worthwhile.

Tracy spent most of his free time alone, reading; but occasionally he joined the rest of the cast in the evenings, and he even enjoyed a couple of weekend benders. The cast was mostly male, and included Robert Ryan, Walter Brennan, Russell Collins, Dean Jagger, John Ericson, Lee Marvin, and Ernest Borgnine.

In *Bad Day at Black Rock* Tracy comes to Black Rock to present a posthumous medal to the father of a Nisei soldier but finds that the Japanese farmer was long since murdered. The story was suspenseful and grim, a curious and unusual picture.

Dore Schary produced the film personally. Because *Bad Day at Black Rock* was such an offbeat project, several months passed before M-G-M knew it had a critical and commercial success. While awaiting its release, Tracy almost became involved in a movie with Humphrey Bogart. He nearly took on the part of the father in *The Desperate Hours*, in which Humphrey Bogart played the lead that Paul Newman had played on the stage. A dispute over who would get top billing ended the plan, however.

Fredric March accepted the role Tracy might have taken and March ultimately came out the best in the reviews, for Bogart was badly miscast and looked poor for perhaps the first time on film.

Tracy decided it was time to see some more of Europe, particularly Italy, where David Lean was filming *Summertime* in Venice, with Katharine Hepburn as the star. Tracy could not shake the *Hollywood Reporter's* 'rambler', whose latest rumor was that he was about to buy a villa in Florence and spend most of his time there. The trades also reported that Tracy had told friends he would not renew his M-G-M agreement. The studio, meanwhile, announced that Tracy would follow *Jeremy Rodock* with still another Western, *The Law and Jake Wade*, completing his commitment.

When Tracy returned to Hollywood, the M-G-M publicity department asked for interviews to help promote *Bad Day at Black Rock*. Tracy said he'd cooperate if they got him a date with Grace Kelly, whom he had never met. When he heard Grace Kelly would be thrilled to meet Spencer Tracy, he backed off. He had been joking but he had to go through with it. Tracy and Miss Kelly had their 'date', escorted by Emily Torchia and Morgan Hudgins, also of M-G-M.

It was an innocent enough evening, but in Hollywood anything can make for gossip. Soon Tracy was listed as the latest — along with Gary Cooper, Clark Gable, and Ray Milland — to fall for Grace Kelly. Other accounts reported that Miss Kelly was thoroughly charmed by Spencer Tracy. They did hit it off. Not long afterward M-G-M announced that Grace Kelly would play opposite Tracy in *Jeremy Rodock*, and *Variety* suggested that this was to soothe Tracy, who had not been happy about his assignment.

Grace Kelly had played Gary Cooper's bride in *High Noon* before joining M-G-M, and had since done well for herself and for the studio. But Alfred Hitchcock, who borrowed her for *Dial M for Murder* and *Rear Window* gave her better material than M-G-M did. When Paramount borrowed her for *The Country Girl*, for which she won an Oscar. Grace Kelly decided to take a stand. She flatly refused to be put in a couple of poor pictures, and one of them was *Jeremy Rodock*.

The part opposite Tracy was not particularly large or interesting, and the picture as a whole didn't please her. The studio quickly recovered and offered her a new version of Molnar's *The Swan* which Grace Kelly accepted; it was, ironically, the story of a girl who marries a prince.

Grace Kelly's walkout dampened Tracy's enthusiasm for the picture still further. He was anxious to fulfill his obligation to M-G-M so he could start thinking about *The Old Man and the Sea*, and perhaps do his own production of *The Mountain*. Meanwhile the studio gave *Jeremy Rodock* a new leading lady, Irene Papas, a young Greek actress, and a new name, *Tribute to a Bad Man*.

The new title notwithstanding, Tracy did not like anything about the package. The script was weak, and he hardly knew the director, Robert Wise. He didn't know Irene Papas at all, and was unhappy when he heard she stood five-ten in her bare feet, as tall as he.

Tribute to a Bad Man finally went into production in the first week of June in 1955. A large crew arrived at the ranch set constructed in the Rockies near Montrose, Colorado. Tracy checked in six days late, with no explanation to the distraught Robert Wise. But Tracy was in one of his moods. He shut himself off in the motel suite provided for him in town, and dug into the stack of books he had brought with him.

Tracy was pointedly rude to Wise. Before he had shot a single take, he disappeared from the set without warning. No one knew where he was. He was gone more than a week, and was noncommital on his return. One account was that he had been holed up nearby in the little town of Cimarron going over his part. Or he might have been in Beverly Hills consulting his agents. Still another report was that he was getting advice from Katharine Hepburn.

A showdown was approaching between Tracy and Wise. The director, who was riding high at M-G-M after the successful *Executive Suite*, felt he was being enormously patient with Tracy, who seemed to begrudge any time spent before the cameras.

Wise's patience reached a bitter end when Tracy announced he couldn't stand the altitude — the plateau on which the set was constructed was almost eight thousand feet up — and he wanted them to take the set apart and rebuild it lower in the mountains.

Tracy was used to getting his own way, and as a top star he did have some power over his directors. But this was impossible. A rumor spread that Tracy was trying to get Wise replaced by another director. Perhaps Tracy was just trying to work his way out of doing the picture; if this was the case, it was an expensive way to do it.

Howard Strickling, the studio publicity chief and a vice-president, arrived on the scene to negotiate a peace. Strickling was one of the few Tracy friends left with any power at

M-G-M, and he was diplomatic in taking care of the company's interest first. He talked with Tracy privately, talked with Wise, and then the three met together. The news dropped on June 25.

Tracy was fired.

Wise wanted Tracy out of the picture and Dore Schary, by telephone, backed Wise up. It was something Tracy obviously had not expected. James Merrick, the unit publicist, saw Tracy break down, sobbing; and despite the trouble Tracy had caused, Merrick felt sad, for Tracy was 'one of the guys who put M-G-M on the map'.

The news service releases said Tracy left the film because of an 'artistic disagreement' with Wise, but the New York *Enquirer* made it a headline story that Tracy was fired outright after an 'epic bender'. The facts were blurry in any case. The only sure thing was that Tracy was through at M-G-M, after twenty years, two months, and two weeks.

Tracy's role in *Tribute to a Bad Man* was taken by James Cagney. Irene Papas towered above him, but that was the least of the problems. When it was released, it quickly proved to be a flop.

*   *   *

Tracy had been humiliated, but he was free. After meetings with Schary and other members of the studio's executive board, his M-G-M contract was terminated. He checked out without the usual round of farewell handshakes.

Along Hollywood Boulevard people said that Tracy was washed up, sick, and would never make another picture. Ironically, at the same time, *Bad Day at Black Rock* was doing well all over the country, it was an entry in the 1955 Cannes Film Festival, Tracy was named Best Actor, and he was a sure bet to pick up another Oscar nomination. Smart alecks said the Oscar would be a sure thing if his 'retirement' became official.

But after the shock wore off, Tracy sat down with Bert Allenberg and formulated a package for *The Mountain*. He was not interested in becoming an independent producer, but he knew he had something to sell. Paramount bought the deal. Tracy named the director, Edward Dmytryk, who had made *Broken Lance*, and from the cast of that picture came Robert Wagner as Tracy's co-star. The principal female role was taken by Tracy's longtime friend, Claire Trevor.

Paramount shot *The Mountain* in color and in Vista-Vision, and did not scrimp on the budget. The Troyat novel centered around an ascent of Mont Blanc and the film crew went to the scene. Production was headquartered in Chamonix, on the French side of the mountain.

Tracy said that *The Mountain* proved the *ridiculous* lengths man would go for art's sake. The location shooting was a three-month ordeal with no respite, physically very exhausting. Tracy was bothered by the altitude and worn out by climbing the mountain for the camera, but he was earning $200,000 for his labor and felt he shouldn't complain; besides, the picture was his own idea.

There were many anxious moments, such as the time Tracy, Robert Wagner, and a few crewmen were stranded in a *téléférique* — the air-suspended cable car — when the mechanism stalled. For several hours the cab dangled by the mountainside twelve thousand feet up, and Tracy spent the time looking straight downward, transfixed.

In the summer of 1956, production of *The Old Man and the Sea* was ready to begin at last. Leland Hayward had arranged the financing and distributing with Warners and had hired Fred Zinnemann as director, a choice endorsed by Tracy with real enthusiasm. Tracy met with reporters before leaving for the filming in Cuba, and intimated he was about to start his final film. *The Mountain* and *The Old Man and the Sea* had each promised to be an extraordinary adventure in movie-making. They were the ones he had wanted to do, and no other projects had been planned afterward. At the time Tracy had no inkling that *The Mountain* would be a failure, notable only for its dullness, or that the production of *The Old Man and the Sea* would be fraught with difficulties.

The script was written by Hemingway and followed the

novella faithfully. Not only was Tracy in every scene, but most of the time he was to be alone at sea in his tiny boat, watching for the marlin, not speaking a word.

Tracy was content with Fred Zinnemann, but Leland Hayward was not.

The venture began as a spirited international curiosity. While Hayward, Zinnemann, and Tracy were getting ready in Cuba, Ernest Hemingway was fishing off the west coast of South America for a huge marlin to use in the picture. These beginnings received more press coverage than any other film the world had ever had.

Tracy was put in a rambling fourteen-room villa off the coast of Cuba, with a full crew of servants. He entertained some of the native Cubans to get the 'feel' of the fishing community, and he struck up a friendship with little Felipe Pazos, who played the boy in the film.

Only a little footage had been shot three months later when Zinnemann left the picture; some said he had disagreed with Hayward on a technical matter and had resigned, others that Hayward had fired Zinnemann because he wanted to change Hemingway's story. Tracy was not involved in the flareup.

'It's a matter between Hayward and Zinnemann,' Tracy said. 'I don't know what it's about. Maybe it's the schedule, and maybe Fred just couldn't stand my face.'

Tracy was instrumental in naming John Sturges, who had directed *Bad Day at Black Rock*, to succeed Zinnemann. Sturges ran into trouble with the weather and was unable to get much usable footage. Tropical storms and rain interfered with shooting on the water, and besides, Hemingway had not pulled in his big marlin.

Days and weeks passed in idleness. At last the production shut down until an artificial ocean, stocked with an artificial fish, could be built at the Warner Brothers studio in Burbank.

Tracy was understandably depressed when he returned to California. His mood wasn't helped by the failure of *The Mountain*. Katharine Hepburn was a life-saver. She got Tracy back to work on another picture.

Tracy and Miss Hepburn had not worked together in almost five years, although most of their free time had been spent together. In 1956 20th Century-Fox wanted Katharine Hepburn for *The Desk Set*, which had been a successful Broadway comedy with Shirley Booth. Miss Hepburn was doing well, having followed her moving performance in *Summertime* with *The Rainmaker*. She suggested Spencer Tracy for the leading male role in *The Desk Set*, and the studio was glad to meet Tracy's going price. A Hepburn-Tracy picture couldn't miss.

Walter Lang, who had directed Betty Grable and Dan Dailey Technicolor musicals, turned out a lesser picture than those Tracy and Hepburn had done with the Kanins and Cukor, although it was a pleasant enough movie, with moments of high comedy.

The Desk Set was only a moderate box-office success, but it restored Tracy to an even keel, so that he was once again ready to begin work on *The Old Man and the Sea*.

Upon returning to Hollywood, Tracy learned from friends at Romanoff's the well-kept secret that Humphrey Bogart was sick, and probably had cancer. During Bogart's last months Tracy and Miss Hepburn visited him regularly at the Holmby Hills house where he and Lauren Bacall had spent most of their eleven years of marriage.

Tracy and Miss Hepburn had their last visit with a brave, joking Bogart on a Saturday night in January of 1957. When Bogart became visibly tired, they got up to leave. Miss Hepburn kissed Bogart, and when Tracy took his hand Bogart said, 'Good-bye, Spence.' Miss Hepburn told Joe Hyams, Bogart's biographer, that he had always said 'Good night' before, and that as they were leaving the house Tracy looked at her and said, 'Bogie's going to die.'

Bogart lapsed into a coma the next day and died the following Monday morning.

*   *   *

Warner Brothers had made an ocean out of 750,000 gallons of water. The huge mechanical fish was made out of rubber.

Tracy came back to *The Old Man and the Sea* to find more delays and technical complications, and the unpleasantness of his own personal rift with Ernest Hemingway.

'This picture is becoming my life's work,' Tracy said in the fall of 1957. 'By now there isn't a chance to make back all the money we will spend, so we're just concentrating on making it worthwhile.

The Old Man and the Sea finally cost almost six million dollars, nearly two-thirds of it spent in Cuba although the location footage amounted to only twenty per cent of the final print. Tracy's remark to Joe Hyams that he would gladly sell his interest in the project for fifteen cents was widely quoted.

'If I'd known what trouble it was going to be, I'd never have agreed to it. This is for the birds.' Tracy was also unhappy because the long schedule prevented him from doing another movie that interested him, John O'Hara's *Ten North Frederick*. After the Hemingway project finally wound up, he went to work in a screen adaptation of another runaway best-seller, Edwin O'Connor's *The Last Hurrah*. Both John Ford, the director, and O'Connor insisted that only Tracy would do.

The atmosphere on the set of *The Last Hurrah* at the Columbia studio was nostalgic. Production began early in 1958. It was the story of a Boston-Irish politician named Frank Skeffington, a dead ringer for Boston's notorious mayor, James M. Curley. (Curley later sued unsuccessfully on the grounds of invasion of privacy.) The story deals with Skeffington's final bid to succeed himself, an effort that ends in defeat and death. Most of Tracy's Irish friends were in the cast — Pat O'Brien, James Gleason, Frank McHugh, Ed Brophy, and Wallace Ford, and the old-timer Donald Crisp, who had acted in *The Birth of a Nation*.

Tracy was in the midst of his Wednesday night circle once again, and making a good film at the same time. The picture was both comical and poignant, and Tracy thought it a significant film for him to make.

'I've joked about retiring but this could be the picture. I'm superstitious — you know that's part of being Irish — and I'm back with John Ford again for the first time since I started out with him twenty-eight years ago. I feel this is the proper place for me to end. Even the title is prophetic.'

Columbia worked fast on editing *The Last Hurrah*, and it was ready for release at the same time as *The Old Man and the Sea*, in the fall of 1958.

The Last Hurrah received good reviews. The reaction to *The Old Man and the Sea* was as uneven as its production history. Some complained that it looked like a low-budget project rather than a multimillion-dollar undertaking. *Time*, in the same week it praised Tracy for *The Last Hurrah*, found his acting and everything else about *The Old Man and the Sea* lacking — it was a literary property about as suitable for the movie medium as *The Love Song of J. Alfred Prufrock*. Most reviewers were disappointed and agreed the film was too literary, but almost all respected Tracy's performance as the old man. A few critics called the film a classic. Paul V. Beckley in the New York *Herald-Tribune* started his review by calling it 'one of the great films of our generation'. Luckily Mr. Beckley was able to recognize a surprising number of pictures as among our generation's great films; he gave film companys' advertising staffs their best quotes during his brief tenure as the *Herald-Tribune* critic.

Early in 1959 many people thought that Spencer Tracy would win a 1958 Academy Award, and thus become the first person to be named best actor three times. And it didn't matter much which role he won it for. It would probably be *The Last Hurrah*, which had been cited by the National Board of Review for Tracy's acting and John Ford's directing. Hemingway didn't help by remarking that in *The Old Man and the Sea*, Tracy's performance looked like the work of 'a rich, fat actor'. The picture was already obviously a financial disaster.

The Academy ignored *The Last Hurrah*, however, and Tracy was nominated for his role as the fisherman. He still was the favorite to win, but lost ground when he made some salty remarks about the Academy and the awards ceremony that got into the papers. And David Niven won, for *Separate Tables*.

As usual, Tracy did not attend the ceremony, and was criticized for it. By now he didn't care. Watching the show on television he stared in amazement when the ceremony ended early and no one knew what to do with the remaining twenty minutes of air time.

'My God, what have we come to?' Tracy said, as Jerry Lewis, the master of ceremonies, herded a collection of stars on stage, most of whom had just lost out on awards, for a group-sing.

When asked why he had voted for David Niven instead of for himself, Tracy grinned. 'It's my integrity. There are six, maybe seven of us out here who still have it. It doesn't count much.'

He was tired after ten years as Hollywood's film father, working around the world beyond his physical capacity. His hair was now snowy white. But he grew restless, and he told Abe Lastfogel of the William Morris office to be on the lookout just in case an interesting part came up.

CHAPTER EIGHT

THE GRAND OLD MAN: 1960–1966

THE love story of Spencer Tracy and Katharine Hepburn was Hollywood's big secret. Although Hollywood fed on scandal, for almost twenty years nothing was said about the romance. In a town where nothing was sacred, this story seemed to be in a special category.

Even their close friends did not try to discuss the situation with either one of them, and certainly not with the press. Their relationship was simply accepted. George Cukor expressed the prevailing attitude: 'These are two great stars, they are highly respected, they are very good friends.'

Gossip columnists stopped dropping hints about an affair early in their relationship. Hepburn-Tracy stories did not appear in the fan magazines. Even when *Confidential* magazine and others of its type dredged up near-libelous material about many figures in the mid-1950's, their private life remained uninvaded.

Metro-Goldwyn-Mayer's policy was to ignore the romance. Its publicity releases stated that Tracy was married and living at home. The fact that he was living apart from his family was never announced by the press.

M-G-M executives tolerated but hardly encouraged the Tracy-Hepburn relationship. Not once did studio staff writers write a screenplay for the star team, despite their seven films together at M-G-M, and they never 'assigned' the two to the same picture. Miss Hepburn requested Tracy as her co-star in *Without Love*, he asked for her in *The Sea of Grass*. The stories written specifically for them were always the work of the Kanins, who were not on the regular studio payroll.

What Hollywood thought really made no difference. They were not 'Hollywood people'. Tracy, of course, had been more interested in living it up in the years before they met, but Miss Hepburn never tried to be a part of the Hollywood scene. Their life together was their own, whether they were walking in the Hollywood hills, relaxing in New England, or touring Europe.

As years passed and more people became aware of their deep feeling for each other, there was some speculation as to why they never married. People assumed that Tracy had asked for a divorce and had been refused; but Spencer, not Louise, was the Roman Catholic.

Perhaps Katharine Hepburn liked it the way it was. She had dominated her husband during her brief marriage when she was very young. Her well-publicized romances in the 1930's involved strong-minded men, but the relationships would fall apart when marriage seemed to be the next step.

Miss Hepburn said, 'I don't believe in marriage. It isn't a natural institution — if it were, why sign a contract for it? One of the few happy marriages, perhaps the only truly happy marriage I've known, was my parents'. They never argued about "things", for my mother never wanted "things" the way most women do. They only argued about ideas.'

Spencer Tracy was a diamond in the rough, a natural talent. These qualities were most important to her. When Katharine Hepburn described the sort of relationship she and Spencer Tracy often acted out on the screen, she might have been talking about their private relationship as well.

'The woman (in the films) is always pretty sharp. She needles the man, a little like a mosquito. Then he slowly puts out his big paw and slaps the lady down, and the American public likes to see that. In the end he's always the boss of the situation, but he's challenged by her. That — in simple terms — is what we do.'

Tracy was steady and calm, whereas Miss Hepburn would take off on giddy intellectual flights or be seized by sudden enthusiasms. They were very different, but complementary: together savoring nature, enjoying the arts and each other's company.

In the New York *Post*, Helen Dudar described Katharine Hepburn as tough, brave, and blunt, but also as tender and fragile as an apple blossom; and she remembered Miss Hepburn saying that Tracy was probably the only man who was man enough to counteract her individualistic femininity. A friend quoted Miss Hepburn: 'To most men I'm a nuisance because I'm so busy I get to be a pest, but Spencer is so masculine that once in a while he rather smashes me down, and there's something nice about me when I'm smashed down.'

Acting was their common ground. Each was captivated by the other's ability, and their happiest times were spent working together. Garson Kanin said, 'Here were two who brought out the best in everyone and in each other, personally and professionally.'

Another Tracy friend, also a writer, said in 1960, 'What would have happened to Spence if Kate hadn't is a dark thought. He was thrashing about, unhappy, and she put his talent in focus so he could understand it. He's a queer bird with his own way of doing things, and it took a brilliant girl just to begin to see inside him.'

Miss Hepburn's presence had a steadying effect on him. He left his shell when she was around and took obvious enjoyment in listening to her. Miss Hepburn did most of the talking because, as she explained, Tracy was not interested in intellectual debates.

'Spencer sees the ludicrous side of everything,' she said. 'That's why the Irish have the miseries. They see themselves as clowns falling through life. He worships entertainers, vaudevillians, the ones who tell the great wonderful stories. If you get him going he can be pretty funny himself.'

Their friends knew little or nothing of the time they spent alone together. The two avoided people and had no need of confidants. In an article on Tracy, J. P. McEvoy pointed out the actor's ease around familiar faces but his discomfort with strangers, particularly crowds of them. Much later Joe Hyams characterized Miss Hepburn as a lady of great authority but one who was at the same time painfully shy, and unhappy about being photographed or even watched by strangers.

Katharine Hepburn originally wanted to act opposite Tracy because 'he's the most economical actor I know and I'm the most uneconomical; I give my all, and he conserves.' According to Miss Hepburn, 'When Spencer first laid eyes on me, he said to Joe Mankiewicz, "Not me, boy. I don't want to get mixed up with anything like that!" You see, Spencer doesn't approve of women wearing trousers.'

But for a quarter of a century they were, as Helen Dudar observed, 'a quiet durable, faithful, oddly matched couple everyone in Hollywood knew about, and — uniquely — no one ever gossiped about.'

*   *   *

Humphrey Bogart's death marked the beginning of the end of an era. By 1960, Ronald Colman, Tyrone Power, Paul Douglas, Errol Flynn, and Mario Lanza were all dead. Many thought that Tracy would be next. People who didn't like him said he had withdrawn into himself because he was afraid of dying. Although he would outlive Clark Gable and Gary Cooper by many years, he had begun his long and losing struggle with poor health.

Tracy had been renting a small guest cottage on George Cukor's estate for several years. Sometimes close friends visited him, but he seldom went out. His 'retirement' was generally accepted, and it was thought that he would take on another picture only as a favor to some director he cared about.

Surprise and skepticism followed the news that Tracy would star in a Stanley Kramer picture. Tracy was an old-fashioned actor, from the days when movies told a story; Kramer was the new wave and his pictures had a message.

The picture was *Inherit the Wind*, a drama based on the Scopes trial. Tracy played the part of the lawyer, modeled after Clarence Darrow, that Paul Muni had played on the stage, and Fredric March, with whom Tracy had never acted, played the character based on William Jennings Bryan. It was an important picture worthy of its fine cast.

Stanley Kramer was in his middle forties and had been making films for two decades. He had already worked with Fredric March, and also with Grant, Bogart, and Cooper — as well as with the younger actors with their different styles, such as Brando and Sinatra.

His first anxious moments with Tracy were recalled by Kramer in a good memoir of Tracy that appeared in *Life*. The shooting of *Inherit the Wind* had begun, and Tracy had delivered a speech that had not been intelligible. When Tracy was asked to do it over, he gave Kramer a dead-eyed stare for a full minute, and then carefully articulated in the slowest possible monotone, 'Mr. Kramer, it has taken me thirty years to learn how to speak lines. If you or a theater arts major from U.C.L.A. wants to do this speech, I am quite willing to step aside.'

Kramer said, 'Then he picked me up, shook me a little, dusted me off and said, "All right, we ought to try it again."' Kramer contended that Tracy was showing who was boss — he always did what was requested of him after that.

To newsmen, *Inherit the Wind*, became their favorite haunt, although the set was officially closed. Tracy and March had a grand time trying to outdo one another, both for the cameras and for the reporters and studio workers who came to see them in action, Gene Kelly, playing a character based on H. L. Mencken, said, 'I finally stepped out of my class. I just can't keep up with this pair.'

In a courtroom scene, during a long speech by Tracy, March vigorously wagged a fan; when March was speaking, Tracy sat and listened thoughtfully . . . and picked his nose. Stanley Kramer recalls that every take of this friendly battle brought down the house.

March mentioned that he was impressed by Tracy's ability to memorize long speeches. Katharine Hepburn, who was knitting in her usual seat, watching the shooting, said, 'It's his concentration — his theatrical background, you know.'

Fredric March, who unlike Tracy, had spent long periods of his career on the stage, bowed to Miss Hepburn and said, 'Thank you, Mrs. Shakespeare!'

In the film March's wife was portrayed by Florence Eldridge, who is also married to him in real life. They planned to travel around the world when the shooting was over. March showed Tracy the route, which included Far Eastern ports that Tracy had not visited. Had it not been for another script that interested him, Tracy and Katharine Hepburn might have made the trip, too.

During the 1960's Tracy no longer avoided columnists, although he was still outwardly cantankerous toward them. Now he enjoyed getting the better of them.

'What keeps us up? What else but talent?' Tracy put himself with Gable, Stewart, and Cooper in an exchange with reporters. 'Bogie said the difference between the seventeen-year ball player and the three-year one is simply the ability to manage talent.'

The writers liked to get Tracy going about movie actors in the Rock Hudson era. 'Pretty-faced no-talents are always around in this business,' he said. 'They don't last, and they're not missed, for a new crop comes in and it's the same asparagus.'

Unexpectedly, Tracy gave his new director good publicity. 'Stanley is a lot like Irving Thalberg, very smart and really in love with the movie business, only warmer than Thalberg and not so much driven by money. If a Kramer picture makes a good profit, that's fine, but he is mostly trying to make good pictures. Stanley is as good a director as I've worked with . . . and I've had some of the best.'

Tracy, in fact, accepted an invitation to star in the next Kramer film. But before he could do *Judgment at Nuremberg* there was *The Devil at Four O'Clock*, the project that kept Tracy from following Fredric March around the world. Reporters had a field day watching Tracy with Frank

Sinatra, his co-star in *The Devil at Four O'Clock*. Sinatra, who called Tracy the 'Gray Fox', also was used to first billing and emphasized that he gave away the top spot only to Tracy.

The two men worked very differently, and everyone expected fireworks. Tracy was on the set early, Sinatra arrived when he chose, and seldom before lunch. Sinatra was a spontaneous worker, Tracy was tightly disciplined. Luckily their strong personal affection made for peace. Tracy called it 'a Sinatra picture'. He would say, 'Sinatra is the star!' sarcastically, but underneath he was pleased.

Reflecting on an actor's autonomy in the days of 'independent' productions, Tracy said, 'Nobody at Metro ever had the financial power Frank Sinatra has today.' He said his own days as a box-office favorite were over. He shrugged and looked quizzically from under his brows, as if hoping for a contradiction.

'The truth is I'm old, so old that everything has changed. Not just the movie business but the whole country.'

Part of *The Devil at Four O'Clock* was filmed on location in Hawaii, and Katharine Hepburn accompanied Tracy. Looking at some stills with Tracy and director Mervyn LeRoy, Miss Hepburn said, 'Spence, these are wonderful character studies!' Tracy, without looking at the prints, said, 'Kate, those aren't character studies, they're just pictures of an old man.'

Inherit the Wind was a success, but *The Devil at Four O'Clock* was a dud, which surprised Tracy. He had stopped seeing his own pictures, as he had aged so much it was painful. Perhaps he was thinking of *The Mountain* when he said, 'Actors should not choose their own pictures. I tried to get out of doing some films that turned out great, and a few I thought I liked went sour. Maybe I've earned the right to be wrong.'

He also probably felt he had earned the right to speak his mind about various aspects of the movie business. He was tart enough about the Academy Awards. Tracy gave Joe Hyams enough salty opinions about the Oscars to be a thorn in the flesh of the proponents of the Academy of Motion Picture Arts and Sciences. Year after year he refused to attend the ceremony, and while his absence had not made much difference during the 1940's, it became another matter when the show was televised, beginning in the mid-1950's, and Tracy was often one of the nominees. The movie industry liked to show off its big guns for the home audience, but Tracy refused the invitation regularly, and usually had a few choice words.

'I can't get time off during the day to go to a ball game, so why should I give my own time in the evening to go to the Academy Awards?'

He was nominated again for 1960's *Inherit the Wind*, although Burt Lancaster won, for *Elmer Gantry*.

'We try to be better than television and can't even give it a good show,' Tracy said, as he watched the Awards once on television.

'In the old days you paid four dollars to see Laurette Taylor and it was something special. Now stars are refereeing football games, and opening drugstores, and they don't mean a damn thing to the public. It's a shame.'

Tracy acknowledged the thrill of winning his Oscars. 'Sure I was happy. It meant I'd made the grade. If you work it right, you keep the position you've earned. I don't need to win another one. I need another award like I need ten pounds.'

Tracy said the nominations were an honor, but he thought the honor should end there. 'How can you compare performances — how can you say Judy Holliday in a comedy is better than Gloria Swanson in a dramatic part?'

* * *

He called *Judgment at Nuremberg* 'the best script I've read in years' and admired Stanley Kramer for having the guts to make it. He was disappointed when Laurence Olivier dropped out of the film; he would have played the most prominent German jurist being tried for war crimes at Nuremberg. Olivier was replaced by Burt Lancaster, who, although rated as a major star, was outclassed. The remarkable *Nuremberg* cast included Marlene Dietrich, Maximilian Schell, Richard Widmark, and in cameo roles, Judy Garland and Montgomery Clift.

After completing *Judgment at Nuremberg*, Tracy told a small gathering that he had just made the finest picture of his career, and he was going to retire. Later he amended this — he would make no more pictures 'except the good ones that Stanley does'.

He had had his doubts about *Judgment at Nuremberg*, however. At New York's Idlewild Airport, shortly before takeoff for shooting on location in Berlin, Tracy abruptly changed his mind and got off the plane. United Artists officials were frantic, then watched at a distance as Katharine Hepburn talked to Tracy for several minutes, and planted a little kiss on his cheek. Tracy turned and walked back to board the plane. A United Artists man said Tracy was now so difficult that only Miss Hepburn could handle him.

Tracy, though, could help others. Stanley Kramer recalled the way he handled the emotionally unstrung Montgomery Clift during the filming of Clift's single, long sequence. Clift was coming apart, unable to remember his lines, and Tracy 'grabbed Monty's shoulders and told him he was the greatest young actor of his generation, and to look into his eyes and play to him, and to hell with the lines.' Clift received his fourth and last Academy nomination for *Judgment at Nuremberg*.

Tracy attended the world premiere in Berlin in December of 1961, with Judy Garland and Maximilian Schell. It was his final ceremonial film function. Earphones were attached to each seat in the theater, so one could hear the dialogue in any of several languages.

Midway through the more than three hours of the film, an upset stomach forced Tracy to leave the theater. When he returned to the United States a week later he was pale and drawn.

The Berlin reviews had been mixed; one critic called it 'a

fair and human statement', while another said it was 'much too easy on the Nazis'. But Berlin audiences had broken into spontaneous applause when Tracy, as the American judge, told defense counsel Schell that logic did not always make deeds right. In America the reviewers were almost unanimously favorable, the only harsh ones being those who had already singled out Stanley Kramer as a whipping boy.

Tracy, Schell, Clift, and Judy Garland all were nominated for Oscars. Again watching the ceremony on television, Tracy sank farther into his chair when Schell, making his acceptance speech said, '... but most of all I wish to thank that grand old man ...'

* * *

In January of 1962, while *Judgment at Nuremberg* was playing first-run engagements around the world, a story by Bill Davidson about Tracy broke in an issue of *Look* magazine. For the first time the people of America were being told that Tracy used to drink too much, that he had a mean streak, that he had not been living with his wife for years, and that Katharine Hepburn was something more than a frequent co-star of Tracy's.

The film colony generally, and especially those people close to Tracy, felt betrayed. Bill Davidson was quickly persona non grata. In fairness to Davidson, he tried to deal objectively with the facts, but the problem lay in his having dealt with them at all. Davidson probably worked hard on the story and may have been proud of his accomplishment, and bewildered by the response to it. Joe Hyams, for once, conjectured that the Tracy article may have been a factor in steering Davidson away from writing about Hollywood.

According to Davidson, Tracy's life was separated into five areas: his family, his involvement with Miss Hepburn and her circle of friends, his Irish drinking friends, his career as an actor, and his frequent solitude. Davidson, who had pieced the story from interviews with many Tracy associates, pictures Tracy as a man tormented by the five different lives, by the conflicting demands they made on him.

The days of the Irish clique were over, his career also seemed to be ending, but there was considerable speculation about Tracy's family life. According to Davison's article, Tracy telephoned his wife almost every day and visited her often; he was proud of his son's skill as a cartoonist and of Susie's talent for music. Perhaps inadvertently Davidson implied that Tracy's separation from his family was mostly his own fault. (Not mentioned in the *Look* article was the fact that Tracy's last known drinking spree was touched off by John Tracy's divorce and the full coverage given to it by newspapers.)

Louise Tracy's attitude toward him was a mystery. Romano Tozzi, in a *Films in Review* career story on Tracy, said Louise was sympathetic to Tracy's relationship with Miss Hepburn, and quoted her statement that Spencer needed to lead his own life. She was certainly charting her own course. Her work with the clinic absorbed all her time. The New York *Journal-American* called her 'one of the great women of the American progress, in the humanitarian tradition of Clara Barton and Jane Adams'. That was in 1956 when she won the Save the Children Foundation award. She already had four honorary degrees.

Aside from family matters and the revelation that Tracy had traveled all over with Katharine Hepburn, an aspect of the *Look* piece that fascinated the reading public was a painfully detailed account of the final blowup with M-G-M. Davidson's principle source of information was Jim Merrick, the studio publicist who was temporarily embarrassed by the article. The fact that almost six years after it happened the story was full of surprises even for Hollywood indicated how effectively M-G-M had smoothed over the incident at the time.

In 1962 Tracy returned to M-G-M, not to appear in a film but to provide the soundtrack narration for the company's Cinerama super-western, *How the West Was Won*. His commentary and three unrelated stories provided the excuse for using just about every star at M-G-M in a Western spectacular. It was a small challenge for Tracy, but it did heal some old wounds. Few at the studio had survived all the changes. Mannix, Strickling, and a few others remained on the scene, but television had claimed many of the old-timers. Schary stayed at M-G-M for only two years after Tracy left.

When Tracy did act again it was for Kramer. He accepted *It's a Mad, Mad, Mad, Mad World* before reading the script, because it was Kramer's and because most of the great American comedians were in it — Jonathan Winters, Phil Silvers, Milton Berle, Jimmy Durante, and Sid Caesar were only a few.

Tracy was weak, pale and old-looking while making *It's a Mad, Mad, Mad, Mad World*, and he couldn't cope easily with the heat of the desert shooting location, Kramer made few physical demands on Tracy and limited his working day to six hours.

But he had a grand time making the picture because he loved the other actors and they loved him. Tracy didn't allow himself to drink with them, though he would have a glass of milk with a single ice cube. (His only alcoholic vice now was a single glass of beer every night. Many assumed he was drinking a good deal, because he never made a point of being on the wagon. Hollywood writer-bookseller Gene Ringgold, for instance, said shortly after Tracy's death, 'He was okay on the screen, but just another Irish lush offscreen.' In point of fact, Tracy hadn't been drinking for years.)

The movie project was an attempt to make the biggest and greatest comedy on the screen. It was certainly less than that, but it returned a good profit on an investment of almost seven million dollars. Tracy thought it was 'a good one to go out with', but no one believed him anymore.

*   *   *

In the later days of his movie career Tracy was known as 'The Pope' to some other actors and to writers who covered actors. Tracy attributed the title, which he secretly enjoyed, to David Niven. His whims were law. Other actors knew not to munch sandwiches or play cards on the sidelines while a scene was being shot. Tracy could be relentlessly hard on actors he thought were lazy or not particularly dedicated. Otherwise he got along well with most of his fellows, and to dedicated young actors — Jeffrey Hunter, John Ericson, Bernie Hamilton — he would be most helpful, even paternal.

He was crusty about giving interviews, but it was getting easier for a reporter to see him. He used to say he didn't want to talk about acting or about the old days, but that was in truth exactly what he wanted to talk about.

Tracy's favorite newsman was Joe Hyams, the New York *Herald-Tribune* Hollywood columnist he had 'inherited' from Humphrey Bogart. Tracy liked Hyams because he didn't ask silly questions. Hyams said that with Tracy, questions were not necessary. 'You didn't have to ask him for a story. He'd give you one.'

Tracy, for all his gruffness, usually liked talking about his profession.

'What is a star? Who the hell knows? I know a lot of good actors who are not stars, and maybe some stars who are not good actors. Gable was a star, all right, and he put it on the line that he was *not* an actor . . . but he made an impression with what he *did*.'

He talked about actors' salaries as if trying to get rid of his guilt.

'Yes, a star makes an awful lot of money, but usually he earns every cent of it in the loss of many joys most people take as a matter of course. Really, though, money is a fallacy. An actor's real treasure is his competence. I've known an actor to complain about incidentals when he was making maybe a hundred thousand a picture, or about ninety-nine thousand more than he needed. Many actors, when they get into the money, seem to forget that a responsibility goes with it. I don't mean a responsibility to the publicity department, but to the audience.'

When I asked if actors were 'just like other people', Tracy said, 'Is anybody? Can any member of any profession be just like everybody else? Of course not. There's so much ham in most actors, they exaggerate their failings because they're so damned spectacular about everything they do.'

Even now that he was no longer with M-G-M, Tracy would not knock the studio system that had made him rich and famous.

'I miss the friends I made over the years at Metro, and I only did a couple of pictures there I didn't like. But I got the shivers last time I visited the place. The people I knew are mostly gone, a lot of them dead.

'The way the studios operated, though, was good for a young actor. Hell, you were always working, and that's the way to master a profession. Actors today, they play one part in a television series for years. How can they grow? They can't. That's why actors today are not as good as they were. Acting in stock was no big deal, but it trained people for the acting profession, and now that's all gone.'

Tracy was sad and sardonic when he said that now most of his public appearances were made at funerals. He and James Stewart and Robert Taylor were shown in a famous photograph taken at the Clark Gable funeral and published in *Life*. The end of the era was mirrored in their tired faces.

Later Tracy said, 'I just can't watch the pictures that Bogie and Gable and Coop made anymore. It takes too much out of me, and there's not much left to take out.'

He did not talk about the stars who had died, nor could he be made to talk about himself, his personal life. He would always come back to talking about acting.

'George M. Cohan told me to read the heart into the play, and I try to do that. But I don't try to invent a personality because you *can't* do that. Personality is what you *are*. Personality, I suppose, is "star quality" if anything is. I have not seen any good actor give a performance in which part of the personality didn't emerge. Olivier is the best, and damned versatile ... but when I see him I know it's Olivier. Personality. It's all an actor has to give ... that, and his instinct.'

Tracy fielded questions about his 'retirement' with relish.

'I always announce my retirement until the next picture comes. As Paul Muni said, acting isn't a thing you get too old to do. You know, Eddie Leonard made 471 curtain speeches announcing he had retired, and they say Sarah Bernhardt stopped acting 178 times.'

Not every reporter could avoid asking the 'ridiculous questions' that wore out Tracy's patience. He was quick to dispose of them.

Q. Mr. Tracy, where have you found your greatest fulfillment as an actor,
A. In the cashier's office.
Q. What do you believe is the most useless pastime in Hollywood?
A. Staying awake.
Q. What do you look for when you read a script for the first time?
A. Days off.
Q. If asked to advise young actors, what principal advice would you give?
A. Learn your lines.
Q. What do you find attractive in a woman?
A. I'll give you thirty seconds to think of a better question.

*   *   *

Katharine Hepburn curtailed her own stage and screen activities in the 1960's to look after Tracy in his days of failing health. Between *Suddenly, Last Summer* in 1959 and *Guess Who's Coming to Dinner* eight years later, she made only one screen appearance, a brilliant study of the tortured mother in the Eugene O'Neill *Long Day's Journey into Night*, in 1962.

On July 21, 1963, Tracy drove his Thunderbird to Miss Hepburn's rented beach house at Malibu. They were going on a Sunday picnic. Shortly after his arrival he found it difficult to breathe. Miss Hepburn telephoned the Zuma Beach fire department, and a rescue unit arrived to give

Tracy oxygen. While waiting for the ambulance, Miss Hepburn telephoned Tracy's wife and brother.

During the twenty-five-mile ride to St. Vincent's Hospital, Tracy said, 'Kate, isn't this a hell of a way to go on a picnic?' Miss Hepburn smiled, patted him on the forehead, and said, 'Next week.'

The first radio flash reported a heart attack but Karl Lewis, Tracy's physician, diagnosed it as pulmonary edema. After the first hours, Tracy's condition was listed as 'good', but he stayed in the hospital two weeks.

Miss Hepburn rented a hilltop house in Beverly Hills near Tracy's vine-covered cottage on the Cukor grounds. They spent almost every day together, and if they had to be apart, they talked on the telephone. If they did not dine together, Miss Hepburn sent a home-cooked dinner in a basket from her house to his.

Tracy did not have strength enough for a new film role, but he thought he could do a 'cameo' part in *Cheyenne Autumn*, the film projected as John Ford's last Western. In December of 1963, however, it was announced that Tracy was physically unable to report, and was withdrawing from the assignment.

Almost a year later he felt strong enough to get back. He had found a script he really liked, *The Cincinnati Kid*, about an old poker player taking on a young challenger. Announcement that Tracy would return to M-G-M to star in the film was front-page news all over the country, and Steve McQueen's assignment as his co-star was also news. Tracy thought McQueen one of the most interesting new stars.

Jubilant throughout the preparations for *The Cincinnati Kid*, Tracy said, 'Now I'm playing 'em one at a time.' He would do more pictures if he could, but he wasn't going to plan too far ahead. But when the time came to start production, Tracy's doctors advised him against it. He was not well enough to go through with it. Edward G. Robinson (his *Cheyenne Autumn* replacement) therefore picked up another good part. 'I was ready for the fight,' Tracy said, 'But I couldn't make the weight.'

When Stanley Kramer purchased the movie rights to Katherine Anne Porter's best-selling *Ship of Fools*, speculation was high that Tracy would take the role of the ship's doctor, but after *The Cincinnati Kid*, few people thought that Tracy would ever appear in another film. He was a regular guest on the set of *Ship of Fools*, jokingly calling himself a 'special adviser to Mr. Kramer' and telling people he was taking his apprenticeship as a director. He was amused when the Louella Parsons column swallowed it whole and announced that Spencer Tracy was going to become a movie director.

'I couldn't be a director because I couldn't put up with the actors,' he explained. 'I don't have the patience. Why, I'd probably kill the actors.' Looking at *Ship of Fools'* Elizabeth Ashley, he added. 'Not to mention some of the beautiful actresses.'

Vivien Leigh was one of the *Ship of Fools* stars and Tracy renewed a longstanding friendship. He also befriended Oskar Wener, who played the doctor.

Shortly afterward, in September of 1965 Tracy entered Good Samaritan Hospital for a prostatectomy. Complications developed after the operation, and for several days he was in critical condition. He seemed to be recovering, but on September 17, he had a relapse and the hospital staff alerted a priest to be on call. Tracy recovered, but he spent weeks in the hospital. During the crisis Louise Tracy and Katharine Hepburn kept a bedside vigil by turns.

When he left the hospital, Tracy went into total seclusion. He had few visitors — his brother regularly, Stanley Kramer often — and received few telephone calls (his telephone number was always kept secret). George Cukor had a Hungarian couple who worked for him look after Tracy's needs. Cukor was noncommital about his famous tenant, saying only, 'He's good with the rent.'

Tracy's name dropped out of the papers because there was little to report. He narrated a thirty-minute color film short. *The Ripon College Story*. He had never done any work for television, but he became interested in a series of six historical specials projected by producer David Wolper called *The Red, White and Blue*, and agreed to be the host. The ABC network wanted Tracy but not the show, and the deal fell through.

Tracy could be seen briefly now and then, perhaps driving to Louise's hilltop house near Pickfair for a visit. He was a frail man, who looked older than his years. He took long, slow-paced walks in the hills, sometimes alone, often with Katharine Hepburn. They flew kites together on warm, windy days.

Despite his separation from Hollywood, Tracy was alert, often inexplicably so, to everything that was going on in the film colony. George Cukor said, 'Spencer had an insatiable curiosity, and remarkable antennae for gathering news. He loved tidbits and gossip of all kinds.'

Although he seldom went out, Tracy didn't want to be forgotten. George Cukor said he always 'wanted to be asked'. At the time of the Mia Farrow-Frank Sinatra wedding reception, Tracy hadn't been out of his place for weeks.

'He had no thought of going,' Cukor said, 'but was appreciative of the invitation. Then he thought he might go, and he vacillated back and forth. Finally he did attend the reception, and stayed only a little while, but of course he was the hit of the affair. He always enjoyed himself once he arrived somewhere . . . but he just hated to *go*.'

CHAPTER NINE

THE LEGEND: 1967

STANLEY KRAMER had Spencer Tracy, Katharine Hepburn, and Sidney Poitier signed, sealed, and delivered to *Guess Who's Coming to Dinner* before anybody had seen the script. They liked the idea of a social comedy about a forthright, liberal couple whose daughter brings home a Negro fiancé. Kramer had played Hollywood's favorite game, telling Poitier that he had Tracy and Hepburn before, in fact, he did, and at the same time also telling those two stars that Poitier was all signed up.

The project was a secret in the beginning, then became the top news story in Hollywood. In October of 1966 the announcement was made with great ceremony that Tracy and Hepburn would be reunited in a Kramer project that would also star Sidney Poitier, and would introduce Miss Hepburn's niece, Katharine Houghton, in the role of their daughter. The picture was big news, but the movie community figured it was all wishful thinking. The big question was Tracy's health. Rumours kept circulating that he was sick, that he was close to dying. The odds were he would never even start the picture, much less finish it. One wag made a sick joke at a party by saying he was looking forward to the picture because it would be the first one to co-star Katharine Hepburn and Edward G. Robinson.

There had been no dramatic change in Tracy's condition. He was not much stronger than when he had dropped the idea of *The Cincinnati Kid*. But four years of inactivity had almost destroyed his spirit without improving him physically.

He talked about going out a champion, like Ted Williams. 'Ted connected for a home run and decided to retire while he was rounding the bases. He's enjoying life because he knows he quit at the right time.' Tracy needed to make one more film. Kramer sensed this. He was excited by William Rose's story line for *Guess Who's Coming to Dinner* and also by the hope of starring Tracy in a film once again.

Kramer also knew that if Tracy were to marshal his physical and emotional resources to start a film, he would be depending on Katharine Hepburn. Although Miss Hepburn was most selective in what she liked, she responded immediately to *Guess Who's Coming to Dinner*.

Miss Hepburn's endorsement was all that was needed. William Rose got to work on a screenplay for the screen's finest star team, and at the same time tried to see that Tracy's part was not too physically demanding.

Early in 1967, workers at the Columbia studio in the heart of Hollywood built the set, Matt and Christina Drayton's San Francisco home, within the studio gates. A ten-week shooting schedule was set to begin in February. Tracy was raring to go.

Then he was crestfallen. Insurance companies handling the picture contracts refused to cover Tracy because he was so poor a risk. (Insuring film projects against a star's death was common practice; when Tyrone Power succumbed to a heart attack midway through the filming of *Solomon and Sheba*, full payment was made, the footage was scrapped, and the project begun again with Yul Brynner.)

Tracy assumed this would finish off the picture, or he would be written out of it. Kramer did not hesitate. He would go ahead, and he personally would be liable for the risk. Tracy tried unsuccessfully to talk him out of it, and was moved by Kramer's decision.

The final script was in on February 15, 1967. Four days later, almost on the eve of the scheduled beginning of production, Tracy had another bout with lung congestion. The local fire rescue squad was summoned to his house and again gave him oxygen. Hollywood had something to talk about the next day, for it hit the papers. This time it looked very bad.

A few days later, Tracy recovered enough to think about his plans for the picture. He told Kramer he did not believe he was up to it. His biggest worry was Kramer's faith in him and his willingness to gamble.

'Spence, nobody wants you to do it if you're not up to it,' Kramer said. 'There are no obligations. It isn't too late to call the whole thing off, and I will, if you can't make it. But I'm not going to make the picture without you, and that's final.'

Tracy gave Kramer a long sharp look.

'Okay,' he said quietly. 'Let's go.'

There was a little press conference and Tracy said yes, this was going to be his last picture. He had already retired a dozen times. This time, however, there was no doubt that he meant it. The big question was, could he get through it? Tracy's own wavering confidence seemed critical.

Now a new Katharine Hepburn took over, gracious and helpful to the newsmen whom, in earlier days, she had treated as her enemies. She was saying things like 'Most people get grumpier in their old age; I get nicer.' Partly this was for Katharine Houghton, but George Cukor thought 'Katharine's great show of diplomacy was a means of helping Spencer. She established an atmosphere within which he could work well.'

Tracy was an almost legendary tyrant, and many studio workers on all levels either avoided him, consciously, or were assigned so that they had no contact with him. Kramer did not want Tracy to have to cope with distractions. He needed all his strength for acting.

Kramer scheduled Tracy to begin work at ten o'clock each morning and wouldn't let him work past four in the afternoon. Kramer said that half a day with Tracy was more productive and more rewarding than a full day with any other actor he knew. The shooting schedule was arranged to work around Tracy as much as possible. William Rose's script had different characters pairing off for duologue scenes. The picture stayed on schedule, and Tracy didn't miss a day.

Sidney Poitier recalled later, 'We all were concerned about Spence every day, although no one said anything. He was ill, that was painfully clear. But he thrived on the picture; I'm sure of that.'

Kramer, too, said that Tracy actually looked better and acted more chipper during the making of *Guess Who's Coming to Dinner* than he had in years, and had much more vigor than while making *It's a Mad, Mad, Mad, Mad World*. Miss Hepburn was in constant attendance, an affectionate nurse and co-worker who kept Tracy's mind away from his troubles. She was his adjutant and drillmaster; but as always in their personal relationship, she also did as she was told. And their communication sometimes bordered on the fantastic. Consider an incident that occurred on the set of *Guess Who's Coming to Dinner*. Miss Hepburn had finished a scene and had scurried off to her dressing room. When it was time to shoot Tracy in close-up she reappeared, now in slacks, and sat in a director's chair, preparing to 'feed' lines to Tracy. He does not see her, because she is behind him and to one side, out of camera range. She props her feet on a setpiece and begins. Tracy stops her. Very slowly, he asks her if she intends to sit there with her feet up like that. He does not turn to look at her. She inhales and says nothing. He then tells her, slowly, that they can begin when she puts her goddam feet down and sits like a lady. He still has not seen her. He does not move. She sticks out her tongue at him, wrinkles her nose, and drops her feet. With a little smile, she adopts a ladylike posture. They start to work.

The working script of *Guess Who's Coming to Dinner* zeroed in on the well-known strengths of Spencer Tracy's acting. The climactic scene was a long, barely-interrupted Tracy speech, more than a thousand words in length, bringing a Negro and a white family to a common understanding.

The script could only have been written for Tracy, for many scenes required acting without words.

From Scene No. 104:

He stops and stands there, staring at nothing with a fierce intensity as he thinks, perhaps, of what Mary Prentice has said. Then he shakes his head several times, as if to say, that can't be true, she can't be right. she's wrong, of course I know how they feel, I haven't forgotten anything . . .

Or from Scene No. 106:

Matt Drayton hasn't moved. He simply stands there in the darkness, not noticing or reacting to some sounds from the bay. But his expression is no longer so fiercely intense. He seems to be wondering, to be uncertain . . .

And then, Scene No. 110:

Now he stands staring vacantly up into the night at where, when he was a boy, heaven was said to be. His glance moves slowly but with the speed of light from star to star as he recalls exactly what it was like to love Christina as he first loved Christina. And it's true: he *had* forgotten, and he knows it. He stands there, and his expression now reveals a kind of astonished wonder . . .

At that point the script permits Matt Drayton to speak, and for the only time on film, Spencer Tracy says, 'I'll be a son of a bitch . . .'

Hollywood and Columbia Pictures and Stanley Kramer were struggling to get Spencer Tracy through one more movie — his seventy-fourth — but Tracy did more than get through. He delivered a blue-ribbon performance as rich in understanding and sympathy as it was in skill. Most viewers would say that the highwater mark of the film occurred during Tracy's long speech when, after talking to the black man and the white girl, he turned to Katharine Hepburn and said, 'If what they feel for each other is even half what *we* felt' — his voice cracking — 'then that is everything.'

Tracy's big scene was out of the way when, on the final Monday of the shooting schedule and with only four days to go, Tracy said to Kramer, 'You know, I read the script again

247

last night, and if I were to die on the way home tonight, you can still release the picture with what you've got.' He already had his reward; but the last week's chores would be met.

Production ended on May 26, with much emotion. The sequence in the drive-in had been slated for the wrap-up. And that was that.

There was, of course, the on-the-set party to celebrate the windup. Tracy considered going, even though his doctors didn't advise it, but he changed his mind. He was exhausted; but he was also full of triumphant emotion, and afraid to show if off in public.

However, Miss Hepburn attended, which was more unusual, for she was much less apt to turn up at *any* function. But she mixed with all the company, freckles shining, her niece in tow. During the dinner with its eulogies, Stanley Kramer paid tribute to Tracy as 'the greatest of all motion picture personalities'. At that point Miss Hepburn rose from her chair, and the long-legged figure in the white slack suit strode to the microphone and surprised her fellow workers by thanking them for their cooperation.

'I don't think you people realize how dependent we are on you for the encouragement you give us. These are the things that make up our lives. You are the people who make an actor able to act, and I don't know how many of you realize that. But I want you to know that I shall be everlastingly grateful to you all. And I know that your help . . . made a hell of a lot of difference . . . to Spence.'

While cast and crew were applauding, Spencer Tracy was resting in his house, talking on the telephone to Garson Kanin. 'Did you hear me, Jasper? I finished the picture!'

Kanin said that in the course of the past year he had telephoned Tracy no less than two hundred and fifty times, and this was the only time that Tracy had called *him*. In his remarkable Tracy memoir published in the New York *Times*, Kanin said Tracy was gleeful, excited, relieved, and slightly incredulous.

George Cukor, keeping a close watch, said Tracy was

'Very, very happy, and very, very tired . . . he just wanted to rest.'

He passed the final days that way, resting. His closest friends, considerate of his need, deferred their visits.

*   *   *

On Saturday morning, June 10, 1967, he died. Up and around early as usual, he was stricken shortly before 6 A.M. Ida Gheczy, his housekeeper, found him, but Tracy was dead before Carroll Tracy arrived with Dr. Mitchell Covel. The official cause of death was heart failure. His sixty-seven years had been full and strenuous. Garson Kanin offered a E. Lewis quote as one of Tracy's favorites: 'You only live once . . . and if you work it right, once is *enough*.'

Louise, John, and Susie Tracy arrived at the cottage shortly after Carroll Tracy. George Cukor notified Katharine Hepburn, and they arrived together afterward, accompanied by Ross Evans, Tracy's business manager in recent years.

The film colony long had been braced for Tracy's death but had been encouraged by his well-publicized return to the cameras. Hollywood was shocked, stunned. Unkind feelings toward Tracy, generated during his difficult later years, evaporated, and the entire film colony mourned him.

His death was front-page headline news around the world. The New York *Times* in a lead story said Tracy 'symbolized the justice-driven American man of action . . . whose trademark of taciturn, unglamorized confidence remained a durable salable commodity.' Later Bosley Crowther said that Tracy's death 'breaks one more strong and vibrant cable on the slowly crumbling bridge between motion pictures of this generation and the great ones of the past'.

Requiem low mass was said at the Immaculate Heart of Mary Roman Catholic Church in Hollywood. The mass was recited by Monseigneur John O'Donnell, Tracy's technical adviser on *Boys Town*. The family pew was occupied by the actor's wife, son, and daughter. Mrs. Tracy was accompanied to the funeral by M-G-M's Howard Strickling.

The eight pallbearers were George Cukor, John Ford, Garson Kanin, Stanley Kramer, Abe Lastfogel, William Self, James Stewart, and Frank Sinatra. The long list of honorary pallbearers included many stage and screen associates, polo pals, college friends, and dignitaries. George Murphy was an usher. The funeral was attended by six hundred people, and burial was at Forest Lawn Cemetery.

Katharine Hepburn did not attend the funeral. She was conspicuous by her absence, but less so than she would have been if present. She paid her respects to Mrs. Tracy, and soon departed for Connecticut to visit with her family.

Charles Champlin, the Los Angeles *Times* motion picture editor whose periodic coverage of the *Guess Who's Coming to Dinner* filming had buoyed Tracy's spirit and confidence, wrote a tribute two days after the actor's death that most Hollywood folk thought captured the unusual Tracy-Hepburn relationship. Champlin said: '(this last) film, as an idea, seems one which only Tracy and Miss Hepburn could have carried. And as a gesture of their personal idealism, it is a remarkably fitting legacy, both of a great career and of an association as beautiful and dignified as any this town has ever known.'

The last will and testament of Spencer Tracy was simple and direct. His income, listed at 'more than $500,000', was willed to his wife and offspring. His wardrobe, paintings, and automobiles went to his brother. Louise Tracy was named executrix.

*　　　*　　　*

The controversy over *Guess Who's Coming to Dinner* began during the November press and industry previews; premieres were slated on both coasts for mid-December to qualify the picture for the 1967 Academy Awards. Some of the first viewers declared it a very fine, very bold film. Others found the picture treacly, sentimental, and contrived. The most common criticism was that it was 'old-fashioned'.

The range of opinion pointed up how swiftly the movie business, and film content, was changing. At the time of its inception it had indeed been a courageous step for commercial films. But the time of its release it was already out of date. Praise for Tracy was unanimous, however, and Miss Hepburn and Poitier also were well received. The only acting that drew any negative response was that of Katharine Houghton, who had to work with a badly written role.

If Kramer and the executives of the Columbia Pictures Corporation were less than happy about the general tone of the reviews, they had reason to be ecstatic about the commercial return. Certainly the picture was right for its time as a mass-marketed product. It was an 'audience' film that would benefit by word-of-mouth publicity. Besides having Tracy and Hepburn, it had the unforeseen gift of Sidney Poitier, already riding high in popularity because of *To Sir with Love* and *In the Heat of the Night*. *Guess Who's Coming to Dinner* was a blockbuster. It was financially the most successful picture of Spencer Tracy's thirty-seven-year career.

Tracy's final performance marked the end of the era of great stars, and his final picture marked the turning point for movie scripts. It was one of the last big-studio glossy pictures whose story could have been lifted from a slick magazine. Kramer, once the great hope of the avant garde, now was called Establishment; *Bonnie and Clyde* and *The Graduate* were the 'new cinema'. At the 1967 Academy Awards, the two styles were in competition. *Guess Who's Coming to Dinner* and *Bonnie and Clyde* led the nominations with ten apiece. That Tracy would be named had been a foregone conclusion, but Katharine Hepburn also received a nomination, and Kramer's film was placed in competition for every major award.

The Oscar ceremony was scheduled, as usual, on a Monday — always a bad night for attendance at the movie houses. The event was postponed until the following Wednesday, April 10, because of the assassination of Dr. Martin Luther King, Jr.

The tragedy cast a pall over the ceremony at the Santa Monica Civic Auditorium, and emcee Bob Hope — also thought by many to be a relic of the old Hollywood — was badly off form.

Bonnie and Clyde scored only with the best supporting actress award for Estelle Parsons. *The Graduate*, the other surprise blockbuster of the new wave, earned the award for best director for Mike Nichols. *Guess Who's Coming to Dinner* was getting nowhere until the announcement came that the William Rose screenplay was the winner, which didn't please those who admired *Bonnie and Clyde*.

Only the two top acting awards and the best picture selection now remained. Of the ten nominated stars, eight were in the audience. The only ones absent were Tracy and Miss Hepburn. She appeared on the program via a film clip — but was out of the country, working. After Tracy's death she hurled herself into a back-breaking schedule, taking starring roles in two prestige efforts to be filmed abroad — Eleanor of Aquitaine in *The Lion in Winter*, and the title part in *The Madwoman of Chaillot*. She was also confirmed, long in advance, for the title role in the Alan Jay Lerner Broadway musical *Coco*.

Rod Steiger was announced winner in the best actor category. Tracy would have approved the choice of Steiger, although they were not friends — if they had met at all. Despite the fact that Tracy became impatient with most method actors, he admired much of Brando's work and all of Lee J. Cobb's, and in 1965 he told England's Robert Haight he had voted for Steiger's performance in *The Pawnbroker*. Steiger was cited for *In the Heat of the Night*, also named best picture in what seemed like a compromise between the old and the new cinema.

But there was one more dramatic moment. It was anybody's guess who would be voted the best actress — it might be Dame Edith Evans, or Faye Dunaway, or Anne Bancroft, or Audrey Hepburn. Sidney Poitier opened the envelope. He took a breath and called out, 'Katharine Hepburn'.

Again a winner, after thirty-four years.

Tracy would have liked that, too.

CHAPTER TEN

THE ACTOR FOR HISTORY

In the very brief period since Spencer Tracy's death, more and more people are aware that the era of the movies is over. The age of *film* is here. The motion picture is the art form of today, of Now. The old studio system is dead, or close to it. Nostalgia has kept it alive beyond its time. In the Good Old Days, the movie was king. No other entertainment form has exerted so strong an influence on a nation, or will again. The Hollywood movies ruled American life and thought during two tumultuous decades between the coming of the talkies and the coming of television: it dictated the nation's habits and shaped its mores.

It was thought that television would destroy motion pictures, but television merely freed the movies to find new techniques and new sophistication.

The mythology of stars created by the studio system during the early years of talkies governed film content into the 1950's. When television became popular, many supposedly indestructible superstars fell by the wayside. Only a hard core of strong masculine stars survived, but soon Bogart, Gable, and Cooper died, and Cagney retired. James Stewart and Cary Grant were still on the scene, but they had joined the group slightly later, after the system's foundation had been laid. Among the heroes who had been on the screen since the first talkies, only Spencer Tracy survived. His death deprived the screen of its most distinguished performer, and ended the era.

The studios built their successful stars into small gods. Without the system, a 'movie star' will be less imposing in the future than he was in the 1930's and 1940's. Spencer

Tracy was a product of that system, which based stardom on the qualifications of ability, durability, identification with a quality product, and the X-quality of individuality. On these bases, Tracy was the screen's biggest star, and no one is likely to come along to challenge him.

Bogart, Gable, Cooper, and Tracy all were screen heroes who shaped their own fates rather than being victims. As stars, they were caught in the conflict between acting and projecting an image. If a star kept his popularity over a period of years, he more than likely always played himself to some degree. Fredric March was one who did not; his every role was an original creation. But March became merely a respected veteran star, and not the twentieth-century folk hero that Cooper was, and that Bogart and Tracy still are.

Cooper, Bogart, and Gable all were effective actors when each was in his own type of part. But Tracy was the only one to play so many different sorts of roles. He had the range of March, the personality fidelity of Cooper, the presence of Bogart. A consistent dramatic actor, he was also one of the screen's few creatively comic actors.

His triumph was his singular naturalness before the camera. His insistence that he always played Spencer Tracy wasn't a fair statement. If he was always himself, there was a special joy in each reincarnation. Father Flanagan is not, after all, the Father of the Bride, but both are distinctly Spencer Tracy. His comedy is strengthened by reality, and in his drama there is a richness of natural humor. His Manuel in *Captains Courageous* is a marvelously human comedian in a realistic situation.

We may marvel at the consistent distinction of his career. Most stars' popularity dipped up and down, but Tracy's never failed him. As years passed and screen heroes tried to stay young, Tracy exploited his age and became the only genuine major character star, in contrast to Gable and Bogart, who to the end of their careers were leading men involved in the same romantic and dramatic situations that had made them stars.

Tracy was constantly depreciating himself and his craft,

passing off his success as luck. He knew better, but tried to keep his vanity, his fierce ego, and his professional pride from being obvious.

America liked Spencer Tracy, but he was embraced warmly in other parts of the world. Abroad he was considered the representative American actor. He was championed in the Soviet Union, and one of the more eloquent prose eulogies was penned in *Izvestia* by the eminent Sergei Gerasimov. In part, it read:

> By remaining true to himself, Spencer Tracy opened for many persons the best traits of his people. Soviet audiences came to love him for his manly serenity, his just, kind and somewhat sad view of the intricate world around him. He was one of the greatest artists of contemporary world cinematography, and I would even say that he was not merely an actor, so diversified and important was his part in the esthetic self-determination of film art. He will live, think, and speak from the screen to audiences of many countries, and they will always be grateful to him for the truth of his art.

But what will happen to the Tracy legend? Will he become another Gary Cooper — the myth dying with the man — whose films hold no interest for the new generation? Or will he, like Humphrey Bogart, gain more and more acclaim after his death?

The answer is, probably, he will be somewhere else, in between.

The younger generation are Bogart's people. Although he died in 1957, Bogart is very much of the 1960's: cynical, existentialist, self-reliant. They also identify with John Garfield, who was the precursor of James Dean and also, to some extent, of the young Brando and Paul Newman: rebellious youth bucking the odds imposed by an unfair society. The sociology of the Garfield films has a relevance today. The Cooper and Gable romances do not.

Tracy means more to his own generation, and to the one

that preceded it. A good representative of his time, he was an even stronger image of an earlier time. He was the pragmatic American who, though still respectable today, is out of fashion, obsolete. Katharine Hepburn called him a sturdy oak buffeted by the wind — a throwback to an age of rugged heroism. Tracy was that vanishing American, the self-made man. He was what we imagined our grandfathers to be.

Of his prewar films only *Captains Courageous* and to some extent *Fury* hold up today, except, of course, for *The Power and the Glory*, which was never reissued or released to television and therefore remains unseen by many young people. Charles Champlin says. 'It is the bright, tart, sophisticated comedies he did with Miss Hepburn that we'll remember perhaps longer, because the parts and personalities — cocky, talky, forceful, volatile, charming, kind — seemed in those films to coincide perfectly.' And today even such trifles as *Without Love* and *The Desk Set*, only ordinary pictures in their day, have that special allure.

Historically, Tracy was really the first modern actor on the screen. He was studied and copied by younger actors. He was an influence on styles as different as Montgomery Clift's and Steve McQueen's. Yet no other actor could duplicate Tracy in voice, movement, or sheer personality. James Cagney said, 'There was only one Garbo, and there's only one Tracy. Do you notice how mimics and comedians are always imitating me and other actors? Well, nobody imitates Tracy. Nobody can. What other actor can you say that about?'

*   *   *

Tracy, who felt the only thing an actor owed the public was a good performance, hoped to be remembered. He died with some of his goals unrealized. He had his two Oscars, but felt a loss in having never been cited by the New York Film Critics. He once remarked that he had been on the cover of *Life* three times but had never made the cover of *Time* except as a character in *State of the Union*.

Undoubtedly his private life with its storms and calms drove him to work harder. Katharine Hepburn said, 'I think Spencer and Laurette Taylor were the best actors I've ever seen. They both were Irish and both had problems in their lives, but they were so direct. They had concentration.'

Tracy's mania for concentration and for perfection estranged him from his family, and in later years from old friends. He became a misunderstood man, sitting for days at a time in the silence of his rented cottage with its spartan furnishings, where, in George Cukor's words, 'there was the air of a place where a man might do penance'.

For many years all of Tracy's other burdens were augmented by his feeling of guilt for having left the stage; but in the last years and particularly through his association with Stanley Kramer, he saw that there could be true nobility in movie-making.

That was why the last movie — and his living to complete it — was so important to him. He had at last accepted his life and his work.

He once said, 'I have no complaints. I've had wonderful friends, I've done something I've enjoyed and had more money than I needed ... and I've had a home.'

Perhaps in those last days after his final movie was finished, Spencer Tracy could say to himself, it's been a good life.

SPENCER TRACY'S FILMS

1.

UP THE RIVER
(Fox)

October 1930. Director, John Ford. Original screenplay, Maurine Watkins. 92 minutes.

St. Louis	Spencer Tracy
Judy	Claire Luce
Dannemora Dan	Warren Hymer
Steve	Humphrey Bogart
Pop	William Collier, Sr.
Kitty	Joan Lawes
Frosby	Noel Francis
The Warden	George Macfarlane

2.

QUICK MILLIONS
(Fox)

April 1931. Director, Rowland Brown. Screenplay, Rowland Brown, from a story by Courtenay Terrett. 95 minutes.

'Bugs' Raymond	Spencer Tracy
Daisy DeLisie	Sally Eilers
Dorothy Stone	Marguerite Churchill
'Arkansas' Smith	Bob Burns
Kenneth Stone	John Wray
Jimmy Kirk	George Raft
'Nails' Markey	Warner Richmond

3.
SIX CYLINDER LOVE
(Fox)

May 1931. Director, Thornton Freeland. Screenplay, William Anthony McGuire, from his play. 81 minutes.

William Donroy	Spencer Tracy
Monty Winston	Edward Everett Horton
Marilyn Sterling	Sidney Fox
Gilbert Sterling	Lorin Raker
Richard Burton	William Collier, Sr.
Margaret Rogers	Una Merkel
Harold Rogers	Bert Roach
Janitor	El Brendel

4.
GOLDIE
(Fox)

June 1931. Director, Benjamin Stoloff. Screenplay, Gene Towne and Paul Perez, from the screenplay, 'A Girl in Every Port'. 74 minutes.

Bill	Spencer Tracy
Goldie	Jean Harlow
Spike	Warren Hymer
Constantine	Lina Basquette
Dolores	Maria Alba

5.
SHE WANTED A MILLIONAIRE
(Fox)

February 1932. Producer, John W. Considine, Jr. Director, John Blystone. Story and screenplay, William Anthony McGuire. 80 minutes.

Jane Miller	Joan Bennett
William Kelly	Spencer Tracy
Mary Taylor	Una Merkel
Roger Norton	James Kirkwood
Mrs. Miller	Dorothy Peterson
Mr. Miller	Douglas Cosgrove
Humphrey	Donald Dillaway
Morther Norton	Lucille LaVerne

6

SKY DEVILS
(United Artists)

March 1932. Producer, Howard Hughes. Director, Edward Sutherland. Story and screenplay, Joseph Moncure March. 79 minutes.

Wilkie	Spencer Tracy
Sergeant Hogan	William Boyd
Mary	Ann Dvorak
Mitchell	George Cooper
The Colonel	Billy Bevan
Fifi	Yola d'Avril
Innkeeper	Forrester Harvey

DISORDERLY CONDUCT
(Fox)

April 1932. Producer-director, John W. Considine, Jr. Original screenplay, William Anthony McGuire. 83 minutes.

Phyliss Crawford	Sally Eilers
Dick Fay	Spencer Tracy
Olsen	El Brendel
Jimmy	Dickie Moore
Tom Manning	Ralph Bellamy
James Crawford	Ralph Morgan
Tony Alsotto	Frank Conroy
Helen Burke	Sally Blane

8

YOUNG AMERICA
(Fox)

May 1932. Director, Frank Borzage. Screenplay, Sonya Levien, from a play by John Frederick Ballard. 74 minutes.

Jack Doray	Spencer Tracy
Edith Doray	Doris Kenyon
Arthur Simpson	Tommy Conlon
Judge Blake	Ralph Bellamy
Grandma Beamish	Beryl Mercer
Nutty	Raymond Borzage

| Mabel Saunders | Anne Shirley |
| Maid | Louis Beavers |

9.
SOCIETY GIRL
(Fox)

June 1932. Director, Sidney Lanfield. Screenplay, John Larkin, Jr., from the play by Charles Bearden. 78 minutes.

Johnny Malone	James Dunn
Judy Gilett	Peggy Shannon
Briscoe	Spencer Tracy
Tom Warburton	Walter Byron
Curly	Burt Hanlon
Olive Converse	Marjorie Gateson

10.
THE PAINTED WOMAN
(Fox)

September 1932. Director, John Blystone. Original screenplay, A. C. Kennedy. 73 minutes.

Tom Brian	Spencer Tracy
Kiddo	Peggy Shannon
Captain Boynton	William Boyd
Robert Dunn	Irving Pichel
Jim	Paul Rulien
Collins	Murray Kinnell
Yank	Stanley Fields

11.
ME AND MY GAL
(Fox)

December 1932. Director, Raoul Walsh. Story and screenplay, Barry Connors and Philip Klein. 90 minutes.

Don Dolan	Spencer Tracy
Helen Reilly	Joan Bennett
Kate Reilly	Marion Burns
Duke	George Walsh
Pop Reilly	J. Farrell McDonald
Jake	Burt Hanlon

12

20,000 YEARS IN SING SING
(Warner)

January 1933. Director, Michael Curtiz. Screenplay, Robert Lord and Courtenay Terrett, from the book by Lewis E. Lawes. 90 minutes.

Tom Connors	Spencer Tracy
Fay	Bette Davis
Warden Long	Arthur Byron
Bud	Lyle Talbot
Joe Finn	Louis Calhern
Dr. Ames	Grant Mitchell
Mrs. Long	Nella Walker
Billie	Sheila Terry
Dr. Meeker	Arthur Hoyt

THE FACE IN THE SKY
(Fox)

February 1933. Director, Harry Lachman. Screenplay, Humphrey Pearson, from a story by Myles Connelly. 70 minutes.

Joe Buck	Spencer Tracey
Madge	Marion Nixon
Lucky	Stuart Erwin
Triplett the Great	Sam Hardy
Sharon Hardley	Lila Lee
Ma Brown	Sarah Paddon
Jim Brown	Frank McGlynn, Jr.

14

THE POWER AND THE GLORY
(Fox)

August 1933. Producer, Jesse L. Lasky. Director, William K. Howard. Screenplay, Preston Sturges. 108 minutes.

Tom Garner	Spencer Tracy
Sally	Colleen Moore
Henry	Ralph Morgan
Eve	Helen Vinson

Tom Garner, Jr.	Clifford Jones
Henry's Wife	Sarah Paddon
Mulligan	J. Farrell MacDonald

15.

SHANGHAI MADNESS
(Fox)

September 1933. Director, John Blystone. Screenplay, Austin Parker and Gordon Wellesley, from a story by Frederick Hazlitt Brennan. 80 minutes.

Pat Jackson	Spencer Tracy
Wildeth Christie	Fay Wray
Li Po Chang	Ralph Morgan
Lobo Larnegan	Eugene Pallette
Van Emery	Arthur Hoyt

16.

THE MAD GAME
(Fox)

November 1933. Director, Irving Cummings. Screenplay, William Conselman, from a story by Edward Dean Sullivan. 75 minutes.

Edward Carson	Spencer Tracy
Jane Lee	Claire Trevor
Judge Penfield	Ralph Morgan
Thomas Penfield	Howard Lally
Chopper Allen	J. Carroll Naish
Butts McGee	Matt McHugh
Mike	Jerry Devine

17.

MAN'S CASTLE
(Columbia)

December 1933. Producer-director, Frank Borzage. Screenplay, Jo Swerling, from a story by Lawrence Hazard. 97 minutes.

Bill	Spencer Tracey
Trina	Loretta Young
Fay La Rue	Glenda Farrell
Ira	Walter Connelly
Bragg	Arthur Hohl

| Flossie | Marjorie Rambeau |
| Crippled Boy | Dickie Moore |

18.
THE SHOW OFF
(M-G-M)

March 1934. Director, Charles Riesner. Screenplay, Herman Mankiewicz, from the play by George Kelly. 80 minutes.

Aubrey Piper	Spencer Tracy
Amy Fisher	Madge Evans
Mrs. Fisher	Clara Blandick
Mr. Fisher	Grant Mitchell
Clara Harling	Lois Wilson
Joe Fisher	Henry Wadsworth
J. B. Preston	Claude Gillingwater
Frank Harling	Allan Edwards

19.
BOTTOMS UP
(Fox)

March 1934. Director, David Butler. Story and screenplay, B. G. DeSylva, David Butler, and Sid Silvers. 84 minutes.

Smoothie King	Spencer Tracy
Hal Reede	John Boles
Wanda Gale	Pat Paterson
Spud Mascot	Sid Silvers
Limey Brock	Henry Mundin
Louis Wolfe	Harry Green
Judith Marlowe	Thelma Todd

20.
LOOKING FOR TROUBLE
(United Artists)

April 1934. Producer, Darryl F. Zanuck. Director, William Wellman. Screenplay, Leonard Praskins and Elmer Harris, from a story by J. R. Bren. 77 minutes.

Joe Graham	Spencer Tracy
Casey	Jack Oakie
Ethel Greenwood	Constance Cummings
Don Sutter	Morgan Conway

Mazie   Arline Judge
Pearl La Tour   Judith Wood

21.
NOW I'LL TELL
(Fox)

June 1934. Producer, Winfield Sheehan. Director, Edwin Burke.
Screenplay, Edwin Burke, from a story by Mrs. Arnold Rothstein.
73 minutes.

Murray Golden	Spencer Tracy
Virginia Golden	Helen Twelvetrees
Peggy Warren	Alice Faye
Al Moister	Robert Gleckler
Freddie	Hobart Cavanaugh
Doran	Henry O'Neill
Mary	Shirley Temple
George	G. P. Huntley, Jr.

22.
MARIE GALANTE
(Fox)

November 1934. Producer, Winfield Sheehan. Director, Henry
King. Screenplay, Reginald Berkeley, from a novel by Jacques
Deval. 80 minutes.

Crawbett	Spencer Tracy
Marie Galante	Ketti Gallian
Plosser	Ned Sparks
Tapia	Helen Morgan
Brogart	Sig Rumann
Tenoki	Leslie Fenton
General Phillips	Arthur Byron
Sailor	J. C. Flippen
Bartender	Stepin Fetchit

23.
IT'S A SMALL WORLD
(Fox)

May 1935. Producer, Edward Butcher. Director, Irving Cummings. Screenplay, Sam Hellman and Gladys Lehman, from
'Highway Robbery', a story by Albert Kramer, 67 minutes.

Bill Shevlin	Spencer Tracy
Jane Dale	Wendy Barrie
Judge Clummerhorn	Raymond Walburn
Clara Nowell	Virginia Sale
Midge	Astrid Allwyn
Luther	Irving Bacon
Edgar Nowell	Charles Sellon

24.

DANTE'S INFERNO
(Fox)

July 1935. Producer, Sol M. Wurtzel. Director, Harry Lachman. Screenplay, Philip Klein and Robert Yost. 82 minutes.

Jim Carter	Spencer Tracy
Betty McWade	Claire Trevor
Pop McWade	Henry B. Walthall
Jonesy	Alan Dinehart
Alexander Carter	Scotty Beckett
Dean	Robert Gleckler
Dancer	Rita Hayworth
Dancer	Gary Leon

25.

THE MURDER MAN
(M-G-M)

July 1935. Producer, Harry Rapf. Director, Tim Whelan. Story by Tim Whelan and Guy Bolton, screenplay by Tim Whelan and John C. Higgins. 84 minutes.

Steve Gray	Spencer Tracy
Mary Shannon	Virginia Bruce
Captain Cole	Lionel Atwill
Henry Mander	Harvey Stephens
Shorty	James Stewart
Pop Gray	William Collier, Sr.

26.
WHIPSAW
(M-G-M)

December 1935. Producer, Harry Rapf. Director, Sam Wood.
Story by James Edward Grant, screenplay by Howard Emmett
Rogers. 88 minutes.

Vivian Palmer	Myrna Loy
Ross McBride	Spencer Tracy
Ed Dexter	Harvey Stephens
Doc Evans	William Harrigan
Harry Ames	Clay Clement
Monetta	George Ranavent
Wadsworth	Robert Warwick
Dabson	John Qualen

27.
RIFFRAFF
(M-G-M)

January 1936. Producer, Irving G. Thalberg. Director, Robert Z.
Leonard. Story by Frances Marion, screenplay by Frances Marion,
H. W. Haneman, and Anita Loos. 90 minutes.

Hattie	Jean Harlow
Dutch	Spencer Tracy
Nick	Joseph Calleia
Lil	Una Merkel
Jimmy	Mickey Rooney
'Flytrap'	Victor Kilian
'Brains'	J. Farrell McDonald
Rosie	Juanita Quigley
Lew	Vince Barnett

28.
FURY
(M-G-M)

June 1936. Producer, Joseph L. Mankiewicz. Director, Fritz
Lang. Screenplay, Bartlett Cormack and Fritz Lang, from a story
by Norman Krasna. 94 minutes.

Katherine Grant	Sylvia Sidney
Joe Wheeler	Spencer Tracy
District Attorney	Walter Abel

Kirby Dawson	Bruce Cabot
Sheriff	Edward Ellis
'Bugs' Meyers	Walter Brennan
Charlie	Frank Albertson
Tom	George Walcott
Durkin	Arthur Stone
Fred Garrett	Morgan Wallace
Defense Attorney	Jonathan Hale
Mrs. Whipple	Esther Dale

29.
SAN FRANCISCO
(M-G-M)

June 1936. Producers, John Emerson and Bernard Hyman. Director, W. S. Van Dyke II. Screenplay, Anita Loos, from a story by Robert Hopkins. 111 minutes.

Blackie Norton	Clark Gable
Mary Blake	Jeanette MacDonald
Father Mullin	Spencer Tracy
Jack Burley	Jack Holt
Mrs. Burley	Jessie Ralph
Mat	Ted Healy
Trixie	Shirley Ross
Sheriff	Edgar Kennedy
Professor	Al Shean
Della Bailey	Margaret Irving

30.
LIBELLED LADY
(M-G-M)

November 1936. Producer, Lawrence Weingarten. Director, Jack Conway. Story by Wallace Sullivan, screenplay by Howard Emmett Rogers and George Oppenheimer. 99 minutes.

Gladys	Jean Harlow
Bill Chandler	William Powell
Connie Allenbury	Myrna Loy
Haggerty	Spencer Tracy
Mr. Allenbury	Walter Connolly
Mrs. Burna-Norvell	Cora Witherspoon
Mr. Bane	Charlie Grapewin
Graham	Charles Trowbridge

31.
THEY GAVE HIM A GUN
(M-G-M)

May 1937. Producer, Harry Rapf. Director, W. S. Van Dyke II. Screenplay by Cyril Hume, Richard Maibaum, and Maurice Rapf, from the novel by William Joyce Cowan. 94 minutes.

Fred	Spencer Tracy
Jimmy	Franchot Tone
Rose Duffy	Gladys George
Sergeant Meadowlark	Edgar Dearing
Saxe	Mary Treen
Laro	Cliff Edwards
Judge	Charles Trowbridge

32.
CAPTAINS COURAGEOUS
(M-G-M)

June 1937. Producer, Louis D. Lighton. Director, Victor Fleming. Screenplay, John Lee Mahin, Marc Connelly, and Dale Van Every, from Rudyard Kipling's novel. 116 minutes.

Harvey	Freddie Bartholomew
Manuel	Spencer Tracy
Disko	Lionel Barrymore
Mr. Cheyne	Melvyn Douglas
Uncle Salters	Charlie Grapewin
Dan	Mickey Rooney
Long Jack	John Carradine
Cushman	Oscar O'Shea
Priest	Jack La Rue
Dr. Finley	Walter Kingsford
Old Clement	Christian Rub

33.
THE BIG CITY
(M-G-M)

September 1937. Producer, Norman Krasna. Director, Frank Borzage. Screenplay, Dore Schary and Hugo Butler, from a story by Norman Krasna. 80 minutes.

Joe	Spencer Tracy
Anna	Luise Rainer

The Mayor	Charlie Grapewin
Sophie Sloan	Janet Beecher
Jim Sloan	Irving Bacon
Grandpa Sloan	Clem Bevans
Beecher	William Demarest
Mike Edwards	Eddie Quillan

34.
MANNEQUIN
(M-G-M)

January 1938. Producer, Joseph L. Mankiewicz. Director, Frank Borzage. Screenplay, Lawrence Hazard, from a story by Katherine Brush.

Jessie Cassidy	Joan Crawford
John L. Hennessey	Spencer Tracy
Eddie Miller	Alan Curtis
Briggs	Ralph Morgan
Beryl	Mary Philips
Pa Cassidy	Oscar O'Shea
Ma Cassidy	Elizabeth Risdon

35.
TEST PILOT
(M-G-M)

April 1938. Producer, Louis D. Lighton. Director, Victor Fleming. Story by Frank Wead, screenplay by Waldemar Young and Vincent Lawrence. 120 minutes.

Jim Lane	Clark Gable
Ann Barton	Myrna Loy
Gunner Sloane	Spencer Tracey
Drake	Lionel Barrymore
General Ross	Samuel S. Hinds
Landlady	Marjorie Main
Mrs. Benson	Gloria Holden
Sarah	Virginia Grey
Benson	Louis Jean Heydt

36

BOYS TOWN

(M-G-M)

September 1938. Producer, John W. Considine, Jr. Director, Norman Taurog. Story by Dore Schary and Eleanore Griffin, screenplay by Dore Schary and John Meehan. 95 minutes.

Father Flanagan	Spencer Tracy
Whitey Marsh	Mickey Rooney
Dave Morris	Henry Hull
Pee Wee	Bobs Watson
John Hargreaves	Jonathan Hale
The Judge	Addison Richards
The Bishop	Minor Watson
Tony Ponessa	Gene Reynolds
The Sheriff	Victor Kilian
Burton	Robert Emmett Keane
Dan Farrow	Leslie Fenton
Mo Kahn	Sidney Miller

37.

STANLEY AND LIVINGSTONE

(20th Century-Fox)

August 1939. Producer, Darryl F. Zanuck. Director, Henry King. Story by Hal Long and Sam Hellman, screenplay by Philip Dunne and Julian Josephson. 109 minutes.

Henry M. Stanley	Spencer Tracy
Eve Kingsley	Nancy Kelly
Gareth Tyce	Richard Greene
Lord Tyce	Charles Coburn
Jeff Slocum	Walter Brennan
Dr. David Livingstone	Sir Cedric Hardwicke
James Gordon Bennett, Jr.	Henry Hull
John Kingsley	Henry Travers
Sir John Cresham	Miles Mander
Mr. Cranston	David Torrence
Captain Webb	Paul Stanton
Frederick Holcomb	Holmes Herbert
Sir Henry Forrester	Brandon Hurst

38

I TAKE THIS WOMAN
(M-G-M)

February 1940. Director, W. S. Van Dyke II. Story by Charles MacArthur, screenplay by James Kevin McGuinness. 97 minutes.

Karl Decker	Spencer Tracy
Georgi Gragore	Hedy Lamarr
Madame Marcesca	Verree Teasdale
Phil Mayberry	Kent Taylor
Linda Rogers	Laraine Day
Sandra Mayberry	Mona Barrie
Joe	Jack Carson
Bill Rogers	Paul Cavanagh
Dr. Duveen	Louis Calhern
Lola Estermont	Frances Drake
Gertie	Marjorie Main
Sid	George E. Stone
Sambo	Willie Best

NORTHWEST PASSAGE
(M-G-M)

March 1940. Producer, Hunt Stromberg. Director, King Vidor. Screenplay, Laurence Stallings and Talbot Jennings, from the novel by Kenneth Roberts. 126 minutes.

Major Rogers	Spencer Tracy
Langdon Towne	Robert Young
Elizabeth Browne	Ruth Hussey
'Hunk' Marriner	Walter Brennan
'Cap' Huff	Nat Pendleton
Reverend Browne	Louis Hector
Humphrey Towne	Robert Barrat
Lieutenant Avery	Douglas Walton
Lord Amherst	Lumsden Hare
Sergeant McNutt	Donald McBride
Jennie Colt	Isabel Jewell
Jesse Beacham	Hugh Sothern
Webster	Regis Toomey
Wiseman Claggett	Montagu Love

EDISON, THE MAN
(M-G-M)

May 1940. Producer, John W. Considine, Jr. Director, Clarence Brown. Story by Dore Schary and Hugo Butler, screenplay by Talbot Jennings and Bradbury Foote. 107 minutes.

Thomas A. Edison	Spencer Tracy
Mary Stilwell	Rita Johnson
Bunt Cavatt	Lynne Overman
General Powell	Charles Coburn
Mr. Taggart	Gene Lockhart
Ben Els	Henry Travers
Michael Simon	Felix Bressart

41

BOOM TOWN
(M-G-M)

September 1940. Producer, Sam Zimbalist. Director, Jack Conway. Screenplay by John Lee Mahin, from 'A Lady Comes to Burkburnett', story by James Edward Grant. 119 minutes.

Big John McMasters	Clark Gable
Square John Sand	Spencer Tracy
Betsy Bartlett	Claudette Colbert
Karen Vanmeer	Hedy Lamarr
Luther Aldrich	Frank Morgan
Harry Compton	Lionel Atwill
Harmony Jones	Chill Wills
Ed Murphy	Joe Yule
Ferdie	Curt Bois
Baby Jack	Baby Quintanilla

42

MEN OF BOYS TOWN
(M-G-M)

April 1941. Producer, John W. Considine, Jr. Director, Norman Taurog. Screenplay, James Kevin McGuinness. 106 minutes.

Father Flanagan	Spencer Tracy
Whitey Marsh	Mickey Rooney
Pee Wee	Bobs Watson
Ted Martley	Larry Nunn

Dave Morris	Lee J. Cobb
Mrs. Malland	Mary Nash
Mr. Mailland	Henry O'Neill
Flip	Darryl Hickman
Mo Kahn	Sidney Miller
Mrs. Fenely	Anne Revere

43.
DR. JEKYLL AND MR. HYDE
(M-G-M)

August 1941. Director, Victor Fleming. Screenplay, John Lee Mahin, from the novel by Robert Louis Stevenson. 110 minutes.

Dr. Harry Jekyll	Spencer Tracy
Mr. Hyde	Spencer Tracy
Ivy Paterson	Ingrid Bergman
Beatrix Emery	Lana Turner
Sir Charles Emery	Donald Crisp
Dr. John Lanyon	Ian Hunter
The Bishop	C. Aubrey Smith
Mrs. Higgens	Sara Allgood

44.
WOMAN OF THE YEAR
(M-G-M)

February 1942. Producer, Joseph L. Mankiewicz. Director, George Stevens. Original screenplay, Ring Lardner, Jr., and Michael Kanin. 113 minutes.

Sam Craig	Spencer Tracy
Tess Harding	Katharine Hepburn
Ellen Whitcomb	Fay Bainter
Clayton	Reginald Owen
William J. Harding	Minor Watson
Pinkie Peters	William Bendix
Flo Peters	Gladys Blake

45.
TORTILLA FLAT
(M-G-M)

May 1942. Producer, Sam Zimbalist. Director, Victor Fleming. Screenplay, John Lee Mahin and Benjamin Glazer, from the novel by John Steinbeck. 101 minutes.

Pilon	Spencer Tracy
Dolores (Sweets) Ramirez	Hedy Lamarr
Danny	John Garfield
The Pirate	Frank Morgan
Pablo	Akim Tamiroff
Mrs. Torelli	Connie Gilchrist
Jose Maria Corcoran	John Qualen
Tito Ralph	Sheldon Leonard
Paul D. Cummings	Donald Meek
Portugee Joe	Allen Jenkins
Father Ramon	Henry O'Neill

46.
KEEPER OF THE FLAME
(M-G-M)

January 1943. Producer, Victor Saville. Director, George Cukor. Screenplay, Donald Ogden Stewart, from the novel by I. A. R. Wylie. 100 minutes.

Steven O'Malley	Spencer Tracy
Christine Forrest	Katharine Hepburn
Clive Kerndon	Richard Whorf
Mrs. Forrest	Margaret Wycherly
Geoffrey Medford	Forrest Tucker
Freddie Ridges	Stephen McNally
Dr. Fielding	Frank Craven
Orion Peabody	Percy Kilbride
Jane Harding	Audrey Christie
Jeb Richards	Darryl Hickman
Mr. Arbuthnot	Donald Meek
Jason Richards	Howard da Silva

47.
A GUY NAMED JOE
(M-G-M)

December 1943. Producer, Everett Riskin. Director, Victor Fleming. Story by Frederick Hazlitt Brennan, screenplay by Dalton Trumbo, from a short story by Chandler Sprague and David Boehm. 117 minutes.

Pete Sandidge	Spencer Tracy
Dorinda Durston	Irene Dunne
Ted Randall	Van Johnson

Al Yackey	Ward Bond
The General	Lionel Barrymore
Nails Kilpatrick	James Gleason
Dick Rumney	Barry Nelson
Ellen Bright	Esther Williams
Colonel Sykes	Henry O'Neill
James J. Rourke	Don DeFore

48.
THE SEVENTH CROSS
(M-G-M)

September 1944. Producer, Pandro S. Berman. Director, Fred Zinnemann. Screenplay, Helen Deutsch, from the novel by Anna Seghers. 112 minutes.

George Heisler	Spencer Tracy
Toni	Signe Hasso
Paul Roeder	Hume Cronyn
Liesel Roeder	Jessica Tandy
Madame Marelli	Agnes Moorehead
Poldi Schlamm	Felix Bressart
Mrs. Sauer	Katherine Locke
Bruno Sauer	George Macready
Fiedler	Paul Guilfoyle
Gahrenburg	George Zucco

49.
THIRTY SECONDS OVER TOKYO
(M-G-M)

November 1944. Producer, Sam Zimbalist. Director, Mervyn LeRoy. Screenplay, Dalton Trumbo, from the book by Ted Lawson and Bob Considine. 140 minutes.

Lt. Col. James H. Doolittle	Spencer Tracy
Ted Lawson	Van Johnson
David Thatcher	Robert Walker
Ellen Lawson	Phyllis Thaxter
Davey Jones	Scott McKay
Charles McClure	Don DeFore
Bob Gray	Robert Mitchum
Jurika	Leon Ames

277

50

WITHOUT LOVE
(M-G-M)

March 1945. Producer, Lawrence Weingarten. Director, Harold S. Bucquet. Screenplay, Donald Ogden Stewart, from the play by Philip Barry. 111 minutes.

Pat Jamieson	Spencer Tracy
Jami Rowan	Katharine Hepburn
Kitty Trimble	Lucille Ball
Quentin Ladd	Keenan Wynn
Edwina Collins	Patricia Morison
Professor Gouinza	Felix Bressart
Paul Carroll	Carl Esmond

THE SEA OF GRASS
(M-G-M)

February 1947. Producer, Pandro S. Berman. Director, Elia Kazan. Screenplay, Marguerite Roberts and Vincent Lawrence, from the novel by Conrad Richter. 131 minutes.

Jim Brewton	Spencer Tracy
Lutie Cameron	Katharine Hepburn
Brice Chamberlain	Melvyn Douglas
Brock Brewton	Robert Walker
Sarah Beth Brewton	Phyllis Thaxter
Jeff	Edgar Buchanan
Doc Reid	Harry Carey
Selina Hall	Ruth Nelson
Sam Hall	James Bell
Brogden	Robert Armstrong
Major Harney	Russell Hicks

52

CASS TIMBERLANE
(M-G-M)

December 1947. Producer, Arthur Hornblow, Jr. Director, George Sidney. Screenplay, Donald Ogden Stewart and Sonya Levien, from the novel by Sinclair Lewis. 120 minutes.

Cass Timberlane	Spencer Tracy
Jinny Marshland	Lana Turner

Brad Criley	Zachary Scott
Jamie Wargate	Tom Drake
Queenie Havoc	Mary Astor
Boone Havoc	Albert Dekker
Louise Wargate	Selena Royle
Eino Roskinen	Cameron Mitchell
Hervey Plint	Howard Freeman

53.
STATE OF THE UNION
(M-G-M)

March 1948. A Liberty Production. Producer-director, Frank Capra. Screenplay, Anthony Veiller and Myles Connolly, from the play by Howard Lindsay and Russel Crouse. 124 minutes.

Grant Matthews	Spencer Tracy
Mary Matthews	Katharine Hepburn
Spike McManus	Van Johnson
Kay Thorndike	Angela Lansbury
Jim Conover	Adolphe Menjou
Sam Thorndike	Lewis Stone
Samuel Parrish	Howard Smith
Bill Hardy	Charles Dingle
Norah	Margaret Hamilton
Hanrahan	Raymond Walburn
Buck Swenson	Irving Bacon

54.
EDWARD, MY SON
(M-G-M)

June 1949. Producer, Edwin H. Knofp. Director, George Cukor. Screenplay, Donald Ogden Stewart, from the play by Robert Morley. 112 minutes.

Arnold Boult	Spencer Tracy
Evelyn Boult	Deborah Kerr
Dr. Larry Woodhope	Ian Hunter
Bronton	James Donald
Eileen Perrin	Leueen MacGrath
Harry Simpkins	Mervyn Johns
Phyllis Mayden	Harriette Johns

55

ADAM'S RIB
(M-G-M)

December 1949. Producer, Lawrence Weingarten. Director, George Cukor. Original screenplay, Ruth Gordon and Garson Kanin. 101 minutes.

Adam Bonner	Spencer Tracy
Amanda Bonner	Katharine Hepburn
Doris Attinger	Judy Holliday
Warren Attinger	Tom Ewell
Kip Luri	David Wayne
Beryl Caighn	Jean Hagen
Olympia LaPere	Hope Emerson

56.

MALAYA
(M-G-M)

January 1950. Producer, Edwin H. Knopf. Director, Richard Thorpe. Screenplay, Frank Fenton, from a story by Manchester Boddy. 97 minutes.

Carnahan	Spencer Tracy
John Royer	James Stewart
Luana	Valentina Cortesa
The Dutchman	Sydney Greenstreet
Keller	John Hodiak
John Manchester	Lionel Barrymore
Romano	Gilbert Roland
Bruno Gruber	Roland Winters

57.

FATHER OF THE BRIDE
(M-G-M)

June 1950. Producer, Pandro S. Berman. Director, Vincente Minnelli. Screenplay, Frances Goodrich and Albert Hackett, from the novel by Edward Streeter. 93 minutes.

Stanley T. Banks	Spencer Tracy
Ellie Banks	Joan Bennett

Kay Banks	Elizabeth Taylor
Buckley Dunstan	Don Taylor
Doris Dunstan	Billie Burke
Herbert Dunstan	Moroni Olsen
Mr. Massoula	Leo G. Carroll
Mr. Tringle	Melville Cooper
Tommy Banks	Russ Tamblyn
Joe	Frank Orth

58.

FATHER'S LITTLE DIVIDEND
(M-G-M)

April 1951. Producer, Pandro S. Berman. Director, Vincente
Minnelli. Screenplay, Frances Goodrich and Albert Hackett, from
characters created by Edward Streeter. 81 minutes.

Stanley Banks	Spencer Tracy
Ellie Banks	Joan Bennett
Kay Dunstan	Elizabeth Taylor
Buckley Dunstan	Don Taylor
Doris Dunstan	Billie Burke
Herbert Dunstan	Moroni Olsen
Tommy Banks	Russ Tamblyn

59.

THE PEOPLE AGAINST O'HARA
(M-G-M)

September 1951. Producer, William H. Wright. Director, John
Sturges. Screenplay, John Monks, Jr., from the novel by Eleazor
Lipsky. 94 minutes.

James P. Curtayne	Spencer Tracy
Vince Ricks	Pat O'Brien
Virginia Curtayne	Diana Lynn
Louis Barra	John Hodiak
John O'Hara	James Arness
Mr. O'Hara	Arthur Shields
Mrs. O'Hara	Louise Lorimer
'Knuckles' Lanzetta	Eduardo Ciannelli

60

PAT AND MIKE
(M-G-M)

May 1952. Producer, Lawrence Weingarten. Director, George Cukor. Original screenplay by Ruth Gordon and Garson Kanin. 98 minutes.

Mike Conovan	Spencer Tracy
Patricia Pemberton	Katharine Hepburn
Davie Hucko	Aldo Ray
Charles Barry	Jim Backus
Police Captain	Chuck Connors
Collier Weld	William Ching
Barney Craw	Sammy White
Spec Cauley	George Matthews
Mr. Berminger	Loring Smith

61.

THE PLYMOUTH ADVENTURE
(M-G-M)

November 1952. Producer, Dore Schary. Director, Clarence Brown. Original screenplay by Helen Deutsch. 111 minutes.

Captain Christopher Jones	Spencer Tracy
Dorothy Bradford	Gene Tierney
John Alden	Van Johnson
William Bradford	Leo Genn
Priscilla Mullins	Dawn Addams
Coppin	Lloyd Bridges
William Brewster	Barry Jones
Edward Winslow	Lowell Gilmore

62.

THE ACTRESS
(M-G-M)

August 1953. Producer, Lawrence Weingarten. Director, George Cukor. Screenplay, Ruth Gordon and Garson Kanin, from Miss Gordon's play, *Years Ago*. 95 minutes.

Clinton Jones	Spencer Tracy
Ruth Gordon Jones	Jean Simmons

Annie Jones	Teresa Wright
Fred Whitmarsh	Anthony Perkins
Mr. Bagley	Ian Wolfe
Hazel Dawn	Kay Williams
Emma Glavey	Mary Wickes

63.

BROKEN LANCE

(20th Century-Fox)

August 1954. Producer, Sol. C. Siegel. Director, Edward Dmytryk. Screenplay, Richard Murphy, from a screenplay by Philip Yordan. 96 minutes.

Matt Devereaux	Spencer Tracy
Ben Devereaux	Richard Widmark
Barbara Devereaux	Jean Peters
Joe Devereaux	Robert Wagner
Señora Devereaux	Katy Jurado
Mike Devereaux	Hugh O'Brien
Denny Devereaux	Earl Holliman
The Governor	E. G. Marshall
Clem Lawton	Carl Benton Reid
Two Moons	Eduard Franz

64.

BAD DAY AT BLACK ROCK

(M-G-M)

January 1955. Producer, Dore Schary. Director, John Sturges. Screenplay by Millard Kaufman, from Don Maguire's story, 'Bad Time at Honda'. 91 minutes.

John J. MacReedy	Spencer Tracy
Reno Smith	Robert Ryan
Liz Wirth	Anne Francis
Tim Horn	Dean Jagger
Doc Velle	Walter Brennan
Pete Wirth	John Ericson
Coley Trimble	Ernest Borgnine
Hector David	Lee Marvin
Mr. Hastings	Russell Collins

65

THE MOUNTAIN
(Paramount)

October 1956. Producer-director, Edward Dmytryk. Screenplay, Ranald MacDougall, from the novel by Henri Troyat. 100 minutes.

Zachary Teller	Spencer Tracy
Chris Teller	Robert Wagner
Marie	Claire Trevor
Father Belacchi	William Demarest
Revial	Richard Arlen
Solange	E. G. Marshall
Simone	Barbara Barrie
Hindu Girl	Anna Kashfi

THE DESK SET
(20th Century-Fox)

May 1957. Producer, Henry Ephron. Director, Walter Lang. Screenplay, Phoebe and Henry Ephron, from the play by William Marchant. 98 minutes.

Richard	Spencer Tracy
Bunny	Katharine Hepburn
Mike Culler	Gig Young
Peg Costello	Joan Blondell
Sylvia	Dina Merrill
Miss Warriner	Neva Patterson
Ruthie	Sue Randall
Azal	Nicholas Joy
Old Lady	Ida Moore

THE OLD MAN AND THE SEA
(Warner Brothers)

October 1958. Producer, Leland Hayward. Director, John Sturges. Screenplay, Ernest Hemingway, from his short novel. 86 minutes.

The Old Man	Spencer Tracy
The Boy	Felipe Pazos
Bartender	Harry Bellaver

THE LAST HURRAH

(Columbia)

October 1958. Producer-director, John Ford. Screenplay, Frank
Nugent, from the novel by Edwin O'Connor. 107 minutes.

Frank Skeffington	Spencer Tracy
Adam Caulfield	Jeffrey Hunter
John Gorman	Pat O'Brien
Norman Cass. Sr.	Basil Rathbone
Maevis Caulfield	Dianne Foster
The Cardinal	Donald Crisp
Amos Force	John Carradine
Sam Weinberg	Ricardo Cortezz
Festus Garvey	Frank McHugh
Delia	Jane Darwell
Cuke Gellen	James Gleason
Ditto Boland	Edward Brophy
Hennessey	Wallace Ford
Jack Mangan	Frank Albertson
Norman Cass, Jr.	O. Z. Whitehead

INHERIT THE WIND

(United Artists)

December 1960. Producer-director, Stanley Kramer. Screenplay,
Nathan E. Douglas and Harold J. Smith, from the play by
Jerome Lawrence and Robert E. Lee. 118 minutes.

Henry Drummond	Spencer Tracy
Matthew Harrison Brady	Fredric March
E. K. Hornbeck	Gene Kelly
Mrs. Brady	Florence Eldridge
Bertram Cates	Dick York
Rachel Brown	Donna Anderson
Reverend Brown	Claude Akins
The Judge	Harry Morgan
Davenport	Elliot Reid
Stebbins	Noah Beery, Jr.
Mayor	Philip Coolidge

THE DEVIL AT FOUR O'CLOCK
(Columbia)

October 1961. Producer, Fred Kohlmar. Director, Mervyn
LeRoy. Screenplay, Liam O'Brien, from the novel by Max Catto.
109 minutes.

Father Matthew Doonan	Spencer Tracy
Harry	Frank Sinatra
Jacques	Jean Pierre Aumont
Marcel	Gregorie Aslan
Charlie	Bernie Hamilton
The Governor	Alexander Scourby
Camille	Barbara Luna
Dr. Wexler	Martin Brandt

JUDGMENT AT NUREMBERG
(United Artists)

December 1961. Producer-Director, Stanley Kramer. Screenplay,
Abby Mann, from his television play. 189 minutes.

Judge Dan Haywood	Spencer Tracy
Ernst Janning	Burt Lancaster
Madame Bertholt	Marlene Dietrich
Col. Tad Lawson	Richard Widmark
Hans Rolfe	Maximilian Schell
Irene Hoffman	Judy Garland
Rudolf Peterson	Montgomery Clift
Roberts	William Shatner
Emil Hahn	Werner Klemperer
Horst	O. E. Hasse
General Merrin	Alan Baxter
Senator Burkett	Edward Binns
Judge Kenneth Norris	Kenneth MacKenna
Friedrich Hofstetter	Martin Brandt
Judge Curtiss Ives	Ray Teal

HOW THE WEST WAS WON
(M-G-M)

March 1963. Producer, Bernard Smith. Directors, Henry Hatha-
way, John Ford, George Marshall. Original screenplay, James R-
Webb. 167 minutes.

Linus Rawlings	James Stewart
Lillith Prescott	Debbie Reynolds
Eve Prescott	Carroll Baker
Zebulon Prescott	Karl Malden
Rebecca Prescott	Agnes Moorehead
Colonel Hawkins	Walter Brennan
Cleve Van Valen	Gregory Peck
Agatha Clegg	Thelma Ritter
Roger Morgan	Robert Preston
Zeb Rawlings	George Peppard
Abraham Lincoln	Raymond Massey
General Grant	Harry Morgan
General Sherman	John Wayne
Rebel Soldier	Russ Tamblyn
Mike King	Richard Widmark
Jethro Stuart	Henry Fonda
Charlie Grant	Eli Wallach
Marshall	Lee J. Cobb
Julie Rawlings	Carolyn Jones

Narration by Spencer Tracy

73

IT'S A MAD, MAD, MAD, MAD WORLD
(United Artists)

November 1963. Producer-director, Stanley Kramer. Original
screenplay by William and Tania Rose. 160 minutes.

Captain C. G. Culpeper	Spencer Tracy
J. Russell Finch	Milton Berle
Melville Crump	Sid Caesar
Simitar Grogan	Jimmy Durante
Benjy Benjamin	Buddy Hackett
Jimmy the Cook	Buster Keaton
Mrs. Marcus	Ethel Merman

Emmeline Finch   Dorothy Provine
Ding B..   Mickey Rooney
Sylvest.. Morris   Dick Shawn
Otto Meyer   Phil Silvers
J. Algernon Hawthorne   Terry-Thomas
Lennie Pike   Jonathan Winters
and Eddie (Rochester) Anderson, Jim Backus, Ben Blue,
Joe E. Brown, Alan Carney, Barrie Chase, Lloyd Corri-
gan, William Demarest, Andy Devine, Peter Falk, Paul
Ford, Sterling Holloway, Edward Everett Horton,
Marvin Kaplan, Don Knotts, Jerry Lewis, Charles
McGraw, Carl Reiner, Arnold Stang, Jesse White, The
Three Stooges.

74.

GUESS WHO'S COMING TO DINNER

(Columbia)

December 1967. Producer-director, Stanley Kramer. Original
screenplay, William Rose. 108 minutes.

Matt Drayton   Spencer Tracy
Christina Drayton   Katherine Hepburn
John Prentice   Sidney Poitier
Joey Drayton   Katharine Houghton
Msgr. Ryan   Cecil Kellaway
Mrs. Prentice   Beah Richards
Mr. Prentice   Roy E. Glynn, Sr.
Tillie   Isabell Sanford
Hilary St. George   Virginia Christine
Frankie   D'Urville Martin
Peter   Tom Heaton
Judith   Grace Gaynor
Car Hop   Alexandro Hay